NICK HOLDSTOCK spent three and [...] teacher. Since returning he has ha[...] publications such as the *Edinburg[...] Review, [...] and the London Review of Books.* In March 2010 he went back to China to evaluate how the 2009 riots in Xinjiang have affected people's lives. He lives in Edinburgh and is currently studying for a PhD in English Literature. More information can be found at his website:

www.nickholdstock.com.

The Tree that Bleeds
A Uighur Town on the Edge

NICK HOLDSTOCK

Luath Press Limited

EDINBURGH

www.luath.co.uk

First published 2011

ISBN: 978-1-906817-64-0

The publisher acknowledges subsidy from

ALBA | CHRUTHACHAIL

towards the publication of this book

The paper used in this book is recyclable. It is made
from low chlorine pulps produced in a low energy, low emissions
manner from renewable forests.

Printed and bound by
Bell & Bain Ltd., Glasgow

Typeset in 10.5 point Sabon
by 3btype.com

Some sections of this book appeared in different form in
Edinburgh Review, *n+1* and the *London Review of Books*.

For Magda Boreysza

Major cities in Xinjiang

Acknowledgements

THERE ARE MANY people to thank, firstly Jennie Renton for suggesting I approach my publisher. I am also grateful to the Scottish Arts Council for helping fund my trip to Xinjiang in 2010. I would also like to thank John Gittings, former East Asia correspondent of *The Guardian*, for his very helpful and encouraging feedback on an early draft of the manuscript.

Thanks to the following for giving advice, rooms to write in, hands to hold, a slap in the face when required: Ryan van Winkle, Benjamin Morris, Dan Gorman, Yasmin Fedda, Duncan Macgregor, Louise Milne and William Watson.

Thank you Mum and Dad.

I WAS LOOKING at the dome of a mosque when I heard the soldiers. The bark of their shouts, the stamp of their feet. I turned and saw rifles, black body armour, a line of blank faces. We were on Erdaoqiao, a busy shopping street in Urumqi, where a moment before the main concerns had been the prices of trousers and shirts. But the crowd did not scatter in fear at the sight of these armed men. They parted in a calm, unhurried manner, as if this were a routine sight, almost beneath notice. For a moment the street was quiet but for the soldiers' marching chant. As soon as they passed, the salesmen lifted their cries; haggling resumed. But there were more soldiers on the other side of the street, another black crocodile marching through. Policemen stood in twos and threes every hundred metres, outside a bank, a kebab stall, in front of the pedestrian subway. A riot van drove up and stopped at the intersection.

Although this display of force was disconcerting, it wasn't a surprise: nine months before, on 5 July 2009, this street had seen some of the worst violence in China since the Tiananmen Square protests in 1989. Urumqi is the capital of Xinjiang, China's largest province. There has been a long history of unrest in the region, between Uighurs (Turkic-speaking Muslims who account for about half the region's 23 million people) and Han Chinese (the ethnic majority in China). The events of July 2009 marked an escalation in the conflict. During the afternoon of 5 July, around 300 Uighur students gathered in the centre of Urumqi. By late afternoon, the crowd had swelled to several thousand; by evening they had become violent. Official figures put the number of dead at 200, with hundreds more injured. News reports on state television showed footage of protesters beating and kicking people on the ground. Video shot by officials at the hospital the previous night showed patients with blood streaming down their heads. Two lay on the fruit barrow that friends had used to transport them. A four-year-old boy lay on a trolley, dazed by his head injury and his pregnant mother's disappearance. He had been clinging to her hand when a bullet hit her.

By the following morning the streets were under the tight control of thousands of riot officers and paramilitary police, who patrolled the main bazaar armed with batons, bamboo poles and slingshots. Burnt cars and shops still smouldered. The streets were marked with blood and broken glass and the occasional odd shoe. Mobile phone services were said to be blocked and internet connections cut.

There were two main explanations for what had caused these riots. On the one hand, a government statement described the protests as 'a pre-empted, organized violent crime' that had been 'instigated and directed from abroad, and carried out by outlaws in the country'. Xinhua, the Chinese state news agency, reported that the unrest 'was masterminded by the World Uighur Congress' led by Rebiya Kadeer, a Uighur businesswoman jailed in China before being released into exile in the US. Wang Lequan, then leader of the Xinjiang Communist Party, said that the incident revealed 'the violent and terrorist nature of the separatist World Uighur Congress'. He said it had been 'a profound lesson in blood'.

He went on to claim that the aim of the protests had been to cause as much destruction and chaos as possible. Although he mentioned a recent protest in the distant southern province of Guangdong, he dismissed this as a potential cause.

But according to the WUC, this incident was the real cause of the protest. They claimed that the clash in Guangdong province was sparked by a man who posted a message on a website claiming six Uighur boys had 'raped two innocent girls'. This false claim was said to have incited a crowd to murder several Uighur migrant workers at a factory in the area. Rebiya Kadeer claimed that the 'authorities' failure to take any meaningful action to punish the [Han] Chinese mob for the brutal murder of Uighurs' was the real cause of the protest.

The WUC's version of the events of 5 July was that several thousand Uighur youths, mostly university students, had peacefully gathered to express their unhappiness with the authorities' handling of the killings in Guangdong. They claimed that the police had responded with tear gas, automatic rifles and armoured vehicles. They alleged that during the crackdown some were shot or beaten to death by Chinese police or even crushed by armoured vehicles.

The WUC also reported widespread violence in the wake of the protests. Their website claimed that Chinese civilians, using clubs, bars, knives and machetes, were killing Uighurs throughout the province: 'they are storming the university dormitories, Uighur residential homes, workplaces and organizations, and massacring children, women and elderly'. They published a list of atrocities – 'a Uighur woman who was carrying a baby in her arms was mutilated along with her infant baby... over one thousand ethnic Han Chinese armed with knives and machetes marched into Xinjiang Medical University and engaged in a mass killing of the Uighurs... two Uighur female students were beheaded; their heads were placed on a stake on the middle of the street' – none of which could be confirmed. This post was later removed.

There is still much that is unclear about what actually happened during that violent week in July 2009. But however terrible its cost – whether it was a massacre of peaceful protestors, an orchestrated episode of violence, or something in between – it was not without precedent. In Xinjiang, there have been many protests which were either 'riots' or 'massacres', depending on who you believe. The largest of these took place on 5 February 1997, in the border town of Yining. This too was perhaps a protest, possibly a riot, maybe even a massacre. There were certainly shootings, injuries, and deaths.

As for what happened, and why, it was hard to say. At the time there was an immediate storm of conflicting accounts, of accusation and counter-claim. The only chance of learning what had happened was to actually go there. And so in 2001, I did. I got a job teaching English. I stayed for a year. I uncovered a story that is still happening now.

But all of this must wait a moment. First, you must arrive.

The Journey

YOUR TRAIN WAITS in Beijing West one thick September night. The air crowds close around, pressing on your head and chest, desperate to transfer a fraction of its heat.

It will be a long journey. Thankfully you'll be travelling in relative luxury: a padded compartment known as a 'soft sleeper'. You slide open its door and find the other three berths already occupied. You heave in your suitcases. You climb into bed. Beijing lapses into haze and you are far from here.

In the morning you wake to yellow valleys honeycombed with caves. Crops crowd the plateaus, anxious not to waste the space. It's a rehearsal for the desert and it is Shanxi. Or Shaanxi. But certainly not here.

You prowl the train in search of food. The restaurant car is full of people eating fatty meat. You find a seat opposite a middle-aged Han couple. The man is wearing a dark blue suit; the woman's pink sweater is embroidered with flowers in silver thread.

They ask where you're from and going. When you say 'England,' they smile. They frown when you say, 'Yining.'

'That is not a good place,' he says. 'It has a lot of trouble,' she adds.

'What kind of trouble?'

He shakes his head, mutters, looks out the window. Then your food arrives. You eat a plate of oily pork. You go back to bed.

When you wake the plain is a vast grey sheet stretched taut between the mountains. It is such a vacant space that every detail seems important: a man walking on his own, without a house or car in sight; ruined buildings; jutting graves; men in lumpen uniforms who salute the train.

Grey slowly shifts to black; sand firms into rock. Then, in place of monochrome, the space is bright with colour. Purple, yellow, red, and orange, mixed like melted ice cream.

Moving on and further westwards. The sun refuses shadow. You pull into the oasis of Turpan, a green island in a wilderness, its shores lapped by grit. You buy a bunch of grapes from a Uighur woman wearing a pink headscarf. They are almost too sweet.

Hours pass, you slip through mountains, speed through a tunnel of rock. You emerge onto to a plain of blades, white and turning, harvesting wind, chopping it into power.

Now, after 2,192km, you are getting close: this is Urumqi, the provincial capital of Xinjiang. From here it is only another 500km. But this is the end of the train.

During the trip your luggage must have bred with the other bags for now there are more than you can carry. It takes two trips to get your bags from the train, and after this, as you stand on the platform, you wonder what you are doing. Why have you come so far, on your own? What if something happens?

But there is no time for worry. You must move your bags. You grunt and heave, to no avail. They are just too heavy. Then you see a man in faded blue jacket and trousers, a flat cap perched on his head. He catches your eye and comes over. He says he will help.

Staggering through the streets, every building that you pass is either half-built or half-collapsed. Dirt is the principal colour. There is a street where the shops only sell engine parts and the pavement is stained with oil. The shops are cubes that flicker, fade, as men spark engine hearts.

You stop to rest. The sky is grey. Two boys approach with a bucket. In it, a kitten is curled.

'How much will you give me?' says one.

'I don't want it,' you say.

'You can't have it,' says the other, who swings the bucket and laughs.

Two more streets and you reach your hotel. The stone floor of the lobby is wet, as is the stairs, the corridors, where men wander in vests.

In your room the man names a price ten times too high. After you threaten to call the room attendant, he settles for five times too much.

The room has two beds. The other bed is occupied by an old Japanese man. He sits in bed reading a book of Go puzzles, smoking cheap cigarettes. His underpants hang on a line at head height. At night the breath whistles out of his mouth like the wind through a crack in a door.

Next morning you go to the bus station. They refuse to sell you a ticket because you don't have a work permit.

'We can't give you a ticket without it,' says a woman in a baggy black uniform.

'But I can't get the permit until I go there.'

'Not my problem.'

'How I am supposed to get there?'

'Don't know.'

'I'll report you.'

She shrugs. 'Go ahead.'

You raise your voice. You plead. You do not get a ticket.

After an hour of angry wandering you find a car willing to take you. You haggle, fix a price, then wait for two hours while the driver tries to find other passengers.

It is midday when you leave. For the first few hours the road is smooth motorway and all but deserted. Exhaustion segues to sleep; potholes bring you back. Straw-coloured hills rise on both sides, at first distant, then slowly converging, until they funnel the road. You wind between them, seeing only their slopes; then abruptly there is a vista. You are on the edge of a lake so blue and vast you cannot see its far shore. The road follows its edge, till mountains loom, and you begin a hairpin descent. The last of the light straggles into the valley below, lingering in jars of honey on shelves by the side of the road.

You assume the crash position as the car hurtles toward lorries. All you get are panic flashes of the countryside: cotton fields, sheep-speckled hills, tough-looking men on horses. It is three days since you left Beijing. You have the feeling that you are on the frontier of another land, that you have come to the end of China.

It is dark when you reach the teachers' college. A small woman you at first mistake for a child lets you into your flat. The strip light shows worn linoleum, concrete floors, a kitchen with a sink on bricks, no pots or any stove. There are no curtains. The toilet is a hole in the floor.

'What do you think?' she squeaks.

You look around, consider your verdict.

'Very nice,' you say.

Now, at last, you have arrived. Welcome to Yining.

I

THE FIRST THING you need to understand about Yining is that it is a border town; Kazakhstan is an hour away. This alone makes it important. Countries that can't maintain their borders don't stay countries for long.

Yining is located in the north-west corner of Xinjiang ('new land'), China's westernmost province. At 1,650,000km² (about the size of France, Germany and Italy put together), it is also its largest.

Xinjiang is defined by mountains: the Himalayas and Pamirs to the south, the Altai mountains to the north. The Tian Shan ('Heavenly Mountains') slice from west to east, chopping the province in two. And the mountains are not just border markers. The Himalayas and Pamirs steal the moisture from the tropical air that comes up from the Indian Ocean. Little rain falls on the south of the province; the result is the Taklamakan Desert, a vast area of sand and gravel that may contain more oil and gas than Saudi Arabia.

But the mountains are merciful: there's enough snow and glacier melt to irrigate a series of oases that stretch along the desert's edges. These are the towns of the Silk Routes, the old trade arteries between Europe and Asia.

The second thing you need to understand about Xinjiang is that many of its people aren't Chinese.

2

OF COURSE, IN ONE sense all the people in Xinjiang are Chinese. They are all part of the Chinese nation. So in what sense are many of them *not* Chinese?

The difficulty lies in the way that we use the term 'Chinese'. Usually, when we say a person is Chinese it means one of two things: their nationality or their ethnicity. It's easy to conflate the two because China has a clear majority ethnic group, the Han, who make up about 90 per cent of the population. Most of our knowledge about the culture of China – its food, films, art, traditions and language – relates to this group. So when we say that something or someone is Chinese, that thing or person is usually from China and of Han ethnicity. But in Xinjiang there are 12 other ethnic groups that together make up around half of the population; they are thus both Chinese and not Chinese.

The Uighurs (pronounced 'wee-gers') are the largest of these groups, after whom the province is named: officially, it is the Xinjiang Uighur Autonomous Region. The Uighurs are a Turkic people – they belong to the same group of peoples who began in Central Asia and eventually spread as far as Turkey. Uighurs speak a Turkic language (closely related to Uzbek) which is written using a modified Arabic script. The majority of Uighurs are Sunni Muslims, though there are considerable differences between religious practices in the north and south of the province, with the latter tending to be more orthodox.

The second-largest group are the Hui, who are also Sunni Muslims. The Hui are descended from Arab and Iranian merchants who came to China during the Tang Dynasty (618–907AD). Unlike the Uighurs, who are concentrated in Xinjiang, the Hui are distributed throughout the country; almost every major city in China has a Hui community. Unlike the Uighurs, the Hui no longer possess their own language and in appearance are often indistinguishable from the Han.

But despite the large numbers of Hui and Uighur in Xinjiang, Yining is primarily associated with neither. Yining is the capital of the Yili Kazakh Autonomous Region (another of those catchy titles the Chinese government excels at). Over a million Kazakhs live in the north-west of Xinjiang, many of whom are semi-nomadic herders. Kazakhs first came to the Yili valley in the 19th century, seeking refuge from Russian expansion.

Yining is thus the centre of a Kazakh region within a Uighur province of a (Han) Chinese country. I wish that I could say that all these different ethnic groups exist in joyous harmony. But there are problems, not least of which is history.

3

THE CHINESE GOVERNMENT'S position on the history of Xinjiang is admirably clear:

> One thing cannot be denied. Xinjiang has always been a part of China. Since the time of its origins, our great motherland has always been a multi-ethnic nation.

The position of some Uighur groups is similarly clear.

> *One thing cannot be denied. Xinjiang has never been a part of China. Only in recent years have we become a Chinese colony.*

Their different views of the events of 1949 – the year that the People's Republic of China was founded – are equally transparent.

> 1949 was the greatest year in our country's history. It was a year of hope and joy: a year of Liberation.

> *1949 was the worst year in our country's history. It was a year of death and fear: a year of occupation.*

As are their views on the relations between the different ethnic groups.

> Xinjiang is a good example of how the problems of a very different mix of ethnic groups have been solved. They have been united into one big family. The Han nationality has always kept a higher level of development, so many of the other peoples have learned a lot from the Han mode of production and way of life. The Han have selflessly regarded this kind of assistance as their responsibility. They are the big brother of the family. They have helped to develop a once backward region. Life today in Xinjiang is better than ever before!

> *The Han have been sucking our blood for decades. They only know how to take. Our oil, minerals and gas, our homes and our freedom. We are homeless in our homeland, we are orphans in our mother-*

land, we are slaves in our fatherland. Our people are starving in the worst conditions of human misery.

And on those who argue for Xinjiang's independence.

Although national and ethnic unity is the common wish and desire of every person in Xinjiang, we must also admit that ever since Liberation, a small number of separatists, backed by hostile foreign forces, have been determined to sabotage ethnic unity and the integrity of the motherland. These counter-revolutionary terrorists often cloak their separatist slogans in the guise of religion. But these people will never be allowed to break up our glorious motherland.

But we have never given up. An independence movement has existed since the first day of the Chinese occupation. The Uighurs will never stop struggling against the fascist Chinese regime. We will continue to resist this oppression. And one day we shall be free.

But this is not history. This is propaganda. On one side, the Chinese Communist Party; on the other, pro-independence Uighur groups. The latter argue that 'Xinjiang' (a label they reject) should instead be recognised as East Turkestan, a place that has always been the homeland of Uighurs and certainly separate from China. It is tempting to draw a parallel with Tibet; in both cases, the Han Chinese can be viewed as invaders.

However, even a brief study of Tibet's history suggests a more complicated relationship, one where the Han fade in and out, sometimes playing the aggressors, at other times, absent and fragmented neighbours, who were themselves invaded by the Tibetans on several occasions.

The history of Xinjiang is similarly complex. The idea of the region as a single unified area dates back no further than the middle of the 18th century. For most of its history, the region has not been united under any one authority.

There has certainly been a Han Chinese *presence* throughout much of the region's history. The first recorded contact was in the

1st century BC, when the Han emperor sent an envoy in the hope of uniting its tribes against the invading Huns. The Han court later established an administrative centre in Xinjiang between 73 and 97AD. Xinjiang remained under their control until the 5th century, when it was conquered by Turkic tribes. During the Tang Dynasty it was briefly recovered, but after the demise of the dynasty it remained out of Chinese control until 1750, when it was taken by the Qing (who were themselves invaders). It was they who renamed the region 'Xinjiang'. But their presence remained a marginal one, mostly confined to soldiers, officials and prisoners. Many Chinese were said to view the region as 'a kind of purgatory'.

The huge distances between Xinjiang and the centres of imperial power (before the introduction of motorised transport, it took over 100 days to get to Beijing) made it hard for the authorities to maintain control. A succession of riots and uprisings took place throughout the 19th and early 20th centuries, which led the region to acquire a reputation for being China's 'most rebellious territory'. Only since 1949 has the region been fully integrated into the rest of China.

So in the last 2,000 years Chinese control in Xinjiang has been more the exception than the rule: Xinjiang has not *always* been a part of China. But does that mean it has been a Uighur nation?

4

All historical rights are invalid against the rights of the stronger.
ALEXANDER TILLE, *Volksdienst*

IN 1981, A WOMAN'S BODY was found at Loulan, deep within the Taklamakan Desert. She had long golden hair, a European nose, and was very, very old. But the dry sands had treated her well; she scarcely looked her age. You wouldn't have taken her for more than 1,000, though in actual fact she was at least 3,000 years old, perhaps even 6,000.

They found other bodies, some with brown or reddish hair. Who these people were has been debated ever since; even their age is contested. At first, radiocarbon dating suggested they were over 6,000 years old but this finding is likely to have been contaminated by radiation from nuclear testing in the area. More conservative estimates place their age at approximately 3,000 years.

The question of these mummies' identity has become politicised. If they were Uighur (many of whom have light brown or, occasionally, reddish hair) it would provide strong support for the idea that Xinjiang was home to Uighurs long before the Han arrived. This has led to claims that Uighurs have a 6,000-year history in Xinjiang.

The problem with this is that the mummies are no closer to Turkic peoples than they are to Han Chinese. Elizabeth Barber, an expert on prehistoric textiles, argues that the bodies and facial forms associated with Turks and Mongols don't appear in the region until a thousand years after the mummies lived. According to her, the more likely explanation is that these people were originally migrants from central Europe. Any similarities between some Uighurs

and these mummies are thus probably a legacy of old intermar-
riages.

So this is one reason why Xinjiang has not been a purely Uighur
domain for all time. The other is that the earliest Uighur kingdom
was in Mongolia.

5

THE UIGHURS RULED most of Mongolia between 744 and 840AD. Most of the people followed Manichaeism, an early Christian sect based around the distinction between Light (representing the spirit) and Darkness (representing the flesh). Adherence to these beliefs is said to have transformed 'a country of barbarous customs, full of the fumes of blood, into a land where people live on vegetables; from a land of killing to a land where good deeds are fostered'.

One of these 'good deeds' was helping out the Tang, the Chinese rulers at the time, who were struggling with an internal revolt. The Uighur kingdom began to disintegrate at the start of the 9th century, due to war with the Kirghiz, who invaded in 840AD.

The Uighurs fled and established a new, predominantly Buddhist kingdom around the eastern oasis of Turpan, which endured until the Mongol invasion in the 13th century. During this period, the rest of the region was controlled by other Turkic peoples, most of whom were Muslim. At the time, the term 'Uighur' was used to denote someone who was *not* Muslim. After the majority of Uighurs had converted to Islam in the 15th century, the term fell out of usage. However, it was not so much a people who disappeared but an *identity*.

It was not until the 1920s (after Stalin started a craze for ethnic labelling) that the term came back into use. There is some debate over who first reintroduced the term, but it seems clear that by the start of the 1930s, 'Uighur' had acquired its current meaning: a Muslim oasis-dweller.

The term 'Uighur' has thus been used to define populations according to different ethnic and religious criteria. The present notion of 'Uighur' is thus as much a modern creation as 'Xinjiang' itself.

The messy truth appears to be that Xinjiang was little more a Uighur kingdom than a Chinese one. The history of the region is rather that of many different peoples, and shifting bases of power.

But in a sense, whether the Chinese government or Uighur nationalists are right isn't important. What matters is that both believe themselves to be. Thus we have two groups of mutually exclusive views, both laying claim to the same territory; both with too much invested in their particular historical narratives. Which brings us back to the riots.

6

THE FIRST AND greatest problem with the events of February 1997 is that most accounts are from people who weren't present, or from those who were but are far from impartial. Foreign reporters were denied permission to visit the area, and at the time official comment was limited to revealing statements such as, 'There was a protest. It was illegal. Illegal protests are curbed'.

Most foreign journalists chose to portray it as a political protest. An Associated Press report described the events as 'a Muslim march demanding independence'; Reuters described it as 'a separatist riot'; CNN called it a 'protest against Beijing rule'. But there were plenty of alternative explanations. The East Turkestan Information Centre (ETIC) described it as 'a peaceful demonstration demanding respect for human rights'. A number of official Chinese sources later claimed that it was nothing more than random violence, the work of drug addicts, thieves and other 'social garbage'.

Despite their differences, the various sources generally agree on the following: approximately 1,000 young Uighur men marched through the town shouting slogans. The marchers clashed with the police and there were numerous injuries and casualties. Afterwards there were multiple arrests and executions.

It is the details that are disputed. How many were killed? Estimates range from none to 1,000. Who started the violence? The police – who were accused of firing into the crowd – or the protesters? They were accused (as they would be 12 years later, in Urumqi) of looting and damaging property, of attacking Han Chinese.

The Xinjiang regional government claimed the protests had been orchestrated by 'hostile foreign forces' determined to overthrow the government (again, a claim that was repeated in July 2009). Some said the trouble started when police arrested some religious students; others that the protests were triggered by the executions of 30 Uighurs the previous week.

How many were arrested? 100? 500? 1,000? What happened to them? Were they displayed naked in city squares and publicly tortured, as was later claimed by some overseas Uighur groups?

These were the questions I hoped to answer.

Autumn

7

FOR ALL ITS REMOTENESS, Yining is a place that people have heard of. It has been in the *Lonely Planet* guide since the first edition.

> In Yining you won't know whether to laugh or cry. Nothing seems to work and half the population seems permanently drunk.

The guide had mellowed slightly by its fifth edition.

> Yining is a grubby place with a few remnants of fading Russian architecture.

Despite these ringing endorsements, there were already ten other foreigners in Yining when I arrived. Eleanor was the first I met. She was tall, friendly and from Derbyshire, and had already been teaching in the college for two years. She introduced me to some people.

* * *

The bus crawled down Liberation Road, stopping, starting, presenting tableaux: nicotine-coloured apartments; muffled road sweepers waking dust; a donkey pulling a cart of red apples; a crowd gathered round an argument, one man pointing at a crushed bicycle, another leaning against a taxi, slowly shaking his head.

We veered right at a roundabout topped by a stone eagle. A soldier stood outside a concrete gate, a rifle by his side. More turns later we arrived at the town square, which was paved in pink and white tiles.

Two Uighur men were waiting for us, one very tall, one short, both with thin moustaches. The smaller smiled, and said in English, 'Welcome to Ghulja. I'm Murat.'

'Does he mean Yining?' I whispered to Eleanor, but Murat nonetheless heard. He snorted. 'That's what the Chinese call it. We say 'Ghulja'. It means a wild male sheep.'

Ismail was the taller of the two. He and Murat ran an English course in a local school. We had lunch in a restaurant called King of Kebabs. A fat man sat outside threading lumps of meat onto skewers. A cauldron of rice and carrots steamed next to him. When he saw us he stood and boomed a greeting. He shook hands with Murat, Ismail and me, nodded to Eleanor.

Inside was dim and noisy with the sounds of eating. Ismail gestured for us to sit then said, 'This is a good place, very clean. You know, Uighur people are Muslims. We shouldn't smoke or drink. What would you like to eat? Have you had *polo*? It is traditional Uighur food.'

Polo turned out to be the rice and carrot dish I'd seen steaming outside. In addition, there were soft chunks of mutton and a tomato and onion salad dressed in dark vinegar.

'Is it good?'

'Very.'

Ismail grinned and said, 'You must stay for a long time!' After that we ate in silence until Murat said, 'Many Han people make a noise when they eat.'

Ismail chimed in, 'That's just them speaking!'

I kept eating, quietly, a little shocked by the vehemence of their dislike. It also surprised me that they were saying such things to someone they had only just met.

After lunch we strolled through the square. Huge propaganda posters towered overhead. A composite photo loomed above, showing three generations of Chinese leaders: Mao Zedong, Deng Xiaoping and Jiang Zemin (the then-current leader). Next to it was a 20-foot poster showing all 57 ethnic groups in China. They were smiling and wearing brightly coloured costumes. They seemed about to launch into song.

There was a sense of transition on crossing the square. The bright cubes of the Han shops, their handbags, shoes and machine parts, quickly faded into market stalls – to scarves, carpets, glassware, packs of henna, crystal sugar, dried grapes, black tea and other products more reminiscent of a Central Asian bazaar. Bare heads were replaced by a hundred hats, by homburgs, trilbies, flat caps, pork pies, baseball caps and most of all, a boxy, stiffened skullcap called a *doppa*.

Murat turned and whispered, 'Don't tell anyone, but I MUST go to the toilet.'

'OK. Isn't that one, over there?'

'Yes, but I must go home.'

As we watched him scamper off, Ismail cleared his throat.

'It takes him a long time. He has this problem. With his…'

He didn't know the word. Eventually we settled on 'kidney'. Eleanor chose this moment to mention that she thought our phones were bugged. She said that sometimes she heard noises from the other end, and that there had been some dubious coincidences, like going to make a complaint about something and finding that the person in question had already taken steps to nullify her criticisms. At the time I thought she was being paranoid. After a few weeks in Yining, I was not so sure.

When Murat returned he looked pleased with himself, as if he had performed some difficult task well. He suggested looking round the market. As we drew near the entrance – a large faux-Islamic gate – three men selling pictures of Mecca started shouting at us.

'What are they saying?'

Murat laughed. 'They are saying 'Hello Russians!'

There has been a long history of Russian involvement in Yining: Russia occupied the valley from 1871–81; after the 1917 Bolshevik Revolution, the Soviets were granted special trading rights in the area and had a consulate in the town. Following the Sino-Soviet pact of 1924, Russian involvement in the province increased to the point where 80 per cent of the region's trade was with Russia. Sheng Shicai – the warlord ruler of the province from 1934–44 –

relied heavily on Soviet military aid. Russia was forced to withdraw from the province in 1943, after Sheng Shicai shifted his allegiance to the Nationalists. Following their withdrawal, inflation rose and trade virtually stopped. But they were soon presented with an opportunity to re-establish their influence when a revolt broke out among the Kazakhs, who had been especially dependent on trade with Russia. Direct Soviet military aid on the side of the rebels led to the capture of Yining in 1944, and the founding of the East Turkestan Republic (ETR). The Russian presence in Yining remained strong until the Communists took power in 1949. Relations between Russia and China worsened throughout the 1950s, culminating in the Sino-Soviet rift of 1960 and the eradication of Soviet influence from the region.

Today there are few traces of the city's Russian past. Apart from the Russian consulate, which is now a restaurant, there are only a few scattered buildings, some within the teachers' college. Only a handful of Russians still live in the city, running a bakery that makes perfect cakes.

So given that most foreigners in Yining had previously been Russian, it was logical that Eleanor and I should be Russian too. I didn't mind; it made a change from everyone thinking I was American.

The market was dim and busy, full of rows of traders selling leather jackets, wraps and hats, *doppas*, stiff suits, thick jumpers, sensible shoes, armoured trench coats, various fur things. The traders whistled at me, trying to get my attention. Ismail and Murat shook hands with many of them. I asked how they knew them.

'Ismail and I used to do business. We used to sell leather.'

'Why did you stop?'

'Things are difficult now. Business is bad.'

Ismail sighed. 'Many people don't have jobs. Especially Uighur people. Maybe 80 per cent are unemployed now.'

'Why's that?'

Ismail looked at the floor while Murat said, 'In this city, there are some problems. Maybe you don't know. It is difficult.' He coughed then said, 'Please excuse us. We must go and pray.'

It was their third prayer of the day. Eleanor and I drifted round the back streets while they went to the mosque. A group of kids took time from booting a ball around to giggle at us; the braver ones ventured a hello. Two men sat playing chess, their stillness broken by sudden aggression as one slammed a bishop down. Peace returned, and then was broken. The sky showed no sign of being bored with blue.

8

NEXT MORNING THE telephone woke me.

'Hello, Nick?'

'Yes?'

'This is Miss Cai.'

Who?

'I am *waiban*.'

That at least I understood. The *waiban* ('foreign officer') is the person responsible for the safety and welfare of foreigners. I decided she must have been the child-like woman who let me into my flat when I arrived.

'Please come to my office now. I have something to tell you.'

'All right. Er, where's your office?'

'By the gate. On the second floor.'

I went out, got lost, asked for directions, was ignored, tried again, and was finally helped by a boy who took hold of my sleeve and did not let go till we were outside a long, two-storey Russian building. I went inside and climbed to the second floor, wandered down a hallway, tried several doors, till I was looking at a small woman in maroon who seemed to leap up when she saw me while still remaining seated.

'Nick! Hello! Come in! Come in!'

She could not have sounded more delighted: as if we were about to embark on some long-promised picnic.

She began by apologising for the state of my flat, saying that she had wanted to buy some cleaning things but had been unable to because the president of the college was having kidney stones removed. She paused, looked suitably grave; I dutifully asked how he was.

'Better! Much better! Now he can sign the purchase order.'

'That's good,' I said, and thought of asking for curtains, maybe even some bowls.

'And what about your health?' she said, in a tone of pure solicitude.

'Fine, thanks.'

'Good! And your family?'

'Very well.'

These pleasantries went on for a while. Not until things were utterly cosy did she get to her point.

'Nick, the president of our college has asked me to tell you some things. They are very important. As you know, Yining is a border town. This is a safe place, but you must still be careful. There are some bad people who want to cause trouble.'

'What kind of trouble?'

'Some people try to use religion as an excuse for crime. They want to separate from China. They are very bad.'

She frowned at their badness.

'So you must be careful. Your safety is important to us.'

'Thank you.'

'Of course! There are some other things. No one can stay in your house except you or a relative.'

'Why not?'

'It's against the rules. Also, you shouldn't stay out at night.'

'Why?'

'Sometimes there are bad people outside. Another thing is about religion. In our country, everyone has freedom of religious belief. But it is against our law to try to force others to believe something. Some foreigners came to China in the past to do this.'

'Don't worry, I don't believe in any religion.'

'Really?'

She looked sceptical.

'Not all foreigners believe in God.'

This was clearly news to her.

'You don't believe in anything?'

'Nothing.'

'Oh, well, good!'

She backtracked to disbelief.

'But *why* don't you believe?'

'I don't know. Maybe I believe in science instead.'

'Good, good! Oh, there's one more thing. You mustn't go over the bridge.'

'Which bridge?'

'The one over the Yili river.'

'Why not?'

'That's a different county. It's closed at the moment. You mustn't cross the river.'

9

THE SUN SHONE DOWN reprovingly as I cycled over the bridge. The river that ran beneath was swollen but indifferent. Only the mountains encouraged me; they spread their snowy arms. I felt the special joy that comes from breaking rules. I wasn't sure how far I'd get but this didn't matter since I had no idea where I was going.

The road was lined with silver poplars. I dragged the stick of my gaze along their trunks as I pedalled. Tree, tree, tree, what? Something tent-like, white and circular with a horse tethered outside. A yurt, perhaps.

Gradually the heat increased, and with it, a rich smell, as of spice but mixed with engine oil. I passed two other cyclists, their old frames festooned with honking geese, at least 20 on each bike. The cyclists were Uighur, which gave me a chance to practice the one word of their language I knew.

'*Yakshimsis*,' I said, and when they understood, and said hello back, I was unjustifiably smug.

Herds of sheep grazed next to streams; their minders slept or fished. I kept expecting to be stopped but no one seemed anything other than curious, not even the soldiers smoking in a copse of birch. I stopped to watch two Uighur kids trying to catch fish in a leaky jam jar. I popped my gum out, stuck it over the hole, and then we all grinned.

'Where are you from?' said one of the kids in Chinese; he was wearing a blue baseball cap. When I told him, he started laughing uncontrollably. His friend did not laugh and in fact looked very serious. 'There are many wolves,' he said, and refused to believe otherwise.

I cycled on till I was almost killed by a wire strung across the road at head height. Ten feet further on the road was just rough stones. I took the hint and turned onto a small track. The fields were midway through harvest, their contents still their own. Fodder, wheat, and corn were stacked in mounds awaiting transport. I stopped to take a photo of a row of red chillies hanging out to dry.

A family sat in the next field, cooking on a fire. They laughed to see me take a picture of something so ordinary; then they called me over. Three generations were present: several matrons in their 40s; two young girls scampering round; a septuagenarian matriarch. The girls giggled when I said hello, then were hushed by their grandmother. She offered me a seat in their shelter, a three-sided structure made from lashed branches with a rush roof and dirt floor. Most of the space was taken up by a large bed of rugs laid upon thick planks. A shelf ran along two of the walls. On it there were some bowls, a toothbrush, a pile of chopsticks, some string, a chopper, and a very large bag of white powder.

I didn't think they were Uighur, and they certainly weren't Han or Hui. I tried the only other option that I knew.

'Are you Kazakh?' I asked in Chinese.

One of the girls replied, 'No, we're Xibo.'

'Xibo?'

'Yes, there aren't many of us. Most are in Heilongjiang.'

Heilongjiang is a province in the far north-east of China. How did the Xibo end up on the other side of the country?

In some ways the story is similar to that of the Han Chinese in the 1950s, only bloodier. At the start of the 18th century, the Qing government (who were ethnically Manchu, not Han) were in the process of conquering the area, in one sense 'making' Xinjiang. Their campaign was halted in the northern part of Xinjiang (what is sometimes referred to as Jungaria, an area that also incorporates western Mongolia and eastern Kazakhstan) by the Junggar Mongols, who inflicted a major defeat on them. This major loss of face and life prompted Emperor Kangxi to dispatch Zuo Zongtang, one of his best generals. He adopted a slow but sure approach: his soldiers planted crops, waited to harvest them and then moved on, thus ensuring the health of the troops. It took them three years to reach the Junggar plateau, whereupon they exterminated the Junggar Mongols. Afterwards the region was so depopulated that the Emperor had to send 1,000 Xibo officers and soldiers, who took along more than twice that number of family members. The Xibo, along with the remnants of the Manchu army, can be credited with making the area fit for cultivation, mainly through the development and use of irrigation. Today, there are around 35,000 Xibo in the area, most of whom work in agriculture. The other noteworthy thing about the Xibo is that they use the Manchu written script, which is written vertically (unlike modern Chinese), looks like a comb with fluffy teeth, and is still used on street signs in the area.

The sun climbed to its zenith as we sat and chatted. When I stood up to leave, they told me to sit down: lunch was almost ready. I sat and watched the women shred a pile of peppers, tomatoes and chillies to go with a tower of nan bread. Men emerged from the surrounding fields; by the time we ate we were 12.

The salad was moist and delicious, if a little salty. One of the older women asked if the food was all right.

'It's great.'

'Don't be so polite! There's not enough salt.'

She scattered some over the vegetables. For a few minutes we ate in silence. Then one of the men said, 'It needs a little more.'

There were grunts of approval as he threw a handful on. My kidneys began to whine. Hope appeared in the form of steaming tea, poured into bowls with milk. A tub of white powder was passed to me. Taking it for sugar, I put a large pinch in, then drank. Salt. It was salt. My kidneys gave up.

The Xibo's liberal use of salt allows them to consume more of staple foods such as rice or bread, which helps when there isn't much else to eat. Unsurprisingly there is a high incidence of heart disease and kidney failure among the Xibo.

By now I was gasping. I made my excuses and took a photo of

the family that I promised to send. There was some discussion about whether they should write their address in Chinese or Xibo; they eventually agreed on both.

I shook the men's hands, thanked the women, pedalled towards water.

10

BEFORE I WENT TO Yining, I taught in a college in Hunan, a province in southern China. Hunan is quintessential rice-field China: a wet expanse of squares that flash a brilliant green in spring. When one of my students heard I was leaving he said, 'How wonderful! Xinjiang is a good place. You know, our government wants to develop the west. It is a necessary.'

I corrected his grammar, then asked why.

'Because Xinjiang is so... backward. It is very poor. It–'

He was interrupted by another boy. 'Yes, but the Xinjiang girl is very beautiful! And the people there are very good at dancing and singing.'

I asked if they had ever been.

'No, but I want to,' said the first.

'And I've seen it on TV,' said the other.

Most expressed similar sentiments on hearing I was going to Xinjiang. No one I knew had ever been which didn't stop the refrain of 'singing/dancing/beautiful'. It was a crude stereotype but one for which I couldn't blame them. Their newspapers and magazines were full of smiling, dancing, singing Uighurs in shiny, happy costumes, the girls all slight and coy, the men silent and strong. There was nothing to compete with these images: Xinjiang was a three-day train ride away and there were no Uighurs in town. I comforted myself with the thought that at least my students in Yining would be better informed.

11

Xinjiang is famous for her delightful scenes: bright lakes, sweet melons and most of all the Uighurs Dance. The Uighurs are an ethnic group who are good at singing and dancing. It's their practice to sing and dance in gala dress when they meet new friends. The Uighurs Dance is a symbol of their colourful life.

Yang Haimei

THIS GIRL HAD BEEN living in Yining for three years when she wrote this. She, like the majority of my students, was 20, female and Han. Most of them came from new towns in the north of Xinjiang, places like Shihezi, Kuytun and Karamai.

Before 1949, there were around 20,000 Han in the region, less than five per cent of the population. The succeeding years witnessed a demographic explosion as the government encouraged Han from the more populated provinces to resettle in the region. Today there are said to be about six million Han in Xinjiang, about 45 per cent of the population (though these figures are most likely an under-estimate, as the government probably doesn't wish to publicise the scale of Han immigration).

At least a third of these are part of the Xinjiang Production & Construction Corps (XPCC). The XPCC was created in the early 1950s as a way to utilise soldiers from the surrendered Nationalist army. Between 1952 and 1954, 170,000 soldiers were ordered to retire from the People's Liberation Army and then incorporated into the newly founded XPCC. By 1961, a third of the region's arable land was being cultivated on state farms. From 1963 to 1966, 100,000 people were sent from Shanghai alone. Since then successive waves of migration have swelled the ranks of the XPCC, which today stands at around 2.5 million.

The XPCC is a unique institution in China, in that it is administered independently from the Xinjiang provincial government. It has its own police force, courts, agricultural and industrial enterprises, as well as its own large network of labour camps and prisons. Its main unit of production is the state farm or *bingtuan*. The *bingtuans* have had the dual function of developing the region's economy and in quelling unrest; in one of its marching songs the XPCC describes itself as 'an army with no uniforms'.

It is not just the agricultural population that has swelled; the urban population has also increased rapidly in the last few decades: Kuytun grew from a small village to a city of 50,000 by 1985; Urumqi went from 80,000 in 1949 to 850,000 in 1981. In many of these newer northern cities, the Han Chinese became the majority, often living in separate, ethnically defined communities.

So in one way it wasn't surprising that many of my Han students knew little more about Uighurs than their Hunanese counterparts. They had grown up in places that were predominantly Han. But Yining was different. In 2001, the Kazakhs and Uighurs still outnumbered the Han. But after three years in this mixed environment, my Han students had progressed no further than the 'singing/ dancing' stereotype.

It was puzzling, as was the fact that of the roughly 200 students in the English department, all but ten were Han. When I asked other teachers why there were so few Uighur or Kazakh students, I was told that Uighur and Kazakh students weren't interested in learning English. At the time this seemed a little strange, as the Uighur and Kazakh students seemed interested in all the other subjects. But several things prevented me from dwelling on these questions. The state of my flat was one – I still had no stove, curtains or pans. Another was all the strange people I was meeting.

12

OF ALL THE PEOPLE I met in China, both in Hunan and Xinjiang, the oddest were invariably the other foreigners. Whether their eccentricity had pre-dated China, or was something they had developed post-arrival was impossible to say. At first I wasn't too keen on having other foreigners around; it seemed too easy for us to slip into some cosy expat clique. And when I heard there would be ten of them in Yining, I had second thoughts about going. But I shouldn't have worried: it proved easy to muster a clinical interest in them.

I was about to go to bed when there was a knock at the door. I opened the door and a man strode in, tall with brown hair, wearing a check shirt. His left arm was in a sling.

'Did you get the bus?' he said, in transatlantic tones.

'No, I had to get a car. They wouldn't sell me a ticket.'

He raised his good arm then brought his hand down on his knee. 'It's racism,' he said. 'They say it's against the rules, but really they don't know. They're not sure, but rather than check, they just say no. It's everything that's wrong with this place.'

He sighed, looked doleful, quickly brightened. 'So how long did the car take?'

'Seven hours, I think.'

'Wow, that's fast. Six and a half is the record.'

I still had no idea who he was. I asked about his arm.

'I came off my bike in Urumqi. A car pulled out in front of me, I braked sharply then went right over the handlebars, hit the ground and actually heard my shoulder crack.'

His name was Gabe. He had come to Yining to learn Uighur, and had already been there several years. Apart from him, there

THE TREE THAT BLEEDS

were four other foreign students – Brad, Jamie, Lisa and Michelle – all of whom were young Americans.

There was only one other foreign teacher, an English man named Colin who came round shortly after Gabe. We shook hands then he said,

'I thought you'd be taller!'

'Sorry about that!' I said. He qualified as 'short'.

'No, don't worry, just kidding, mate!'

'So, do you also teach here?'

'Yeah, we've been here since '98.'

'We...?'

He pushed his glasses up with his finger, then said, 'My family's here. Susan, Sarah and Adam. Sarah's four, Adam's nearly eight. Got any kids yourself?'

'No.'

'Hey, don't worry,' he said, and brought his hand up towards my shoulder, as if he meant to give me a consoling pat. 'There's plenty of time.'

I made a noncommittal sound.

'Just kidding!' he said. 'Anyway, it's time for Adam's bath. Why don't you come round for a coffee tomorrow? But you might be busy, so hey, no pressure.'

When I said I'd try, he said, 'That would be great.' Then he backed away, and didn't turn for a few moments, as if he was going to say something more. But all he did was smile.

13

ALL MY STUDENTS KEPT a diary in English because a) it was good for their writing and b) it allowed me to peek into their lives. This was a day in the life of Huang Li, a third-year student.

> When I got up I was still tired. But I had to go exercise or pay a fine. I joined the others in the playground and we exercise. Then I went to canteen and ate breakfast. I had to run classroom as I was nearly late. This morning we had four hours class: Russian and Translation. I like learning Russian but it is difficult for me. Translation is boring. I hate Mr Liang. He keep us for extra five minutes so that when we went to lunch canteen was full.
>
> This afternoon we had the physical education. The teacher told us we would have an exam for high jump next week and that we must practice. I am worried about this as I am short girl. After dinner I had to go to meeting. The speaker spoke for a long time about the importance of national unity. Afterwards I went to classroom and study until 11. We hate it but we can do nothing.

Wake, exercise, eat, class, eat, class, eat, class, sleep; always in the presence of others. On any given day, the students had no more than between one and two hours' free time. The question was why.

In Hunan the crushing routine and numerous political activities had seemed an attempt to ensure the students were too busy to start trouble. Yining Teachers' College looked to be more of the same, albeit stricter. There were more political meetings, more performances to prepare for, more compulsory study sessions. I figured it was just border-town paranoia.

The patterns of institutions are easily apparent. You learn the rules then cease to think about them; it is simply how things are. It took me several weeks to notice that there was another dynamic at work, a further set of sub-routines to life in the college.

* * *

The lunchtime bell had rung. A wave of students was already sweeping down the path, chatting, laughing, all intent on food. I was standing on the corner, waiting for Eleanor. The crowd came to the crossroads and spilt. One half carried on towards the canteen; the other half wheeled right. The Han students carried on. The Uighurs and Kazakhs turned right. I stopped one of my Han students and asked where the latter were going.

'To have their lunch.'

'Where?'

'In their canteen.'

'They have their own canteen?'

'Of course.'

It wasn't as strange as it sounded. As Muslims, Uighurs and Kazakhs don't eat pork, whereas Han Chinese do. Most Muslims would refuse to eat in a restaurant that served pork, hence the need for a separate dining hall. It was a piece of segregation that was clearly justified. But afterwards I started noticing other ways in which the students were divided. There were Uighur and Kazakh dormitories; there were Han dormitories. There were Uighur and Kazakh classes; there were Han classes (and for English, a whole department). This was by no means absolute: some courses were mixed, such as computing or politics, but generally, the different ethnic groups were separated.

The division was even stronger in the social sphere. The Han and Uighur students didn't talk to each other or play sport together. They certainly did not date.

But despite this separation, there was little visible rancour. It was more like they were trying to pretend each other did not exist.

14

MURAT WAS ALMOST two hours late. I sat on my sofa fuming. He and Ismail had agreed to come round to teach me some Uighur. When Ismail arrived at ten past two, he seemed cheerful, pleased to see me, certainly not sorry.

'How are you Nick?'

'Fine.'

'What have you been doing?'

'Not much. Just sitting here. Where's Murat?'

'Oh, he said he might be late. He has some things to do.'

I fought the urge to erupt.

'Ismail, do you have a watch?'

'Yes, I have one.'

'What time is it?'

'Twelve o'clock.'

'Are you sure?'

'Yes, look.'

The little hand was on the 12.

'I think your watch is wrong.'

'Really?'

'Yes. Mine says two o'clock.'

'That's Beijing time.'

'What?'

'Beijing time is two hours ahead of Xinjiang time.'

'Oh.'

'Uighurs use Xinjiang time. Chinese people use Beijing time. Twelve o'clock Xinjiang time is two o'clock Beijing time.'

I had forgotten about Xinjiang time. The college ran on Beijing time, so I had set my clocks accordingly. My first lesson was at ten o'clock, Beijing time, which was psychologically preferable to eight o'clock, Xinjiang time. I knew that Xinjiang time was correct, just from the time the sun rose. But Beijing time provided me with the illusion of a lie-in. And yes, it was confusing.

It illustrated how far the Chinese government was willing to go to make a point. To encourage the use of Xinjiang time would be to admit that the place was different to the rest of China. It represented yet another way in which the people of Yining were divided, not just spatially but temporally as well.

Murat announced himself with a cough. He apologised for being late and we got on with our lesson. After an hour my throat was feeling mangled, but I had learnt some conversational pleasantries, plus a couple of Arabic letters. I couldn't remember how to thank them in Uighur, and didn't want to use English, so I used Chinese.

'*Xiexie ni laoshi*!'

Ismail looked pained; Murat said imploringly,

'Please don't speak Chinese. You don't need to with us. Now, Nick, do you have something to do?'

Murat and Ismail held an English Corner every Sunday, where their students could practice their speaking skills. Murat was always keen for me to come, as it encouraged people to attend (though my presence often made some of the students too shy to speak). His students were young to middle-aged men and women; all of them were Uighur. On my first visit one of the more confident students, a young man with a wispy moustache, chose to risk a question.

'What's your impression of Uighur people?'

I said that the people I had met were very nice.

'What about Chinese people? Do you think they're ugly?'

There was general laughter, which was fortunate as it gave me time to both be shocked *and* formulate a reply.

'Maybe some, but then that's true of all people.'

He shook his head, refusing the platitude.

'Chinese people have such small noses. They look like pigs.'

There were laughs and nods. I looked to Murat and Ismail, but they did not seem bothered that such things were being said by their students. Then a thin man with thick eyebrows mercifully changed the subject.

'Do you like football, I do, I like the Brazil team, there's Ronaldo, Rivaldo...'

He rattled off the rest of the squad. I asked him his name.

'I am Tilawaldi. I work in an office, an office of the government, I am busy, so busy and every morning I have to listen to such rubbish, rubbish about the Communist Party and you know President Jiang Zemin, I don't like it, I am so busy, and it is just rubbish, why must they waste our time, they know it is rubbish too...'

He continued in this exhausting vein for another minute, after which I turned to two young women sat next to us, who had remained silent. When I asked them their names, they giggled in reply. After several more questions, and giggles, Tilawaldi undertook to act as go-between. It emerged, between giggles, that they worked in the same office. Both wore identical green sweaters and said they loved Tom Cruise. One was learning English so she could go to America for an operation. I could see ghost marks of stitches under her tights, running down her entire leg.

On the way out I walked next to the young man who admired the Chinese (and their noses) so much. He introduced himself as Erkin, said he was glad to meet me, then asked if I knew about the '97 troubles.

I said I'd heard of them.

'Some people fought with the government.'

'A lot of people?'

'A lot.'

'Did many people support them?'

'Some did, some didn't. It's a big problem.'

I wondered what he was referring to: the fighting or the lack of support for it? Just before we parted, he smiled and said, 'Come to my wedding next week.'

15

A small number of criminals had caused some criminal activities contrary to the national law by beating, rioting and looting. These activities damaged the social stability. To protect the national law, national wealth and people's lives and safety, the law enforcement agencies had to stop these criminal acts with legal procedures.

TANG GUO QIANG, Foreign Ministry

WHAT WERE THESE 'legal procedures'? What happened after the riots?

During the following weeks a full-scale curfew was imposed in Yining and Urumqi. Paramilitary (i.e. from the XPCC) and army soldiers patrolled the streets. Extensive house-to-house searches were reported, plus large-scale arbitrary arrests. According to Amnesty International, between 3,000 and 5,000 people were detained. The prison facilities of the *bingtuan*'s fourth Division, located in Yining, were used to detain protesters, while the remainder were taken to jails outside the city. Many were held without charge for weeks, even months. There were allegations of torture.

The contributions of the XPCC did not escape praise. According to Wang Lequan, 'In recent years, the corps' armed police units have been playing an important role in safeguarding Xinjiang's political stability and unity'.

Meanwhile Deng Xiaoping – who re-opened China to the rest of the world in the 1970s and sent the tanks into Tiananmen Square – was dying in Beijing. Six days of mourning followed. His funeral was held on 25 February 1997. The occasion was marked by wreaths, tributes, very long speeches, and bombs that exploded on three buses in Urumqi. Seven died and 67 were injured. Sirens sounded throughout the city and armed police were posted at bus stops.

When another bomb exploded in Beijing, Uighur dissidents based in Turkey claimed responsibility for the attack. They described it as retaliation against China's 'suppression of pro-independence activism' in Xinjiang and the government's 'refusal to seek compromise through dialogue'. In the wake of the bombing, security precautions throughout Beijing were intensified, with some measures directed at Uighurs. Some Uighurs I spoke to said that taxi drivers had refused to pick them up, and that they had been turned away from many hotels.

Unsurprisingly, these events attracted substantial media attention. In April 1997 the BBC managed to sneak some journalists into Yining. After two days of filming and interviews they were arrested and had their footage confiscated. According to the *Daily Telegraph*, the crew were held for ten days, then expelled to Pakistan. Further arrests were made amongst those interviewed.

The trials of those arrested after the riots began in mid-April. A rally attended by about 5,000 people was held in Yining city stadium, in order to pronounce sentence against 30 Uighurs who were said to have taken part in the protests. Three men were sentenced to death on charges of 'causing injury, arson, hooliganism, smashing property and looting'. They were executed after the rally at an execution ground on the outskirts of the city. According to the World Uighur Congress, their bodies were not given back to their families.

Afterwards, the 27 prisoners who had received prison sentences were driven through the city streets in a convoy of open trucks and buses. While the convoy drove through the streets, a crowd of mostly relatives and friends approached the trucks, either to speak to the prisoners, or perhaps to try and rescue them. The police escort opened fire, reportedly killing three people and injuring ten others. One report in the *Yili Evening News* of 1 May 1997 described the civilians as 'rioters', and said that two had been killed and seven injured. The report also claimed that the armed police had first fired warning shots into the air.

There were more arrests. On the 22 May, the *Yili Evening News* reported that police raids had been carried out in the area. As part of a 'strike hard' action, 61 trucks carrying 248 police officers had been sent to arrest 'violent criminals, terrorists and main religious leaders'. As a result, 84 suspects were arrested.

By June, the authorities had begun to explicitly link separatist activities with religion. The *Xinjiang Daily* reported that a crackdown on underground religious activities had resulted in an official banning of the construction or renovation of 133 mosques. Altogether 44 'core participants in illegal religious activities' were said to have been arrested in the region. In addition, the authorities claimed they had broken up more than 100 illegal classes teaching the Qur'an. The report boasted that 'illegal religious activities were cleaned up... district by district, village by village, and hamlet by hamlet'. In July, Amudun Niyaz, chairman of the Xinjiang People's Congress, publicly called for the 'waging of a people's war against separatists and illegal religious activities'. However, he was careful to add:

> Our struggle against national separatists is neither an ethnic nor a religious problem. It is a political struggle between those who safeguard the motherland's unification and security and those who split the motherland.

Throughout June and July, and well into 1998 and 1999, the executions continued. Another sentencing rally was held in Yining, this time televised. The prisoners were shown standing in military trucks, heads bowed, hands tied behind their back, wearing placards with their names and crimes. They were subsequently paraded through the city streets. In April 1999, Amnesty International reported that there had been almost 200 executions in the region since the protests.

But eventually, slowly, awfully, things began to settle. The government's attention shifted to the Falun Gong (who didn't even merit the label 'religion'; they were described as 'an evil cult'). At times, the governmental rhetoric sounded oddly tolerant.

> We have to take the endurance of the various ethnic groups into consideration. We [the Party] should respect the language as well as the customs and habits of different ethnic groups.

On 1 September 2001, Wang Lequan made the confident assertion that 'Xinjiang is not a place of terror' and was by no means 'a place where violence and terrorist accidents take place very often'.

Then two planes crashed into the World Trade Centre.

16

A precise assessment of the human rights situation in Xinjiang is complicated by the fact that some sectors of the Uighur pro-separatist movement... have not infrequently resorted to violent means in pursuit of national independence. In such a context, the Chinese government clearly has legitimate security concerns in the region.

Human Rights Watch

APART FROM SHOCK and surprise, there were basically three types of reaction to 9/11 from my Han students:

> I think it is the worstest thing. I felt so sad when I heard about all those people killed. I wanted to cry, really.

> When I heard the news I was very happy because for a long time America attacked other countries and told them what to do. They think they are big dogs world policemen but not now.

> At first I was glad because America is a bully but later I felt sorry for all the innocent people that die in the big accident.

The Chinese government wisely chose the first response and pledged support for the air strikes in Afghanistan. In the past China had been generally unsupportive of foreign involvement (e.g. in Iraq and Yugoslavia), either from fear of intervention in Taiwan or Tibet, or because it wished to show support for other repressive regimes it had 'bilateral ties' with. What made the war on terror different?

Bush's you're-with-us-or-against-us rhetoric was obviously important. However, of greater utility to the authorities was the fact that anything that could be labelled as 'terrorism' – international or domestic – was now an acceptable target. Someone must have suddenly remembered all the 'terrorism' that wasn't happening because in October 2001 officials began talking about close ties between Xinjiang separatists and international terrorist forces, in effect suggesting that 'separatism' and 'terrorism' were equivalent.

The arrests resumed. At least seven Uighurs were executed for 'disrupting social order' in the week leading up to the country's 1 October holiday. The *China News Service* reported that police in Urumqi had begun a 'campaign to clear up cases'. Its aim, according to Du Jianxi, Urumqi's Public Security Bureau chief, was to maintain 'public order and stability during the winter and next spring by smashing the bloated pride of violent terrorists'. *Xinjiang Daily* later reported that 166 'violent terrorists' and 'other criminals' had been arrested between 20 September and 30 November. The *World Uighur News Network* put the number detained as high as 3,000.

At the time I had little idea this was going on. I had only been in Yining a few weeks, and after 11 September, was still caught in quadruple take. But a number of things made me realise that the political climate had changed.

The first was when Gabe, Colin and I were summoned to a meeting with the president of the college. Miss Cai wouldn't say what it was about, only that it was 'very important.' We waited in a room with throne-like chairs. When the president entered, we stood. He asked us to sit then informed us that, 'Yining is a border town with many different ethnic groups. You must be careful.' He told us to be alert as there were 'a small minority of separatists' who wished to cause trouble, and that we must not connect with such people, 'nor believe their claims to represent any nationality or religion'. He finished by telling us not to stay out after 11.30pm (Beijing time), in the interests of our safety. As a final flourish, he added that there might be a few Taliban around, and that we were prime targets for kidnapping.

He waited to be thanked for his concern, which Colin and Gabe duly did, then swept regally out.

I didn't take any of this seriously. All I could think of was my upcoming trip, a full week in stone's-throw-away Kazakhstan.

17

FOREIGN RESIDENTS CAN leave China at any time. But to come back you must have a re-entry visa in your passport, otherwise your work permit will be confiscated. Getting one of these isn't difficult: a few forms, a photo, some money and one is quickly yours. But in Yining nothing was simple. There were rules that had nothing to do with the law. Crossing the bridge was one. I later discovered that there was no such 'law' and that the area was not closed: the college simply did not wish me to stray too far.

The re-entry visa was a similar case. I was told I needed the college's permission to even apply for one. First I had to ask Miss Cai, who asked me a number of suspicious questions ('Why do you want to go?', 'What will you do?', 'Who are you going to visit?'). She then agreed to ask the president, who considered it for a week, then said yes, authorising Miss Cai to write a letter to the police giving me permission. I duly went to the police station with letter, forms and photo, explained what I wanted, smiled sweetly, handed over my passport, smiled some more and was told to come back next day. This was a great relief: I had spent a lot of time and money getting the Kazakhstan visa in London. It was only valid for the next two weeks. After this time it would just be pretty paper in my passport.

Next day I was there before the police station opened. The officers stood in rows like children in assembly, some in uniform, some not. A fat man barked the register. I waited patiently. Ten minutes later, when I went in, I was told that my visa wasn't ready.

'What about tomorrow?'

'Maybe.'

Next morning when I went to the police station, I was met by Miss Cai. She grasped my arm and steered me out. Before I knew what was happening we were in a car, moving away from the police station, which still had my passport.

'What's happening? Why can't I have the visa?'

'The situation has changed. We don't think it is safe for you to go.'

'Do you know something I don't? There's no trouble in Kazakhstan.'

Her head flew to one side, her eyebrows raised, her mouth formed a circle.

'No, we do not think it's safe. You must listen to us. We care about your safety. You can go another time.'

I tried to explain that my visa was only valid for this particular week. Miss Cai looked bewildered, then went to ask the president. Half an hour she returned to say that they hadn't been able to get in touch 'with the officer in charge of the case'.

'What do you mean? Is it the college or the police that is stopping me?'

'We're not stopping you. We just suggest that you don't go.'

A petulant outburst ensued.

'SUGGEST? You have STOPPED me from going. I don't care about your suggestions. I want to go and you have STOPPED me. Now, I want two things from you. I want you to provide me with written documentation of the fact that you have stopped me with your reason for doing so. AND I want my passport back. TODAY.'

Despite all their talk of 'concern for my safety', I doubt they were truly bothered. They were just scared of being held responsible, in the unlikely event that I was killed or maimed or kidnapped by one of their imaginary Taliban. It was possible they knew about risks that I did not, but more probable that they were simply paranoid.

When I got my passport back the next day, inside was a crisp re-entry visa, with a cancelled stamp on it. I briefly knew what it felt like to be part of a system with no right of appeal. It made me angry and frustrated. I couldn't begin to guess what it must be like to wake up every day and feel this way. It could make a person angry enough to do something desperate.

18

AUTUMN IS THE ONLY good time to marry in Yining. Winter and summer are too cold or hot; spring is far too wet. But autumn is clear and mild: the sky is an unbroken azure. Cupboards are opened, bedding is beaten. Sheep and horses fatten.

I was flattered that Erkin had invited me to his wedding after just meeting me. He told me to meet him outside a bakery on Liberation Road at 2pm Xinjiang time. When I arrived, I saw Ismail, Murat and six other men waiting, all wearing dark suits with red carnations in their buttonholes. I thought I recognised Erkin among them, and went up to him.

'Hi, this must be a very happy day for you!'

He smiled and looked confused. A voice behind me said,

'Yes, Ali is happy to be best man. But I'm even happier.'

I turned round. It was Erkin. I laughed nervously then asked what time the ceremony would start.

'We've already had it. I am now married!'

The ceremony had taken place that morning at the home of the bride. In most Uighur weddings the bride is absent during the actual ceremony. The bride gives her consent to the marriage beforehand at a private meeting with the *imam* and a witness. During the ceremony only the *imam*, groom, best man and a small number of friends are present. I told Ali, the man I had mistaken for Erkin, that I couldn't imagine many women I knew in Britain agreeing to this.

'It is our tradition. We are Muslims. Although, there are some people in Turpan who don't do this. Sometimes there the woman is also present.'

'Are they Uighur?'

'Yes, but they are not good Muslims.'

This would not be the last time that I heard someone speak disparagingly of Uighurs in other cities. Peter Fleming, writing in the 1930s, argued that these divisions were due to the vast tracts of desert separating the different oases, which 'impose on their inhabitants a parochial and disunited outlook. There really has been no need for the Chinese to put their immemorial colonial policy of *Divide et impera* into practice; nature has done it for them'.

Ali wasn't finished with the bad Muslims of Turpan.

'When a person from Ghulja goes to Turpan, the Turpan people will try and cheat them. If a Turpan person comes here, we won't do this, only tease them a little.'

'How do people know where someone is from?'

'By the way they speak, and sometimes by their *doppa*.'

Some of the towns in Xinjiang have different *doppas*. In Yining, many wear a round red one, in Kashgar, a square green one, and in Hotan, a black one with white embroidery. However, there is nothing to stop someone from Yining wearing a Kashgar *doppa* if they think it looks nice.

Ali asked if I liked Ghulja. I said I preferred it to Hunan and was halfway through the why when he interjected, 'Because there are less Chinese!' I wondered if there were any Uighurs who didn't hate the Han.

A fleet of black cars arrived, each covered in ribbons, bows and plastic bouquets. Ali asserted himself as best man by complaining over the car decorations. He busied himself with the arrangements, trimming ribbons and straightening carnations, fussing like a hairdresser. After ten minutes he announced that we could proceed. Erkin and Ali got in the first car; Ismail, Murat and I followed in the car behind. Seven other cars formed the rest of our convoy.

We made a circuit of the city, each car hooting its horn. We finished at the bridge, where several other wedding parties were already posing for pictures. The photographer was having problems due to the amount of traffic passing over the bridge. No sooner had he got 30 people all looking the same way and smiling, than a juggernaut thundered past. And it wasn't just lorries, but cars, buses, flocks of sheep being driven home from the fields. In the end the photographer had to stand in the middle of the road to get the traffic to stop.

We stood waiting for a space upon the bridge, the thick light of late afternoon pooling on our faces. Murat pointed at the nearest wedding group to us, whose women were wearing very pretty white dresses.

'I hate them,' he said.

'Who?'

'Those people. The ones wearing the dresses. It is not our traditional dress. They should preserve Uighur custom.'

'What about driving round in cars? Is that a traditional custom?'

He thought for a moment, then said, 'This is the 21st century. It is a modern age, there is new technology. We should accept *some* changes. The ones that are good.'

Eventually, the bridge was free. Erkin's wife and her brides-maids arrived, veiled and wearing red- and yellow-striped dresses. We stood and let the camera click until the light had gone. Then we got back in the cars and drove to Erkin's new house, which he (with help from Murat, Ali and Ismail) had only finished decorating the day before. Most of the wedding receptions I went to later were held in restaurants, a far more costly option. This is a fairly modern practice, perhaps attributable to the influence of the Han, for whom the custom has a longer history. For Murat and his circle, this was definitely not an option.

We had problems finding Erkin's house, and so it was dark by the time we arrived. His 'house' was actually three buildings arranged around a courtyard; a wall with a large wooden gate completed the square. A few pink roses bloomed in a corner; bleats came from a clutter of sheds.

I followed Murat and Ali up a few stairs into a small room with a stone floor where we slipped our shoes off. Then we walked into a second, thickly carpeted one where 20 men sat cross-legged on the floor, their backs against the walls. The centre of the room was full of plates piled with bread, sweets and fruit. Erkin was sitting on the far side of the room, facing the door. I asked where his wife was.

'She's eating in another room. With the other women. She will come in after we finish.'

I sat down next to Ali, who made sure that I tasted at least one of every kind of sweet. I was in mid-munch when he asked me what I thought of the 9/11 attacks. I said I thought they were terrible. He nodded in agreement. Then he asked whom I thought responsible. I said maybe Bin Laden, though there wasn't any real evidence of that. He nodded vigorously, then leaned in and whispered,

'Many don't think it was him.'

'So who do you think did it?'

He leaned so close I felt his breath.

'The Chinese.'

I looked at him in amazement.

'Yes. That's right.'

'That would be awful.'

'Maybe, but it could also be good.'

'How?'

'The Americans will fight the Chinese. They will win and then we will be free.'

He laughed but I could tell he was serious. It made me realise how desperate some Uighurs were. But I had no chance to reply because then the *polo* was brought in, steaming platters crowned with massive chunks of lamb. In people's homes, *polo* is often eaten with the hands. At first I had difficulty with this; Ali brushed rice from his sleeve then demonstrated. He scooped a handful to the edge of the dish; pressed it firmly against the side; brought the sticky lump to his mouth.

We ate until we were full, then at Erkin's urging, ate more. Afterwards we sat and held our stomachs. There was a brief lull in conversation, before a stocky, thickset man began speaking. Everyone leant forward to hear.

'Who is he?'

Ali laughed and said, 'He is a funny man.'

There was a roar of confirmatory laughter. Then another, then a third, just to labour the point.

'What is he saying?'

Ali shifted uneasily.

'He is just joking.'

I tried to concentrate on what he was saying, even though the chances of him using any of the ten Uighur words I knew were pretty slim.

'Something something something something *Anglia* something.'

The word sounded familiar. Still the laughter continued. Clearly this was a very funny man.

'Ali, *Anglia* means England doesn't it?'

'Um, yes.'

It was then I realised he was talking about me – no, not only that, he was taking the piss and had been for the last few minutes.

'*Anglia* something something something something!'

What no one bothered to tell me was that this sit-down comedian wasn't some random stranger who had decided to mock me: he had been *hired* for that purpose.

Traditionally, the joker is an integral part of the wedding reception, and will usually pick on a number of people. Sometimes two or three jokers will be hired, who will then make fun of each other. The joker at Erkin's wedding probably saw me as an easy target, for which I couldn't blame him. Unsurprisingly, it's not unknown for jokers to be attacked after weddings.

It was a relief when the joker found other targets. A man's nose was compared to a penis; another man was said to resemble an ape. Ali took great pleasure in translating these quips, saying what a funny man the joker was, the funniest he'd ever heard. He did not think it so funny when the joker singled him out. Ali's face went red, and he made sounds of protest, but everyone, including me, laughed. Eventually, the joker sat back beaming at a job well done.

Ali said a few words in Arabic to announce the end of the meal. The men began a prayer with their palms held upwards, as if they were holding some invisible book. Then they brought their hands to their faces, moving them in a circle as if stroking their (mostly non-existent) beards. Then everyone stood up. We put our shoes on, said goodbye, slipped into the night.

19

NEXT MORNING I HAD the pleasure of a call from Miss Cai.

'Hello, Nick? I tried to call you yesterday. Where were you?'

Perhaps she thought I had nipped into Kazakhstan.

'At a wedding,' I said.

'What kind of wedding?'

'A Uighur one.'

'Oh! How lovely! Did they sing and dance?'

20

ALI MUST HAVE FELT bad about the joker at Erkin's wedding because he rang a few days later with an invitation.

'I will take you to a great man. Meet me at the park.'

The People's Park is on Ahmetjan Road. The street is named after Ahmetjan Kasimi, who was one of the main leaders of the East Turkestan Republic (ETR) based around Yining from 1944–1949. This was not only the street he had lived on; it was also where he was buried. In 1949, he and other leaders of the ETR had been *en route* to negotiations with Mao Zedong – who, by then, controlled the rest of China – when their plane crashed. There were no survivors. The details of the crash were never made public, fuelling speculation that Mao had had them killed.

After the ETR lost most of its leaders, there was little to prevent the Communists taking control of the region. However, the ETR has continued to be invoked by opponents of the Chinese regime, for whom it proves that 'Xinjiang' (or at least some of it) was an independent state prior to the arrival of the Communists. And as leader of that state, Ahmetjan Kasimi was a man worthy of veneration.

Ali was in no doubt of this.

'Ahmetjan was a good man, very kind. My grandfather has told me about him. He would often walk through the streets and ask people if they had any problems. If a person had some trouble, he would always listen carefully, even if it was a little thing. He never got angry or impatient. And what happened? They killed him.'

We walked down a grey concrete path. Signs informed us we would be fined if we walked on the grass. We passed a woman selling dusty bottles of orangeade. She called to us and mimed a drinking motion. A Han boy and girl sat further on, holding hands and gazing in different directions. I stared at the two of them until the girl went pink.

The path wound towards its end. The grass followed, virgin and forbidden. Then the concrete widened to an area the size of a basketball court. A terracotta-coloured column poked the air aside, on which an inscription said in Chinese characters:

> May their spirit live forever! They perished in the service of national liberation and of the people's democracy!
>
> MAO ZEDONG, 1949

On first reading it seemed ludicrous. But then a second sense emerged. Perhaps Mao believed that their death was *necessary* for national liberation.

The official line on Ahmetjan Kasimi and the ETR, propagated in revisionist historical works such as Jack Chen's *The Sinkiang Story*, is that it 'was a national liberation movement deeply influenced by the ideas of Marxism-Leninism... it was one of the great tragedies of Xinjiang and of all China that several of the finest leaders of the revolution perished in an air crash on the eve of the great victory of 1949'. The crux of the argument that the ETR was part of the Communists' struggle to 'liberate' China is that it opposed the Guomindang (the other warring faction) — an argument little more sophisticated than 'my enemy's enemy is my friend'.

The aim of including Ahmetjan and the ETR in the revolutionary struggle is twofold: first, by defining the ETR's opponents in political terms, it diminishes the role of ethnicity as a source of conflict. They were thus not against the Chinese *per se*. Secondly, the ETR would be discredited if its goals were similar to the Communists and thus could no longer inspire notions of separatism.

Three white tiled mounds lay beyond the column. Ali pointed to the middle one.

'That is Ahmetjan's.'

'Whose are the other two?'

'*That* is a Kazakh. That is a *Chinese*. Why they are here I do not know. Perhaps they want to pretend that they were all together. There are many lies here. But I know that things would be different if Ahmetjan had not died. He would not have let the Chinese do what they have done.'

Exactly what Ahmetjan might have done is far from obvious. It is unclear whether he wanted independence or not, and there is very little evidence that he was especially pro-Communist or anti-Guomindang, although he did describe one Guomindang general as a 'Chinese leader who believed that the only way to bring peace to the people of Xinjiang was to put them in their graves'. The closest thing to an endorsement of the new Communist regime was a speech in which he said:

> We must clearly state one thing. Since the day the peace agreement was signed, the Yili party at no point proposed, secretly or openly, that Sinkiang should secede from China. The Yili group has worked hard and will continue to work hard, to accomplish the aims of the agreement.

This, however, was conditional on the granting of real autonomy, which would have included control over education and the economy, neither of which were delivered. It is also doubtful whether he would have approved the massive Han influx into the region. But Ali was sure of one other thing.

'Now there is no one like him. The Tibetans have the Dalai Lama. Who do we have? Who is there to tell people about what is happening here?'

He shook his head violently.

21

THE PRESIDENT'S CONCERN for me stopped at the classroom door. How or what I taught was of no interest to him, so long as it was not political. In the unlikely event that I chose to discuss Taiwan or Tibet, his denial would have been almost too plausible. The person most likely to be held responsible was the dean of the English department, Geng Hui, who I called Mr Geng and sometimes Boss, neither of which he minded, especially the latter.

We met one morning during my first week. It was only just light but someone was nonetheless hammering on the door. After a few minutes it was clear they weren't going to stop. I flung open the door, fully prepared to attack the portly man in his 40s who stood before me. But he got there first.

'Come to the lake!'

'What?'

'Sayram lake!'

I guessed he meant the bluest lake I had passed on the way.

'When?'

'Now!'

'I can't. I'm...'

What was I?

'I'm busy. And, er, who are you anyway?'

He fished a card from his pocket and handed it to me. I read it and felt glad not to have savaged him.

'You should come. A professor from Shanghai will be there too.'

'Right, well, sorry, another time perhaps. But thank you.'

'You're a naughty boy!'

'Ha! Yes, well, perhaps.'

'Naughty!'

'Yes!'

It was during all this grinning that I noticed his hair. Unbelievably black, ultra glossy, it lay across his head in thick sheets. I was mesmerised, until he said, 'Next week you have no class. The students have something to do. You can have a rest.'

This, of course, was wonderful news: time to go exploring and generally snoop around. But I still wanted to know what they had to do that was more important than class.

I didn't find out till several days later, when Zhou Fengma – one of the other Chinese teachers in the English department – invited me round for dinner. Entering her house was like being transported back to Hunan. There were fluffy slippers to put on; the floors were tiled and the chairs so uncomfortable as to be orthopaedic. Plastic flowers stood in vases. A karaoke machine lurked next to the TV. There were also some surprise guests: a group of teenage girls cramming themselves full of grapes. They produced the requisite giggles then turned their attention to some plums. I asked Fengma who they were.

'They have come to practice their English with you. Isn't that wonderful?'

She disappeared into the kitchen, leaving me to try and coax some language out of them. After several minutes of muteness, I retreated to the toilet, where I found a pink plastic bowl that had 'David Beckham' written on it.

The smell of the food drew me out. Fengma had cooked *da pan ji* ('big plate chicken'), a whole bird cut into pieces and cooked with carrots and potatoes. Though the sauce was rich, and the meat tender, the girls only picked at the food, having gorged themselves on fruit. Despite their pleas of fullness, Fengma kept adding food to their bowls. 'Eat more,' she said, 'You are so thin.'

She shifted her maternal attention to me, asking which classes I was teaching. As I told her, she nodded and smiled; while she was distracted one of the girls slipped a chunk of chicken into her pocket. I added that at present I wasn't doing much teaching, as most of my students had 'something to do'.

'Yes, they are busy. They are picking cotton.'

'Cotton?'

'Yes, every year the students help the farmers for several weeks.'

'Do they have a choice? Do they get paid?'

'No, they are serving the people.'

'I bet the college gets paid. Don't you think it's corrupt?'

'Corrupt, oh no! It's not corrupt. Just unfair.'

She smiled as she said this, as if to say that a little unfairness was only to be expected. When I next saw my students, they were lean and sunburnt. Several said, 'Look – we are black!'

They had had to pick a minimum of 35 kilos a day. Less resulted in a fine, more in them being given a little money. I asked if they had enjoyed themselves.

'No, it was very hot and tired. But... *mei ban fa*!'

There is a world of resignation in these words. They are a kind of verbal shrug. They mean that there is no choice, that things must be endured. Whatever grievances had led some Uighurs to dislike the Chinese, they were by no means the only group of people to suffer under the system. The students had plenty of their own troubles too. But it was hard to imagine them engaging in any form of protest.

22

ON MORNINGS WHEN I wasn't teaching I tried to fester in bed. But it was no good; the sunlight stole through the new curtains; warm winds crept through the cracks in the windowpanes, pulling at my eyelids. There was no option but to go outside.

The border road ran past the college gate; Kazakhstan was a right turn away. A right turn, and 90km. I didn't think I could cycle that far; it was just a heading.

The roads were quiet. Few people in Yining owned a car; most made do with a bike or the bus. After ten minutes all suggestions of the city had faded. The white blocks were replaced by flat-roofed houses, painted various shades of blue, their courtyards full of roses. The side roads regressed into coffee-coloured dirt. I stopped to investigate a metal-roofed building that looked like a mosque, though it was different to ones I'd seen before. Its roof had a broader slope, more like that of the Buddhist temples I'd seen elsewhere in China. It also lacked the decorative minarets by the gate that many of the mosques in town had. But there was a prayer hall and lots of Arabic writing, so I was pretty sure it was a mosque. I stopped a Uighur man carrying a hoe on his shoulder and asked,

'This *is* a mosque isn't it?'

'Yes,' he said, then after a pause added, 'It's a Hui mosque.' He did not seem happy about this.

That there were different kinds of mosque, let alone for different people, was news to me. I didn't know that although both the Hui and Uighur are Sunni Muslims, they follow different Islamic legal schools: the Hui follow Shafi'i doctrine, the Uighurs the Hanafi doctrine. However, there are few substantial differences between these schools, and certainly not enough to prevent a person attending a mosque of the other tradition. Later I discovered that the reasons for the Hui and Uighur worshipping separately were far more secular. I got an inkling of this from the next man I asked, a Uighur man leaning against a wall, chewing on a stick.

'That's a Hui mosque isn't it?'

He snorted.

'It's a *Chinese* mosque.'

The tone, if not the meaning, was clear. I continued on. The harvest was almost done, the fields all but emptied. What remained was being shifted on donkey carts piled ten feet high with bushels. Leeks were on the windowsills; the terraces were covered in corn. Red chillies hung from washing lines like socks for miniscule feet.

A light wind lifted the leaves, amongst which were yellow pieces of crepe paper. All of them were round and had a square hole in their centre.

The road ran towards the mountains, whose summits were already white. I overtook a cart full of people who laughed and shouted 'Russian!' I waved then took advantage of my gears. I blurred through a small village and after that there were no more fields or houses. The ground rose and despite the effort of pedalling, I wondered how far I could go, if I might continue for days, at what point someone would stop me.

But if nothing else, I was too unfit for such a journey. Halfway up the hill I had to stop to rest. Panting, I sat on the ground, wishing I had brought water. The earth was covered by small plants with a bleached look; when I tried to pick one it crumbled in my fingers. Crickets jumped and chirped. The city lounged beneath, a spreading rectangle that looked lusher from afar. You couldn't see the dust on the leaves, the rubbish in the streams, just the lines of poplars. I pushed my bike up the rest of the slope.

The ground soon levelled off. But there was a new problem: minor ravines split the earth every hundred metres. They were too wide to jump, and their sides were too steep to risk. The only option was to follow them until they ended, then carry on in the original direction, which by then seemed rather pointless as I had already gone so far out of my way. But I had spotted something that interested me, so I persevered.

Hundreds of brown mounds covered the slopes of the next hill, roughly eight feet tall and six in diameter. As I approached I saw that most of their bases were coated with concrete. Each had a tall stone bearing Chinese characters. I had stumbled into a massive graveyard. There were no wreaths or flowers; instead there were incense stubs, tatters of red firecrackers exploded for luck, small pieces of yellow paper. Their presence in the cemetery helped explain their shape: in ancient China, heaven was thought to be round, while the earth was held to be square. The frail piece of paper was thus the universe in miniature (and yellow).

The graves filled every focal plane. They were so much larger than the graves in western cemeteries, where the dead can be looked down upon. These tombs would not allow that. Each one was tall and wide enough to impose itself, to say I am dead, and you are not; not yet. But I was not afraid, not at all and to prove this to myself I walked further in, reading what little I could, mostly names and dates. After a few minutes the mounds began to thin and then stopped, as if at some invisible boundary. For the next hundred yards there was empty space. Then the graves began again, only they were different: coffin-sized mounds of earth surrounded by fencing. The headstones were smaller, made of wood as well as stone, and covered in Arabic writing. Crescent moons stood at the head and corners of the graves, all of which faced toward Mecca. Once again, the Han and Uighurs were divided; even after death.

A chill wind picked up. I started towards home.

23

MANY TOWNS IN Xinjiang are associated with fruit. Hami has long been famous for melons. In Chapter XXXVIII of his *Travels*, Marco Polo wrote that the towns' people 'live by the fruits of the earth which they have in plenty and dispose of to travellers'. Korla is renowned for its pears; Turpan for its grapes.

Yining is famous for apples. Orchards spread throughout the valley, and even within the city there are walled squares of trees. Carts and wagons stand at roadsides, stuffed with straw and ripe fruit. Some of these apples were known to me – hard little Cox varieties, pappy Golden Delicious – but others were unfamiliar: a small red one with chewy skin but too-soft flesh (which I shamefully disposed of after eating its outside) and a larger scarlet variety, in texture somewhere between a Braeburn and a rock. Its flesh was hard and unyielding; I always feared it would take one of my teeth.

None of these apples would have been accepted by a supermarket. Few were free of pits, pockmarks or entry wounds. Perhaps they were imperfect things, but you knew where they had come from. No one had modified their genetic code or sprayed them with chemicals. The man who sold them to you (or someone that he knew) had grown and picked them himself, perhaps in the same way his father had, and his father before him. Or so I liked to think.

24

I RAN INTO COLIN in the market.

'Hi Colin, you're a vision in blue.'

'Sorry?'

He looked puzzled. As if I had given a wrong answer in class.

'Your clothes. All of them are blue.'

'Oh, I see. It's because you're not an artist. You don't know about colour. This is purple. Not blue.'

'Perhaps.'

'Just kidding! And hey, it's not your fault. We can't all be artists.'

25

WHY WAS THE SHEEP SO angry? What was its problem? Admittedly, it had been tied to the tree outside my window for the last six hours. I had heard its bleating grow from an occasional and placid *baaaaa* to something more frenzied. I looked out the window and saw it tugging at the rope. After a few minutes it gave up and sank down to the ground. When a little girl went to pet it, the sheep lunged at her.

I went to Eleanor's flat to borrow a grammar book. When I returned half an hour later, all that was left of the sheep were some bloody stains. Where it had gone and who had killed it was a mystery. But as the days shortened it became more and more common to see sheep tethered to trees around the campus. Yet I always managed to miss their actual slaughter. A sheep would be there in the morning, looking resigned, then several hours later it would be replaced by a group of Uighur men sitting round a steaming cauldron of mutton. But when I came across a horse, a chestnut-coloured creature standing by the nursery, I knew this was not to be missed. I nipped back to my flat for a book then sat down to wait.

A couple of my students passed and asked what I was doing.

'Just reading.'

'Why do you read here?'

'It's a nice spot, isn't it?'

'Yes. Yes it is. Bye bye.'

I returned to Anna and Vronsky. Five minutes later I heard Gabe's voice. I'd got to know him a bit and found I rather liked him. His energy and enthusiasm were boundless, so much so that he usually ran everywhere, busted shoulder or not. Something told me he would understand why I was sitting there. When I told him he said:

'Yeah, it's quite a sight when they take one down. It takes three or four big guys to hold it. I never realised how much blood a horse has in it, maybe twenty gallons. They have to dig a hole.'

This I would not miss. Gabe paced up and down, struggling to stay in one place. Twenty minutes later four burly men came over, carrying some ropes. Gabe said a few words to them in Uighur and they laughed in reply, then said something else.

'They say you can watch if you want. But you might have to lend a hand if the horse puts up a fight.'

By then I was ready to take it down myself. They were starting to tie the horse's legs when I saw Miss Cai approaching.

'Ah, Nick! Good! Did you know the dean is looking for you? He wants to see you immediately.'

'Can't it wait?'

She frowned at such a foolish notion.

'Are you busy now?'

What could I say? That I wanted to watch them stick a knife into a horse?

'No, not really,' I said.

I thought of asking them to wait, but could imagine the laughter. I ran to the office. The dean wasn't there. I asked the secretary, who said he'd be back in a minute, which naturally turned out to be 20. I waited. I examined the walls. I thought of the horse. When the dean arrived, he greeted me in a surprised fashion. He sat down, lit a cigarette, smoothed his shiny hair and said, 'How can I help you?'

'I thought you wanted to see me?'

He took a long, thoughtful drag. Then he exhaled and said, 'Yes, naughty boy! I wanted to make sure you were okay.'

'I'm fine. Is there anything else?'

'No, no!'

I ran back to the horse, but it was already in pieces. Its guts were neatly piled; its liver lay nearby. A large hole was full of blood and faeces. The head was being skinned. I watched as they removed the tongue. Next the head was bisected in a shower of bone. I felt something under my foot. It was a hoof.

Next day there was little to see but some dark patches of blood, a few shards of skull, and the horse's spine. It was nailed to a tree and swung gently back and forth in the breeze.

26

I HAD FORGOTTEN ABOUT Tilawaldi, even though it had only been a few weeks since I met him at Murat's English class. When Eleanor told me he had invited us for lunch it took a moment to place him – he was the man who spoke without pauses – which didn't stop me from agreeing to go. I wasn't sure I wanted to spend the next year listening to the racism of Murat and his circle, so anyone new was good.

Tilawaldi was a civil servant. Initially this surprised me, but I soon found that many of the educated Uighurs that I met worked for the government. It was no doubt policy to have the Uighurs well represented in authority, although the highest positions were usually filled by Han. It was another of the government's attempts to portray China as one vast happy family where all the different ethnic groups held hands and danced toward the future. The government may also have hoped that this would prevent the minorities from blaming the Han (rather than the mostly Han government) for their troubles.

We took a donkey cart to his house. It was in one of the more affluent suburbs, where although the roads were unpaved, the houses were grander— two-storey affairs, tiled in pink or yellow, with towering gates like raised drawbridges. I later found out that this was one of the streets the BBC crew visited on their ill-fated attempt to find out what happened in 1997.

Tilawaldi was waiting for us outside. He welcomed us then ushered us into the courtyard. Pots of wrinkled pink plants stood round the walls, their blooms like small brains. Sheep sounds came from a small shed. I put my head round the door and saw some black ewes cuddled together. Tilawaldi came up behind me. I searched for animal small talk.

THE TREE THAT BLEEDS

'Have you had them long?'

'No they are not mine they are my father's I bought them to entertain him he is old and has no work he is retired. But we used to have more maybe 6,000.'

'What happened to them?'

'They were taken by the Communists.'

'When?'

'In 1950 we were rich then.'

I guessed he wasn't used to having actual conversations, hence his machine-gun delivery. Otherwise his English was very good, especially given the fact that he'd only been learning for 11 months. In this time he had reached a level of fluency it took my Han students three or four years to achieve. He said he studied a lot, usually after work or when his wife and child were sleeping. But the main difference between him and my Han students was probably motivation. All my students had to look forward to was teaching in an over-crowded classroom. But with good English, and a few connections, Tilawaldi might be able to go abroad, that vague and shining place of money and supposed freedom.

Eleanor and I were shown into a small stone-flagged room where we took our shoes off. We padded into a second, larger room, where a table was concealed under a spread of dried fruit, nuts, sweets, crystal sugar, apples, pears, sugared pastries, little biscuits, grapes and plums. A large cabinet took up the far wall, full of china and glassware. On another wall hung a *dutar*, a long stringed instrument shaped like a stretched tear. Tilawaldi asked us to sit and then called to someone for tea. A woman wearing a headscarf brought in some small white bowls and a teapot. She went out and returned with three large nan which she placed on the now-hidden table.

'This is my wife.'

We said hello. She smiled shyly, looked at her husband, then left. Eleanor asked Tilawaldi how he had met his wife.

'She is very good woman.'

'Yes, but how did you meet?'

THE TREE THAT BLEEDS

'My friend introduced me although she is from this village but I had not meet her before. The first time I saw her it was love and so we married quickly.'

A small child ran in. He had short hair and a doughy body.

'And this is my daughter she is three, you know many people think she is a boy!'

'Oh, really?'

'Yes!'

I chewed on a handful of dates, then asked,

'Is it true that minorities can often have more than one child?'

'We are allowed two only if I have three I will lose my job. But even if I have two maybe it is not so good for me.'

'But will you have another?'

'That's not up to me. Allah will decide.'

The fact that minorities are allowed to have more children (two or sometimes more in rural areas) than the Han (who can only have one) is something that the government frequently produces as evidence that if the minorities experience any discrimination, it is positive.

'So Nick you are English yes? Like Eleanor?'

'That's right.'

He laughed at something to himself, then decided to share.

'When I was in school we learned that in England the workers must work all day and their reward is to be hit by their bosses all day long. Last week I looked in my niece's book. It is still the same!'

His wife re-entered with steaming bowls of *chuchura*, a kind of beef dumpling soup. She laid the food down and left. She did not return except to clear the dishes. In an unkind moment I wondered if she was allowed to do anything other than cooking or bearing children.

Eleanor and I slurped and listened as Tilawaldi continued talking. He said that in Xinjiang 90 per cent of Uighurs were unemployed, and that in his street only two people had jobs. It also emerged that Tilawaldi didn't just work for the government; he was also a member of the Chinese Communist Party (CCP), not an easy club to join.

You had to have a good political record and plenty of *guanxi* ('conn-ections'). However, in 1995 official statistics proclaimed that there were 270,000 Party members from minorities in Xinjiang. These figures intended to convey a similar message to the presence of minorities in government positions, namely that ethnicity was distinct from political affiliation. You could be a Kazakh or Uighur and still love your government and country.

Tilawaldi said he didn't like being a Party member but admitted it could help his career. The downside was that he was scrutinised and expected to set a good example, hence his worries about having another child. There were other problems too. In 1992, Li Peng, the then-Chinese prime minister, had stated that 'as for CCP members, no matter what their ethnicity, all should support materialism and atheism'. In 1996, the Xinjiang Party Committee had ruled that CCP members and cadres 'shall not believe in any religion or take part in religious activities'. I asked Tilawaldi how he dealt with this edict.

'The Communists do not understand religion and so they don't like it. Last year I was in a meeting when one of the Chinese officials offered me some tobacco. I used to smoke and drink but now I am good Muslim. I refused, I said no I am Muslim I do not. He become angry he shout at me he was so angry.'

I wasn't sure he should be saying such things. He may have been in the privacy of his home, but he still didn't really know us. Perhaps he thought that as foreigners (and thus outsiders) we were less likely to tell someone. There was also the sense of an out-pouring, of things long left unsaid.

We finished eating, answered his questions about England ('Do they have many pigeons?' 'Are there problems with guns?'), then said our goodbyes. He told us to come back soon, which we promised to do. But this was the last time that we saw him. Two months later he went to Canada and did not return.

27

THE FRAGRANT GARDEN was the nearest Han restaurant to the college. It was a family affair: the mother served the customers, the father did the cooking, their two sons helped both. A grandfather was usually present too; his task was to sit in the corner and look like he was brooding on something terrible that had happened during the Cultural Revolution.

One evening there were no free tables so I asked three young Han Chinese men if I could join them. They pulled out a stool and we introduced ourselves. I was a teacher from England; they were teachers from Nanjing, the capital of Jiangxi province. They had been in Yining for six months and were about to return. I asked if they had enjoyed their time. They said they had, although they missed Nanjing. Our food arrived and for the next few minutes we just stuffed ourselves.

A group of Kazakhs were at the next table. They took it in turns to poke at a plate of eggs. One of the Nanjing teachers glanced over at them then whispered to his friend that there were a lot of minorities in the place. His friend looked round and smirked. I made an attempt to distract him.

'Do you like the food here?'

'It's okay but I prefer the food in Nanjing.'

'Do you like *polo*?'

'I've never had it.' His friend nodded, in confirmation or agreement.

'Oh you should, it's great.'

'Maybe but I don't like to eat with my hands. I'm not an animal.'

There was much laughter. The Chinese for the dish, *zhua fan,* literally means 'grab food', not the most respectful phrase. I waited for their laughter to finish then said, 'I think they'd give you a spoon. That's what they do in restaurants.'

They looked doubtful. I wished them a good journey.

28

I WAS WOKEN BY the shouting. It was mostly male voices; they sounded nearby and angry. I pulled the bedclothes over my head, hoping it would die down. But after five minutes it had swelled to a roaring. Scenes of civil unrest flashed through my mind: riots, protests, *intifadas*. I quickly dressed and went out.

The night was thick but lightened by a wedge of moon. The shouts were coming from the direction of the dormitories. Perhaps I had underestimated the students. Maybe they had finally snapped, tired of all the petty injustices, all the fines, all the cleaning assignments and political nonsense. Or maybe the Uighur and Kazakh students were staging some kind of protest. I started to run.

The lights were on in all the dormitories. Boys stood at the windows shouting, some in only their pants. They were dragging their tin cups along the bars on their windows in prison inmate-fashion. But they sounded more excited than angry. My hopes and fears subsided. I went round to the dormitory gate and found it locked. I looked into the courtyard and saw a few people running and yelling but no sign of banners, fires or demonstrations. I went up to one of the boys.

'What's happening?'

'Out!'

He was too excited for verbs. Another boy had a go.

'We want to go out! We want to see!'

'What? What?'

He moved his arm above his head and made a whooshing sound.

'Star!'

That night a storm of them swept through the winter sky.

Winter

29

WHAT HAD I LEARNT after two months? I certainly had no kind of explanation for what had happened in 1997; unsurprisingly, the politically sensitive riots didn't come up in conversation much. All I knew was that a lot of Uighurs resented the Han, so much that the two communities tried to function separately. But with the exception of a few cryptic remarks, I didn't understand why so many Uighurs disliked the Han. What had they, or rather their government, done to inspire such hatred? Was it because of Han immigration, the high levels of unemployment amongst Uighurs, or the imposition of Beijing time? There were many possibilities. But after my talk with Tilawaldi, I had a notion that religion was far from the least of them.

30

No state organ, public organisation or individual may compel citizens to believe in, or not believe in, any religion; nor may they discriminate against citizens who believe in, or do not believe in, any religion.

Constitution of the People's Republic of China, Article 36.

IT COMES AS A SURPRISE to many that religion is permitted in China. Communism and religion are thought to be at odds at with each other, and since China is ruled by a Communist government, it seems impossible for the masses to be allowed their opiate. Yet both in theory and in practice, Chinese people are free to follow Jesus, Buddha or Mohammed.

Of course there is a catch; some would say a big one. Citizens can only follow state-approved religions; sects and cults need not apply (and in Chinese these terms mean 'heresy' and 'perverse religion'). Believers must worship in state-registered venues. In order to qualify for registration, a venue must not 'harm national unity, ethnic unity or the social order, harm citizens health or obstruct the national educational system', a fairly broad set of requirements. Registration must be renewed annually, which makes the position of any mosque, church or temple somewhat precarious. All religious appointments (e.g. priests, *imams*) must be approved by the local authorities. Religious publications are also tightly controlled: there are restrictions on importation; religious materials can only be sold at authorised outlets and all scriptures must be approved before printing.

However, these and other restrictions have not deterred believers of all approved faiths who officially number at least 100 million – probably a massive underestimate, as this figure has not changed since the 1950s.

The Communist Party justify the presence of religion through some agile dialectical reasoning, one fine example of which is contained in a small pamphlet entitled *Questions & Answers about China's National Minorities*.

Q. Does the policy of freedom of religious belief contradict socialism?

A. People in China, whether they are religious believers or not, in general love their motherland and stand for socialism. They all work for the country's socialist modernisation programme. So, it is easy to see that the policy ensuring freedom of religious belief for all citizens is in no way against socialism.

Whilst this might sound contrived, it is unambiguous. The interests of the nation must come first; religion is only permitted if it benefits these aims. The Chinese government thus doesn't need to look hard to find a pretext for suppressing any religious activity it does not agree with. It can simply argue that the practice in question is an obstacle to economic, social or political development.

One of the reasons that the Communist Party has managed to retain power in China for so long is that it has prevented the form-ation of many large-scale organisations outside of the state: civil society is still very much in its infancy. The Party fears that any large groups could serve as a rallying point for dissent and opposition, hence the need to limit their formation and control their membership. Religion is thus a political issue anywhere in China, and certainly in Xinjiang.

The association between religion and protest in Xinjiang can be said to begin with the demonstration in Baren (a town in south Xinjiang) in April 1990. Hundreds of Uighur villagers protested in front of local government offices over birth-control policies that limited the number of children a couple could have to two or three. Traditionally Uighurs have large families (as did most Han Chinese before 1949).

As in the Yining riots, there are different accounts of how many died on each side during the protests. According to the Chinese government, 22 died during a 'counter-revolutionary rebellion', including seven police officers. Amnesty International cites reports that more than 50 villagers were killed by mortar and helicopter gunship, most while they were running away. The government blamed the riot on 'ethnic separatists', who 'cloaked themselves in religion'. Their aim was to said to be to deceive some people into taking part 'in their plot to destroy national unity and overthrow the government'. The authorities claimed that the separatists had incited violent 'Islamic *jihad*' by using religious gatherings to brainwash people. Their conclusion was that 'before and after the Baren incident, the diffusion of religious fanaticism coexisted with the spread of ethnic separatism'.

By linking religion with separatism in this manner, the Chinese government could thus target any religious practice it did not approve of, whilst maintaining that it was only doing so to protect national security. When, after 9/11, the authorities began to crack down on 'terrorism', their focus was on Islam.

31

In performing religious work, we must uphold scientific, materialistic views.

YE XIAOWEN, director of the State Bureau of Religious Affairs

I WAS SPOILING MY students' books with red pen when the telephone rang.

'Nick! This is Murat.'

'Hi Murat, how's it going?'

'What are you doing now?'

'Not much, I'm just doing some marking.'

'I phoned you earlier. Where were you?'

'Sorry, I was out.'

'Who were you with?'

'A friend.'

'A Chinese friend?'

'No, a Uighur.'

'OK, good! Are you free tomorrow?'

'I think so.'

'Then I will come to your house at twelve o'clock.'

'OK, see you then.'

'Don't forget the time. Twelve o'clock.'

He talked as if I were one of his students, a total idiot, or both. But I put up with this because there were things I wanted to ask him. There had been reports that the Islamic clergy were being subjected to 'political education', whatever that meant. I figured that if anyone would know, it would be Murat, and not just because he was so demonstrative in his faith, but because his father was an *imam*.

The question was whether he'd be willing to talk about any of it.

So far, he'd been careful to avoid such subjects. I would have to be somewhat disingenuous, to put it politely. Initially I felt bad about this, but after he arrived late, then told me that my house was very messy ('We can say it is disgusting!' he said) my qualms seemed to vanish.

'Murat, I've been doing some reading about Hui people and it says that they're different types of Muslim to Uighurs. Is that true?'

He eyed me warily.

'Yes, well, why do you want to know?'

'I'm just interested. I want to understand more about Islam.'

He looked sceptical. I switched tactics.

'I thought you'd know, given that your faith is so important to you.'

He bristled a bit.

'Of course I know, but it's difficult to explain in English. If you spoke Uighur, you would understand. You would.'

I did not disagree. A week later I went round his house to lend him some books. Murat was talking to someone on the phone and asked me to wait. His father was in the courtyard. We had a quick chat in Chinese, then he went to buy bread. Murat finished his call and came out.

'I just met your father. He seems very healthy.'

'Yes, he is, thanks to Allah.'

'Does he still work?'

'Not really, though for the last two years he has been an *imam*.'

'Oh, has he? You must be very proud. Is it difficult to become an *imam*?'

'Yes, very difficult. You must study and know many things.'

'Who chooses the *imams*? The people in the mosque?'

'Yes, the people in the mosque and also some government officials.'

I feigned surprise.

'Some government officials? Why? Do they know about Islam?'

He snorted. 'They don't know *anything*. But, you know, there was some trouble before. Some young men fought with the police. The government thinks it was about religion.'

'Was it?'

'Perhaps. But then I didn't understand what was happening. When I saw people throwing stones at the police I didn't know why but I knew I should go home. Afterwards the government closed many mosques and *madrasas* [religious schools].'

'But things are better now aren't they?'

'Maybe. But there are new problems. My father must go to some special classes.'

'About religion?'

'No, it is politics. Only politics.'

At the time I felt I had achieved something in getting him to talk about this, but it turned out that it wasn't a secret. In October 2001, the Xinjiang provincial government announced its intention to 'strengthen the management of religious affairs' and 'actively guide religion to conform to socialist society'. Over 8,000 *imams* in charge of key mosques in the province had to attend a ten-day course, the purpose of which was to give them 'a clearer understanding of the party's ethnic and religious policies'. The classes were conducted under the leadership of party and government officials, and proceeded 'from the perspective of guiding religion in adapting to the socialist society and maintaining the lasting political stability of Xinjiang', according to a Xinhua news report. The *imams* were instructed to spread the pearls they had received among local people, so as to 'increase the influence of the training'.

So in addition to all the other restrictions on how and where Muslims could worship, the government was now trying to put words in the mouths of the leaders of their faith. Imagine if someone prevented you from following what you believed in most. You'd want to blame someone, anyone, even if they were not directly responsible. And once your anger had a focus, it might grow and twist till it demanded release.

32

THE WATER RAN COLDER; the snowline slipped; mounds of coal appeared. The old and young swelled with jumpers and vests. Doors were mended, quilts were aired. They stopped making ice cream. The sun struggled to rise, and when it did, the light it mustered was thin.

But by lunchtime it was warm enough to sit outside. A row of restaurants ran along the road behind the college, small places with several tables outside. Most of these restaurants were run by Uighurs. The menu was pretty straightforward: *polo* or *laghman* – noodles with fried beef and vegetables. Everything was freshly made, including the noodles. In the mornings you could hear the bang and slap of dough being pummelled before it was stretched. There weren't any waiters or waitresses; you just put your head round the kitchen door and gave them your order. While you waited you could sip your weak black tea beneath the swaying birches. You might sit and tritely wonder that a place as lovely as Yining could also be so troubled.

It was easy to fall into the pleasant rhythm of sleep, teach, eat, first in the morning, then after lunch, with a *xiuxi* (a rest, more a doze than a sleep), a gentle late-afternoon lesson from four to six, followed by a light supper with a beer or three. All very pleasant, very nice and perhaps capable of carrying on indefinitely, had I not gone to lunch one day and found an army of sledgehammers breaking down the walls of the restaurants. The college leaders had decided they were scruffy (admittedly not the word that Miss Cai used) and had better be removed. The college owned the land that they were on and, since it had an inspection coming up, obviously didn't feel like taking chances.

It would have been tempting to make an ethnic issue out of it. After all, the college leaders were predominantly Han, and the restaurants were owned by Uighurs. But I had seen the same thing many times in Hunan. Small shops and restaurants had to give way to housing developments, or road improvements, and it wasn't a matter of one ethnicity bullying another, just a question of power.

33

IN MONGOLIAN, URUMQI MEANS 'beautiful pastureland', but despite this pretty name the city has had a poor press. In the 1920s one traveller wrote: 'the town has no beauty, no style, no dignity and no architectural interest. The climate is violent, exaggerated and no season is pleasant'. This was before the Communists built it up into the capital it is today, but tourist guides still bemoan its 'drab concrete-block architecture' and the fact that it has 'little to distinguish itself other than the claim to being the furthest city in the world from the ocean'.

It's certainly true that the city doesn't feel like the capital of the Xinjiang *Uighur* Autonomous Region: most of the time you could be anywhere in central or eastern China, not least because three-quarters of the population is Han. In the 1980s the provincial government tried to make the city's buildings look more Islamic, perhaps thinking of tourism. The legacy of this plan can be seen today in the occasional arched window or dome. But what signs there are of Uighur culture – scattered mosques, the Grand Bazaar, Uighur shops and restaurants on the back streets – somehow never seem more than curiosities. Urumqi is a Chinese city and has always been. It was founded as a garrison town, and even before 1949, never had a Uighur majority.

I had first visited the city in the late 1990s, and hadn't been impressed. When I passed through in 2001, on the way to Yining, little seemed to have changed. If I went back in early winter 2002, it wasn't because I had much interest in the place. My reason for doing so was to judge a speech competition at Xinjiang University. Ordinarily, the thought of having to listen to 20 sets of platitudes on the subject of 'Why it is important to learn English' or 'Why I want to be a teacher' would have made me feign illness. But some of my students were going to take part, so it was a good chance to spend time with them. I wanted to know if they were as naïve as they seemed. The classroom wasn't the best place for discussion: anyone who made a political misstep would be reported by the monitor, the student who was class-president and snitch all in one (and in a further twist, had usually been appointed by the class itself).

The other reason for enduring the 12-hour bus ride was that Dean Geng was going. Initially I had thought him affable, but less interesting than his shiny hair. I changed my mind on meeting his son, who was not entirely Han. If anything, he looked Uighur. That he was of mixed parentage was almost unthinkable, a mark of how separate Han and Uighur were. My doubts persisted until I met his wife, who turned out to be half Uighur. She and the dean had met at university, 20 years before, when inter-ethnic marriages had been equally unusual. One rumour had it that the dean had been told to choose between his girlfriend and joining the Communist Party. It was a rumour I preferred to believe.

We assembled as the light was failing. Besides the dean and I, there were four students, all in their final year. The bus station was aflow with people, coming, going, trying to sell things, waiting for someone. Young Uighur boys wandered round with stools and brushes, looking for shoes to shine. The oldest might have been 14. One of them asked if I wanted my shoes done and when I said 'No, thank you', he laughed and said 'Fuck you' in Chinese. Liu Hai, one of my students, shooed him away, which led the boy to say the same to him before running off. We tutted and went on to blame the parents, society, modernity and the education system. Then he said:

'Nick, did you know that in our college, only 3 per cent of the minority students find jobs in the first few months after they leave?'

'Is that all? Are you sure?'

'Yes, I've heard it many times.'

'Why do you think that is?'

'I don't know. It's very strange.' He sounded genuinely puzzled.

Our bus pulled in, leaning heavily to the left. It was one of the new sleeper buses, which meant that they had changed the sheets on the dwarf-sized beds. There were upper and lower bunks, which required a choice between falling out and being stepped upon by the person above. I chose a bed on the lower right side.

Another one of my students, a tall girl with large lips, asked if she could take the bed above. I told her to go ahead.

'Thanks, and you know, your bed is better for you. You have such long legs. You know, when I saw them, I thought at first they were trees.'

Her name was Xiao Mei and she was in one of the classes I hadn't yet taught, as they were busy doing their 'duty' picking cotton. She wanted to be distracted from her motion sickness, and I was soon glad of conversation once night fell and we were hurtling down an unlit road. It was one those rides you can only surrender to, where you reach for whatever is available, whether it be prayer or alcohol, or in my case, progressively odder topics of conversation with a girl I barely knew.

'Nick, what do you think of the G-A-Y, the gay?'

'Well, I think people should be able to do what they want as long as they don't hurt others.'

'Me too, but I think it's wrong if you are still at school.'

The dean lay several bunks away, snoring like an outboard motor. We pulled into a petrol station. As the floodlights leaked in, I noticed something out of place. His central sheet of hair was at an unnatural angle, at least for real hair. I was wondering how I hadn't noticed such an obvious hairpiece when the dean suddenly stirred. I moved my eyes away guiltily but there was no problem. He gave a twitch of such magnitude that he managed to kick the man in the next bed. The man woke and looked around angrily, but the dean had lapsed back into sleep.

I spent the next few hours trying to imitate this Herculean feat. Eventually the void admitted me. I dreamt that I was hurling rocks at people with paper bags for heads. I was summoned back to consciousness by the dean's cheery voice.

'It's time for noodles!'

'Please, Mr Geng, I'm tired. Let me sleep.'

'Get up, naughty boy! We're here!'

He dragged me to a noodle shack. I sat and watched him slurp his way through a mound of *laghman*. I was too cold and tired for tact, so I asked him straight out.

'Why are there so few minority students in our department?'

He paused in mid-slurp, then said through his noodles, 'There are some Hui and Kazakh.'

'But only four Uighurs. Out of 350 students.'

He appeared to consider this, as if it were news to him.

'It is the policy of Xinjiang education commission to restrict college admission for minorities to alternate years.'

'How do they justify that?'

'In our country, minorities need lower exam scores to enter college. So, to make things fair, they cannot enter every year.'

'What are they supposed to do in the odd years?'

'If they want, they can try to go to a better place, like Xinjiang University or somewhere outside of the province.'

'What about those who can't get into those places?'

'They lose the chance.'

So a bit of positive discrimination had to be balanced by restricting entry to alternate years. However, this didn't explain why there were so few Uighurs compared with Hui or Kazakhs.

We took a taxi to a hotel where I was mercifully given a room of my own. I slept until the speech competition, which was in the afternoon, then slept some more. I briefly woke when one boy said that the reason Chinese people should learn English was so that they 'could triumph over foreign countries'. He did not win. Nor did the person that I thought should have, a young Uighur girl who was the only one able to speak English with correct stress and intonation. Afterwards, I told her this, and she smiled and sensibly remarked that it didn't matter. The difference between winning and losing was a dictionary, and not a very good one at that.

There was no bus back until the next morning. The prospect of a long evening loomed. I was just about to get undressed when there was a knock at the door. It was Xiao Mei. She asked if I wanted to go to a bar in town. I asked her what sort of bar, imagining the pink lights and karaoke of most Chinese bars. She said she hadn't been there but she'd heard it was a Western-style bar. I thought of gin and said yes.

The bar turned out to be a café called *The Vine*. It was owned and managed by two Costa Ricans, who had opened it several years before, in response to the growing number of foreign students and teachers in Urumqi. However, there were also a few Han Chinese there, sitting drinking tea. Xiao Mei admitted that she hadn't a clue what to get, so I ordered two slices of cake. I tried to get a beer but was told that they preferred not to sell it.

I returned to my seat, pondering (and mourning) the lack of alcohol. An anodyne tune was playing in the background. I strained to catch the words.

'Jeeeeeee-sus, Jeeeeeee-sus, what a beautiful name!'

After this chorus, I pondered no more. Xiao Mei was busy picking at her cake, clearly trying to work something out. Finally she appeared to come to a decision.

'Nick, what do you think of Colin?'

'Er, well, I don't know. Why?'

'Some of us are scared of him.'

'Afraid?' Irritated I could understand, but afraid?

'Yes, sometimes he is angry with students. He is too direct, he tries to make us talk or think about difficult things.'

I tried to be professional.

'Well, isn't it the job of a teacher to make students think?'

'Maybe, but he sometimes tries to tell us what we should think.'

I didn't like where this was going and tried to change the subject. I asked Xiao Mei why she thought so few minority students were able to find work after graduation. Her reply was multiple choice.

'You know, minorities need lower scores to enter college, so maybe they aren't as good as Chinese students. But maybe there are some other reasons. They spend a lot of time smoking drugs and going out with their lovers. Or perhaps the Uighur leather industry is not so... competitive. They make their coats from single pieces of leather but others use lots of smaller pieces.'

'Do you think that there is any discrimination against them?'

'Yes, sometimes. Many Han look down upon the Uighurs and think they are behind, no... *backward*.'

She sat back, evidently pleased with the word (it was also a favourite of Miss Cai's). I asked Xiao Mei if she had any Uighur friends.

'No, but I like some Uighur men. They have nice eyes and high noses, like yours. But there is a problem, their taste, no.' She pulled a face. 'Their *smell*. They have a disease under their arms, really.'

It was almost a nice change to hear a Han being rude about the Uighurs. It brought a kind of balance to the prejudice. And in some very politically incorrect way, this directness was preferable to all the talk of Uighurs being colourful and charming.

We left, as the music was beginning to grate, especially one song in Spanish that consisted of a man proclaiming 'Jesus! Jesus! Muchas gracias!' On the way back Xiao Mei said that the girls of Yining were 'very open'.

I looked at her inquiringly. She may have blushed in the dark.

'You know, many of them are not Virgos.'

'Oh, er, well, I'm a Leo.'

It was her turn to look bemused.

'No, Virgo, it means they have not... made love. A Virgo.'

Some mistakes are almost too enjoyable to correct. On that occasion I did, perhaps because I still felt guilty for not working harder to improve the pronunciation of a girl who used to talk about using a fuck and knife.

When we arrived back at the hotel, I prepared to say goodnight. Xiao Mei smiled broadly then said, 'Won't you be lonely in that big room on your own? Do you want some company?'

I stared at her, trying to work out if she was actually propositioning me. Her offer was probably meant innocently enough, nothing more than friendly concern for her teacher. But I didn't spend long wondering; I said goodnight then fled.

34

THE SEPARATION BEGINS EARLY. In Yining, and in all Xinjiang, there are different schools for Han and Uighur children. This division arises as much from linguistic factors as it does from ethnicity. The Han schools use Mandarin Chinese, whereas the Uighur schools use the Uighur language. But the separation is far from absolute: some Uighur children are educated in Chinese schools. These students are known as *Min Kao Han* ('minorities tested in the Han language'), whereas Uighur students in Uighur schools are *Min Kao Min*. No Han students are educated in Uighur schools, as they would have to learn Uighur to do so.

The main reason for the existence of *Min Kao Han* students is that a high level of written and spoken Chinese is needed for virtually any professional career. Most learning materials, especially in medicine, science and computing, are only available in Chinese. Another reason is that English is seldom taught in Uighur schools, or at least not to the same level as it is in Han schools. The justification for this is that for Uighurs, Chinese must be their second language.

So this was another explanation for why few Uighurs studied English in the college. Most Uighurs didn't get the chance to study it at school, unless they were *Min Kao Han*. And indeed, all *four* Uighurs in our department had studied in Han schools. They were all in the same class, which despite being predominantly Han, nonetheless had an eclectic ethnic mix. There were a couple of Uzbek girls, two Kazakh boys, three Hui girls, a Kirghiz boy, and of course the Uighurs. They had entered college in 1999, so according to the 'alternate years' explanation that the Dean had offered, the new 2001 classes should have contained a similar number of minority students, perhaps around 20. There were three.

The '99 class had a different atmosphere from the other classes. They were either comatose or manic. In the former state, they were like 45 total strangers who had mistakenly wandered into the same room. Questions fell unanswered; their gaze was fixed to desks or the floor. There was no sense of class unity. And in the Chinese classroom – where the majority of students are pathologically afraid of making a mistake and thus 'losing face' – this is generally fatal to any attempt to produce the supportive atmosphere necessary for language practice.

Yet there were times when the '99 class surpassed every other class. One evening all the students were told to hold a party in their classroom. The other classes duly pushed their desks against their wall, bought apples and sunflower seeds, blew up balloons, drew pretty pictures on the blackboards and devised a programme of riddles and games (musical chairs, pass the parcel and some game that involved hopping with a mop). When the time came for the party to begin, they dutifully sat behind their desks, safe in the knowledge that their monitor would steer them through the evening's joy. The games began, the seeds were cracked, they clapped and passed parcels. They were 18 going on eight.

The class of '99 were also having a party, but without the aid of seeds or mops. Instead there was loud Turkish music, its beat so heavy and percussive that it was like a blow. Their desks were also against the walls, but only so that people could dance. The whole class was getting down, bar a few sulky girls who sat in a corner, perhaps mourning the absence of parcels. Rosmimet – one of the Uighur boys – stood at the front, shouting and punching the air. He was DJ and MC and fully in the house.

It was hard not to attribute their successes as a class to their ethnic mix. Yes, it created tensions and there were no doubt grievances and misunderstandings but there was also a dynamism to them, an energy that when present made teaching almost bearable.

35

Freedom of religious beliefs is not freedom for religion.
Xinjiang Daily, May 1996

THE CHILDREN WERE PLAYING at dragons. They chased through the morning air, trying to scorch each other with their new cold fire. When they tired of that, they threw bangers. For several weeks the Uighur children had no other purpose than to cause explosions. No peace escaped destruction; every quiet was detonated.

Spades bit into the mounds of coal; the heating began to stir, causing pipes and radiators to clank complaints at being woken. The last leaves fell, new views appeared. Buildings showed their age. To look up was to move in time: first, the bright boxes of the Han at street level, then above them, a flourish of Arabic or an arched window, and higher still, perhaps a fragment of Cyrillic or a sloping eave. And on 17 November, the holy month of Ramadan began.

I rang Ismail to invite him for lunch.

'No, I can't.'

'Oh, are you busy?'

'No, this is a special time for us. It is *Ramazan ul mubarak*. We cannot eat or drink all day.'

'Will all Uighurs being doing this?'

'Most, maybe 80 per cent.'

The festival of Ramadan takes place during the ninth month of the Islamic calendar (which being lunar rather than solar, falls on different dates each year). The observation of Ramadan is the third of the five *rukhns* ('pillars') of Islam, the cardinal rules that all Muslims must follow. It is thus an integral part of any Muslim's faith.

Ramadan is a time to improve self-control, a period in which to grow stronger by enduring weakness. It is thus a time of prayer and fasting: nothing should be eaten or drunk between sunrise and sunset. Sex and smoking are also prohibited during these hours. Some are sensibly exempt from fasting: those pregnant, ill or menstruating. Fasting is supposed to diminish the preoccupation with one's bodily needs, allowing attention to be focussed on spiritual matters. The experience of hunger is also supposed to encourage feelings of sympathy for the less fortunate; acts of charity (*zakat*, which literally means 'to grow') are especially important during Ramadan.

But although this was a major event for most Uighurs, I wouldn't have known it was Ramadan if Ismail hadn't told me. Nothing looked to have changed. There was none of the commercial frenzy associated with Western religious festivals, no Ramadan cards or gifts. The restaurants weren't as busy, and one or two closed for the month, but that was all. People got on with their fasting quietly.

They had good reason to be discreet. The observance of Ramadan is banned in schools, hospitals and other state institutions. Students and workers in these places were encouraged to break their fast and also discouraged from attending the mosque. Some students in the college said they had been threatened with expulsion if they refused to comply. But there had been no official proclamation in the newspapers or on television regarding the counter-revolutionary nature of Ramadan. Those I spoke to said that they had just been told in a meeting with their superiors.

And in the absence of any official statement, rumours thrived: there were stories of name checks in canteens; of students being marched to their cafeterias; of lunchtime banquets sprung upon Muslim officials; of long and tedious meetings whose sole purpose was to see who would drink or eat from the orchards of fruit placed thoughtfully on the tables.

One can only speculate about the reasons for the ban. In the wake of 11 September, the government may have felt that anything Islamic had become fair game, especially given their rigorously established link between religion and separatism. But it is also possible that they saw Bush's war on terror as a chance to make people choose between their jobs and their faith.

Government workers like Tilawaldi had been forced to make similar decisions long before the Ramadan restrictions. Officials are not allowed to wear *doppas* or have beards. *Doppas* are part of Uighur tradition but don't have any religious significance; perhaps the idea was that ethnicity had to defer to nationality. The case of beards is far more clear-cut; we all now know that any Muslim (or Arab) sporting a long beard must be a militant fundamentalist with a pack of plastic explosive secreted in his lower intestine. At the time, I disagreed with the government's approach. If the Islamic terrorists weren't allowed to grow their beards, how could they be identified? However, if left alone, they would incriminate themselves. But perhaps those in power thought the beard was the *cause* of such beliefs. It was hard to say.

36

THE GIVING OF ALMS, known as *zakat*, is another of the five *rukhns* of Islam (the other three are acceptance of the creed that there is no God but Allah and Mohammed is his Prophet, praying five times daily, and making the pilgrimage or *hadj* to Mecca at least once in a lifetime). Muslims should give 2.5 per cent of their income to those in need throughout the year, not just during Ramadan. This sounded fine in theory, but I wondered how it worked in practice, in Yining. So I called Murat.

We arranged a time to meet, once I had agreed to visit his class. It occurred to me that our 'friendship' was one of pure utility, an exchange of my native tones for his insight into the religious sphere. Maybe all relationships are based on mutual use, but if this is true, it is knowledge best forgotten: it's hard to carry on a 'friendship' when plainly aware of your motives, especially if they are less than sparkling.

We met outside the college after lunch, then walked towards the square. He asked me some questions about phrasal verbs, then some about grammar, and I did my best to answer them. After 15 minutes of being quizzed, I felt I'd earned the right to say:

'Well, I've also got a few questions. I've been reading about the *zakat*.'

'Ye-es?' he said, cautiously.

'The *zakat* is money that Muslims have to pay to help the poor.'

'That's true.'

'But who do they give the money to? Do they give it to the mosque?'

'There are eight types of people. The first is the very poor, those in poverty who are Muslims, who believe in Allah. The second are a bit like the first. The third is the *imam*, sometimes he will need some help.'

'What about family and friends?'

'You can't give *zakat* to your family. Your friends, you can.'

'Do many Muslims in Ghulja give it?'

'Yes, all. You know it is very important in our religion.'

We walked on a bit, slipping and sliding on patches of ice. There was something puzzling about this, but it was hard to think without falling over.

'Most Uighur people in Ghulja don't have jobs. Perhaps 70 per cent. So is it difficult for them to give the *zakat*?'

'Yes, that's right. You only have to pay if you can afford. Perhaps if your income is more than... 6,000 yuan a month.'

'Well, I doubt that most people earn that much.'

'No, most don't.'

I could have left it there, but something in his certainty irritated me. I was tired of hearing about what a good Muslim he was and how terrible the less devout were. So I continued

'That means most people don't pay the *zakat*.'

'No, they don't.'

'And do you?'

'No, I don't have enough money.'

'Oh.'

We walked on in silence. It began to rain, a rare event that would usually have filled me with joy. We took shelter in a restaurant and ordered some kebabs. They arrived fatty and lukewarm. Neither of us said anything. I took this opportune moment to ask if I could come to the mosque one Friday. He was understandably less than thrilled and asked why. I started to explain but he cut me off.

'Actually it is not permitted. But if you convert, you could.'

'There's no chance of that. I want to understand, not believe.'

'But you should believe.'

I blundered on.

'Well, you think that, but I don't. But I realise how little I know, and I would appreciate some help trying to understand.'

He was quiet after that, and I wish I could say that we wrapped things up harmoniously, with me apologising for being so blunt, and him for being unhelpful. But it was a long time until I saw Murat again.

37

MY FLAT WAS NICE for ten minutes a day. This was when the sun crept in with promises of warmth. Then my plastic-covered sofa gleamed while the dust did a dance. But it did not last. The north-facing aspect of the building, coupled with the row of trees outside, meant that a Stygian gloom pervaded. I had to switch on the lights when I got up, even in summer. They stayed on all day, dimming and brightening as the power came and went, as if the place's former glories were attempting to get in touch.

The linoleum kept tearing; the power sockets were at head height; and the neighbours! The woman who lived above me was visited most nights by a man who kicked her door then shouted her name while slamming his body against it. He was definitely drunk, and may also have been her husband. Below me were a Han family from Sichuan province who did their cooking directly under my window. If I forgot to close my window at lunch or dinnertime, my flat would fill with the acrid smell of burning oil and chilli. But I should have counted myself lucky; at least I had four walls.

38

NOMO LIVED IN A burrow above the river. He had hollowed out part of the cliff and lined it with blankets. It was a one-room burrow but that made it snug. An old red armchair stood outside it: this was what had led me to scramble down the cliff.

He was washing socks in a biscuit tin. Some cooking pots lay by the fire. A collection of shirts and trousers hung from a poplar's branches. My mind emptied but my mouth still spoke.

'Nice place you got here,' I said in Chinese.

'Thanks.'

'How long have you lived here?'

'18 years.'

'Isn't it cold in winter?'

'No, not bad.'

He wore a pair of khaki slacks, the knees of which were patched in different colours. His four jumpers all had holes but in different places. A red Coca-Cola cap completed his outfit. He looked lean but otherwise healthy. I tried to work out his ethnicity and failed.

'Are you Hui? Or Xibo?'

He shook his head. 'Zang.'

At least that's what it sounded like. It was hard to understand his Chinese; the fact that he was missing a few teeth didn't help either. I thought I knew most of the ethnic groups in China but I'd never heard of the Zang. I asked him to repeat himself, but he just said Zang again.

'Have you got a cigarette?' he asked

'Sorry, I don't smoke.'

This was a huge disappointment. I fished through my pockets for something else to give him. There was only money or some lemon sweets. I offered him the tin. His eyes sparked at the sight and he held out both hands. I shook six or seven into his cupped palms, and Nomo stuffed them all into his mouth. He sat down on a stump, smiling and sucking with evident pleasure while the river hurried past.

After he finished the sweets, Nomo stood and shuffled away, beckoning me to follow. We wound along the bank in single file. Blue-winged birds darted by the water's edge; insects crept on its skin. A quiet droning could be heard, mechanical and far off.

Nomo stopped by a pile of branches. He looked around, saw no one was watching, then began clearing them away. Gradually, he exposed a black tarpaulin weighted down with driftwood. He pulled it to one side. A pile of bottles glinted green. I looked at him quizzically.

'They are my money.'

'Uh huh.'

But he wasn't crazy. People pay for rubbish in China: glass, paper, cardboard, metal and plastic. If there's one thing common to all places in China, it is the sight of people stooping to fill sacks with bottles and cans. You couldn't call it a job: no one employs them. But the three yuan (about 25 pence) paid for each sack – by factories and businesses – can mean the difference between starving and not. And the good people of Yining made life easier for him: Han, Uighur, Hui and Kazakh alike, all threw their rubbish everywhere except into a bin.

The droning began to rise, growing harsh and insistent. Nomo hid the bottles under their cover. He put his hands over his ears and shook his head vigorously. A speedboat smashed into view, its life-jacketed passengers screaming with satisfaction at having paid to risk their lives. The driver was trying to give them their money's worth, twisting the wheel left and right, causing the boat to tilt at 45 degrees. They saw us, waved, then went back to screaming.

Nomo asked me to stay for supper. Although I was curious to see what he might produce, I decided I was capable of getting an upset stomach on my own.

39

I AM DRAWN TO places of worship. Perhaps from a secular fascination with an activity that I struggle to comprehend. Or out of a refusal to be excluded (even though it is I who have done the excluding). With churches, this is seldom a problem. It's all right to saunter in, rub the brass, read the stones. But mosques seem less inviting to the unbeliever. Partly because one should make preparations: you must take off your shoes and be suitably clean. There is also not that sense of entitlement that comes from Christianity's being (until very recently) an integral part of one's culture. I did not feel I had the right to just walk into a mosque. I needed to be invited. However, after Murat had said that it was forbidden for me, as a *kafir* (unbeliever), to enter, I gave up, accepting it as one of the costs of atheism (and no worse than eternal damnation). I resigned myself to just admiring their outsides.

In Yining, there were plenty to look at. The authorities may have been 'strengthening their management of religious affairs', but they hadn't closed the mosques. In addition to at least 50 functioning mosques in the city, a grand new one was under construction near the square, financed by a Saudi businessman. When finished, it would be the largest in Yining, and possibly Xinjiang.

By the middle of November it was -10C. In the city, most people's houses were heated, which meant that as soon as you went outside, you wanted to go back in. Thermal vests and leggings became *de rigueur*; every now and then you glimpsed flashes of white at the neck or ankle, like teasing hints of some superhero costume. The older Uighur men donned trench coats and felt hats and looked distinctly Sicilian. Farmers stomped about like pantomime villains, scowling beneath fur hats, shod in knee-high leather boots, with several thick green army coats hanging cape-like from their shoulders. It became impossible to tell the sex of the young; they were just parcels of clothes not to be opened till spring.

But no matter how cold it got, I had to walk through the streets: there was always something worth seeing. One afternoon the first act was a road sweeper, accompanied by cart and broom. Several furry lumps were wedged behind the handle of the cart. I looked closer, and saw they were rabbits. The sweeper smiled and rubbed his stomach.

A humming filled the intermission. I had heard it before; it always seemed loudest at twilight. I guessed it was the overhead electricity wires, whining at the sudden demand for power. The next act followed, a man sharpening knives upon his bicycle: the turning pedals spun a grindstone against which the blades scraped and sparked. There was a short line of women waiting, most of them clutching meat cleavers.

The main act was a small mosque. Two towers rose on either side of its gate. The colour had faded from the wooden posts but they still looked strong. I entered a swept-clean yard. A raised colonnade ran along the far wall, with strips of green matting on top of the brick. A pair of black shoes lay to the right of a small door. It opened and a Uighur man came out, dressed in a blue padded jacket, wearing a black *doppa*. He was stooping, either from age, or the lowness of the door. When he saw me he stopped and stared in a manner that did not seem welcoming. But instead of telling me to leave, he asked (in Chinese) where I was from. When I told him, he said, 'England? They also face south when they pray.'

Then he saw me shivering and said, 'It's cold. Come inside.'

I slipped off my shoes and followed him in. A bare entrance hall fed into the main prayer room. There was something familiar about this arrangement; it was like many of the Uighur houses I'd been in: the small atrium, the larger sitting room. Did they build their houses like their mosques or their mosques like their houses? Either way, it suggested something that ran deep.

The *imam's* pulpit stood in the corner, painted the same blue as the Uighur houses. A picture of Mecca rested in a niche on the north wall. I asked how old the mosque was and the man said about 100 years. It suddenly occurred to me that he might be the *imam*. When I asked him he smiled, his teeth glinting like rows of golden sweetcorn.

'No, I just look after the place.'

'How often do you pray?'

'Five times a day.'

'If a man doesn't come five times, is this a problem?'

'Perhaps. We all have *djinns* [spirits] who watch us. One here and one here.' He patted his shoulders. 'They see what we do and they tell Allah. But a man is still a Muslim, whether he comes once or five times.'

This sounded like a different interpretation of Islam to that preached by Murat and his friends, one that seemed closer to the sentiments of the founder of the Hanafi school, Abu Hanifa, who reportedly once said that anyone who professed faith was a Muslim, and that it was up to Allah to judge them.

Hanifa, an Arab of Persian origin, was born in Iraq in 699AD. During the early part of his life he was mostly occupied in business, especially the sale of textiles. According to his hagiographers, his business flourished due to his scrupulous honesty. As he grew older he developed an interest in religious learning, which led him to study with many renowned *imams*. Hanifa established a *madrasa* in Kufa at which he lectured. His opinions came to be respected, especially his use of reason to settle theological questions. He saw Islamic law as an organic thing in which changes would be necessary as society changed.

As his fame grew, a number of rulers tried to enlist him in the service of their regimes, usually by offering him the post of chief *qadi* (judge). Hanafi always refused these appointments in a bold and unequivocal manner, and it was this that proved his undoing. In 763AD, al-Mansoor, then ruler of Baghdad, again offered him the post of chief *qadi*. Hanifa refused, claiming that he felt himself unfit for the position. Al-Mansoor tried to insist, accusing him of lying. Hanifa is said to have replied that if he were lying, then his claim to being unfit was doubly correct. The incensed ruler had him thrown in prison where he died two years later. It is said that he was mourned by so many that his funeral service had to be held six times. The Abu Hanifa Mosque was later built in the Adhamiyah neighborhood of Baghdad, where it still stands.

The caretaker apologised and said he had to go: his brother was coming round with a sheep. For my part I remembered that I had to teach. My thoughts turned to the thrilling topic of the future present. We shook hands, then he put his hand on mine. 'Come again,' he said. 'You are welcome.'

40

I MAY NOT HAVE been Colin's biggest fan but there was one thing we had in common: neither of us wanted to spend all our time teaching Han kids from *bingtuans*. I had, perhaps unreasonably, expected to have a few more Kazakh and Uighur students, given that they made up almost half the population. The problem was our contracts: they clearly stated that we were not to teach anyone who was not a student in the college, which, given the ethnic make-up of our department, made it virtually impossible for us to teach anyone other than the *bingtuan* kids. But the solution was simple: we ignored our contracts.

To give Colin credit, he had been running an evening class for Kazakh and Uighur adults for the previous few years, what he called his ' KU class'. Various other teachers, including Eleanor, had taught this class in the past, but it was nonetheless something Colin had initiated and been mostly responsible for. What made it possible was the permission of the dean, who was perhaps not unsympathetic, given his wife and son. However, he didn't permit the use of the department classrooms purely from the goodness of his heart. None of the teachers got paid for their work, and all the KU course fees went directly to him. Given that the course didn't technically exist, there was nothing to stop him from keeping the money (though this is not to say that he did).

Once word got round that the course was set to start again, there was plenty of interest. About 40 people signed up, too many for one class, but about right for two. Eleanor and I agreed to teach one class and Colin the other. All that was left to arrange was when we would meet and who would be in which class. Colin suggested that we meet the students later in the week, and that he would tell us when.

A few days later a friend of Eleanor's invited us round for lunch. She mentioned that she had invited Colin as well. The day passed with no sign of him. When we returned to the college in the early evening, we ran into Hamit and Yusuf, two of our prospective students. They said hello and asked why we hadn't been at the meeting.

'Which meeting?'

'The one to arrange the class.'

When confronted, Colin maintained that he didn't know about the lunch and hadn't been invited. We knew it was a lie but said nothing. It was hard to understand why he had contrived to have the meeting without us, especially since we were certain to find out.

But at least the course was going to take place. My students looked to be an interesting bunch. Among them were four teachers, two doctors, a gynaecologist, a chemist, two farmers and a man who made saddles. Most of them were in their 30s; all were married with children. They couldn't have been less like my 'official' students. I dared to hope they might be able to tell me what was going on.

41

MISS CAI HAD BEGUN to obsess me. Although she had no real power of her own, she was nonetheless my point of contact with those who did. So for me at least, she was an important person, yet one that I knew nothing about. Even her age was a mystery. Sometimes she looked to be in her mid-20s; at others she seemed in her late 40s. There was the always the sense of a performance, of words chosen with care. I wondered if there was anything behind her well-fashioned mask.

It didn't take much digging – her name dropped into a few conversations, always in an admiring fashion – to discover that 20 years before, when still a student, Miss Cai had embarked on a torrid affair. The man was her teacher, and he was married. He also had a daughter little older than her. In the end he left his wife and married her (Miss Cai, not his daughter). In present-day China, this would be a mild scandal; in the 1980s, it must have been out-rageous. The fact that some of my Han students knew suggested it was far from forgotten, or perhaps forgiven.

In an attempt to heal relations after the Kazakhstan episode, I gave her a bilingual edition of *Animal Farm* I had bought in Urumqi. I was initially surprised to see a book whose main message was of the potential dangers of socialism, until I remembered that its warning could not apply to China, where the dream of a socialist utopia was fast becoming a splendid reality. I presented it to her on my return. Her first reaction was shock.

'For me?'

'Yes, for you.'

'Really?'

'Yes, really.'

'Thank you very much! Oh, this looks very interesting!'

'It's about socialism.'

'Oh, good! You know, that is my major. I want to do a post-graduate degree.'

She looked at the back of the book, then rummaged through her handbag. She extracted a ten-yuan note and placed it on the table.

'There you are. And thank you.'

'What's that for?'

'The book. That's the price isn't it? Did it cost more?'

'No, no, it's a *present*. You don't need to pay me.'

If she had seemed shocked before, now she looked terrified. We had another of the 'for me?' exchanges, then she sat back, beaming and confused. I could see she was about to ask why, so I nipped in first.

'Do you like reading much?'

'Yes, especially classic literature. Do you know *Kongzi* [Confucius]?'

'Why do you like that?'

'Everyone's position is clear, you know who they are and what they will do. Modern books are too confusing.'

'But maybe the characters are more realistic, more like people.'

She smiled at me; I smiled back. She started to say something but then the telephone rang; when the call was over I could see that the mask was back. It would have been easy to make much of these personal scraps, to extrapolate a story of youthful transgression and subsequent ostracism; of a life lived in fear of ever stepping outside the boundaries again. A desire that might lead her to accept a job where nothing more was needed than to follow orders and keep her mouth shut.

42

IF THE POLITICAL was taboo with my Chinese students, it was immediately apparent that the same would not be true of the KU class. Even the simplest activity could elicit a remark that would require the subject to be changed. A simple warm-up exercise could quickly become a political minefield.

'So Hamit, which person would you most like to meet and why?'

'The future leader of the Uighurs who will unite us.'

'Right, well, let's try to keep to actual people. What about you, Yusuf – can you think of some person from history?'

'Yes, I would most like to meet Sadur.'

There were murmurs of approval.

'Who was he?'

'A great man! He fought the Chinese.'

'All right, please turn to page 45.'

It was difficult because although I was interested in these kinds of opinions, I realised that the only thing more dangerous than running a secret class for Uighurs was running one that was a focus for dissent. After all, this was taking place in English, in a classroom in the English department; if another teacher, or a good student, heard something like the exchange above, we would all be in trouble.

I wondered what motivated them to make such comments. Most of the class seemed to agree about the misfortunes of the Uighur people. If they weren't trying to convince themselves, perhaps their comments were directed at me. They, and many other Uighurs, seemed to view themselves as a people overlooked by the world, especially compared with the Tibetans, who through the Dalai Lama had managed to make themselves a cause *par excellence*. Whenever I mentioned that I hoped to write a book, the response was enthusiastic, a chorus of 'tell people about us'.

I wanted to tell them they were wrong, that there were people who had heard of Uighurs and, more importantly, who cared. But apart from a few Central Asian scholars and human rights organisations, they were a people whose name could only evoke a blank. But there were people intent on changing this, people with the power to make a difference.

43

This is a very good opportunity to intensify the fight against separatists in Xinjiang... China is also a victim of terrorism.

ZHU FENG, director of the International
Security Program at Beijing University.

WHEN THE CHINESE GOVERNMENT started talking about having its own 'terrorists' after 9/11, it was perhaps in the hope that this would defer any criticism of its policies in Xinjiang. Even repressive regimes need to justify their actions, and the notion of harsh laws being necessary to combat dangerous elements (and thus protect civilians) is a well-worn excuse.

But this seldom does the trick; there are still those tiresome do-gooders who insist on poking their nose into such sovereign concerns. And indeed, in early November 2001, Mary Robinson – the then-UN Human Rights Commissioner – had meetings with Jiang Zemin where she expressed concerns about the new crackdown, sensibly warning that it might produce further resentment and lead to further terrorism. The Chinese president is said to have 'listened carefully', though not to have offered a comment. But a response soon followed.

On 14 November, Foreign Ministry spokesman Zhu Bangzao gave a press briefing on Uighur separatism. He listed ten organizations based in Afghanistan, elsewhere in Central Asia or in Xinjiang, that he said were fighting to end Chinese rule over the region. Not only did he argue that some Xinjiang separatists had received training in Afghanistan before being sent to China, but also that the East Turkestan Islamic Movement (ETIM) was in fact supported and directed by Osama Bin Laden. It was claimed that Hasan Mahsum, the leader of the ETIM, had met Bin Laden in 1999 and 2001, and received promises of 'an enormous sum of money'. Bin Laden's aim was apparently to launch a 'holy war' with the aim of setting up a theocratic Islamic state in Xinjiang.

So Uighur separatists were not simply domestic troublemakers, but also part of the international web of death run by the terrorist *du jour*. To criticise China's attempts to crackdown on them would thus be tantamount to questioning the whole war against terror. No action against them could be called excessive; all their rights were forfeit; they were on the side of evil.

The government also took the opportunity to update history. The 1997 riots were no longer the work of 'social garbage' and other criminal elements. Instead it became a 'serious riot' perpetrated by the East Turkestan Islamic Party of Allah, during which 'the terrorists shouted slogans calling for the establishment of an Islamic kingdom'. The claims of vandalism and of innocent civilians being attacked were also repeated.

Most Uighur independence groups denied the accusations of links to al-Qaeda and the Taliban. In a January interview with Radio Free Asia's Uighur service, Hasan Mahsum – the leader of ETIM and China's most-wanted terrorist – said his organization's goal was to liberate Xinjiang from Chinese rule, but he denied it was engaged in violent acts or received help from al Qaeda. 'We don't have any organisational contact or relations with al Qaeda or the Taliban. Maybe some individuals fought alongside them, but we don't have any organizational ties with them. We don't get any financial assistance.'

A spokesman for the East Turkestan Information Centre said, 'China is now trying to characterize Uighurs as being intent on setting up an Islamic state but our goal is actually a secular democratic government. Osama bin Laden represents extremist Islamic thinking and has nothing to do with Uighurs'. He also chose to add, presumably as proof that Uighurs were not Islamic fundamentalists, 'our men often drink beer and our women wear miniskirts'.

Oddly, this failed to convince the Chinese government. An

editorial in *China Daily* argued that the pro-independence groups had 'demanded that their members not publish radical remarks for the time being, in order to avoid being linked with the terrorist organisations by the countries in which they are located'. Whilst there might have been some truth in this allegation, it was also impossible to disprove: those who made radical remarks were terrorists; those who did not were well-disciplined terrorists.

There were also reactions from more objective sources: 'It is quite possible there would have been meetings between some of Bin Laden's followers and militants in the Uighur movement,' said Paul Wilkinson, director of the Centre for the Study of Terrorism and Political Violence at St Andrews University. 'I suspect it's very small scale and the links so far are modest, but I don't doubt the Bin Laden network would be interested in making those connections'. The tone of the international media also changed. Before there had been talk of Xinjiang as a remote place where human rights abuses took place; now it was 'a hot bed of Muslim unrest' (AFP), and 'China's restive north-west' (Reuters).

The rhetoric of both sides was in place; the only thing missing was proof. Yes, some Uighurs had been arrested in Afghanistan, and yes, it was *possible* that there had been meetings between some Uighurs and members of al Qaeda, but this was far from conclusive. Crucially, there was nothing to tie the Uighurs fighting in Afghanistan to any of the bombings or riots in Xinjiang except their ethnicity. And if that were proof of guilt, then all Uighurs were terrorists. Unfortunately, at the time, a great many people were using the same cracked logic: He is a terrorist and he is Muslim, so if he is Muslim, he must be a terrorist.

After 9/11 much was made of the importance of *jihad* in Islam (usually wrongly translated as 'holy war' when it only means 'struggle'). However, for the majority of Uighurs, the school of Islam they follow preaches against acts of terror. Abu Hanifa forbade the killing of women, children and the elderly, sentiments that were not accepted in Europe for several more centuries.

But whilst this is true of most Uighurs, there are undeniably some, especially in south Xinjiang, that follow a more conservative interpretation of the Qur'an. One that compels the women to wear veils, *burqas* and *chadors*. One not dissimilar to Wahhabism, the form of Islam practiced in Saudi Arabia and the one to which Bin Laden adheres.

Wahhabism is the name given today to the ideas of Ibn 'Abd al-Wahhab (1703–1792), who along with Muhammed Ibn Saud, led a militant reform movement in Arabia. Ibn 'Abd al-Wahhab's teachings drew heavily on those of the medieval theologian Ibn Taimiya, who argued that the practices of Muslims were not distinct enough from those of non-Muslims. The ways of the Prophet Muhammad and his community were the only ones deemed acceptable. Ibn 'Abd al-Wahhab led an uncompromising campaign against any ritual innovations or practices not sanctioned by the Prophet. Music, poetry, silk, gold and dancing were all banned because of *hadiths* ('traditions' or reported sayings and actions of the Prophet) condemning them. However, in theory anything not explicitly forbidden by the Qur'an or in *hadiths* was acceptable, which allowed the Saudi regime to introduce such innovations as the radio, television and telephone, albeit not without some resistance from those who argued that the only practices acceptable were those explicitly sanctioned by the Prophet. In 1962, the Muslim World League was founded for the specific purpose of spreading Wahhabism throughout the world.

Two factors may have encouraged the growth of Wahhabism in south Xinjiang. The first is its proximity to Pakistan, where Wahhabism has grown in influence since the 1980s: people, goods and ideas stream along the Karakoram highway (at least when it is not closed by snow or landslides).

The presence of ideas, however, is not the same as their acceptance. But poverty can help to prepare the ground: when China was 'opened' to the world in the late 1970s, cheaper, better products flooded in. Domestic industries struggled to keep up, not least the agricultural. In Xinjiang, at least 75 per cent of Uighurs are involved in farming or husbandry, especially in cotton production. From 1991, many former Soviet countries started selling their cotton cheaply on the world market, undercutting Chinese prices. Previously, the government had subsidised farmers' losses, but this policy abruptly ended. The tightrope and the safety net had been simultaneously removed.

Discontent grew and with it mosque attendance. To be a believer became a form of protest: it was what the Han were not. It was around this time that the bombings and major protests began. First in Kashgar in 1989, where there was a bus bombing, then the Baren riots in 1990, then another bombing in Urumqi in 1992, one in Kashgar in 1993 and a riot in 1995 in Hotan.

All of these incidents, bar the Urumqi bombing, took place in the south-west corner of Xinjiang. They clearly form a context to the riots in Yining. However, this is not to say the events of February 1997 were motivated by the same frustrations, nor that they were orchestrated by the same agencies. But you couldn't rule it out.

44

The ethnic groups in Xinjiang have always had the glorious tradition of loving and safeguarding national unity and Islam is a peace loving religion. The Chinese government's crackdown against the 'East Turkestan' terrorist forces is not directed at any particular ethnic group or any particular religion but at criminal activities of violence and terrorism.

China Daily, 2002

THE CHINESE GOVERNMENT clearly had no wish to be misunderstood. It was probably in the same spirit of clarity and forthrightness that they choose to amend the provisions of the Criminal Law in December 2001. Although the term 'terrorist organisation' was not clearly defined, this did not stop the penalties for leading or organising such a group from being increased. A new clause was added to punish those who disturbed social order by assembling in public places, obstructing traffic, or preventing agents of the state from carrying out their duties. Such wanton acts of lawlessness could result in 'public surveillance' or up to five years in prison. Taking part in any kind of protest or demonstration, however peaceful, could lead to imprisonment.

Once the government had spelt out all that could not be done, the crackdown commenced in earnest. There were more patrols by security forces in the major cities. Surveillance was increased at airports and railway stations, and there was closer monitoring of vehicles entering the province. Yang Si, head of the *bingtuan* armed police, said that rapid-reaction forces should be ready for increased separatist activity in the region, and that police in Xinjiang should concentrate on separatists and other 'criminal religious personages'.

Leaving aside the minor question of evidence, let's assume that the Chinese government were right: that the people who blew up the buses did so as a result of their religious beliefs, and that said people did have links to al Qaeda or the Taliban. Would this have justified the general campaign against religion and peaceful dissent? Whatever the Chinese government's claims to the contrary, the crackdown was inevitably aimed at a particular ethnic and religious group; it was hard to imagine these measures affecting many Han Buddhists. The fundamental question was surely the extent to which it is acceptable to violate civil liberties in order to maintain national security (a question people were asking of other countries besides China).

However, at the time I was asking myself a quite different question: Did I know any 'terrorists'?

45

OF COURSE NOT. Or at least I hoped not. A more sensible question was, 'What did the Uighurs that I knew think of the war on terror?'

As part of the KU class, I held an English Corner at my house, so that people could practice conversation in a more informal setting. One frozen December morning we were talking about dreams. I asked if anyone ever had recurring dreams.

A small man with a pinched face said, 'In my dream I often pray to Allah.'

'Do you always use the same words?'

'Yes. Sometimes I am without clothes.'

'When you're praying?'

'No, then I am in the street.'

His name was Yusuf. He sold saddles, stirrups, bridles, and bits, all made by him and his brother. He had been learning English for a year and a half but was already as fluent as the best of my Han students (most of whom had been learning since secondary school). This was doubly impressive, as he hadn't been to school when he was young.

After a few others had related their dreams, Yusuf said he had a question for me.

'Go ahead.'

'I don't know. Maybe I should not.'

'It's fine, really.'

'OK!' he said, then smiled broadly. 'Nick, what do you think of bin Laden?'

The room went quiet. I took a few moments to think, then said, 'I don't think he's good. I think it's wrong to kill people. But I also think that Bush is wrong.'

He nodded.

'And what do you think?'

'Oh!' He brought his hand to his heart. 'I'm so proud of him!'

I spluttered out a why.

'He has done much to help Muslims.'

'How has he helped Muslims?'

'He has given much money for education. He has helped people to learn. He is very good.'

'But what have they learnt? Science? Technology? Something useful? Or how to hate others? And what about the people he's killed? Is that right?'

Yusuf scratched his ear. 'Maybe it is OK.'

There was a brief silence. Then Hamit, one of the young doctors, spoke up, glancing around at his peers.

'No, *we* don't think so. A leader should help improve the people's situation. Their health, the conditions. If he do that first, we think he is good. But he does not do this. We think he is wrong.'

Yusuf slowly shook his head. I wondered where this was going, whether there would be some drawing of lines, talk of 'good' and 'bad' Muslims. But it was neither the time nor place for such accusations. Instead the conversation shifted to the pressing subject of whether I should shave off my attempt at a beard.

'It is too terrible,' said Yusuf, and Hamit quickly agreed.

46

THE TEMPERATURE DROPPED to -15C. In the mornings, on the way to class, my nasal fluid froze. My wet hair filled with ice.

But there were compensations. Horse sausages were everywhere, thick brown coils that hung outside windows like luxury bird feeders. The Uighur restaurants filled with stews and soups: there was *ulgre*, a thick tomato broth with noodles (and if you asked nicely, a poached egg). There was the dumpling soup, *chuchura*, stuffed with coriander and chilli. There were also sheep heads and hooves that you had to suck. Best of all, claimed a new friend of mine, was a dish called *isip*.

Rukiye was a teacher in the history department; he was also a student in the class that did not exist. We discovered a mutual interest in snooker and arranged to play. Before I met him I didn't know that Yining had any snooker halls. There turned out to be lot, most of them in basements. People played pool, snooker and a game with 15 reds and a black. The tables were surprisingly good. It was almost something Han and Uighurs did together, in that they shared the same space, although they didn't actually play against each other.

We had to wait for a free table. My eyes drifted over framed photos of former world champions: Davis, Hendry, Taylor and Parrot. There were other pictures. A bare-chested man embraced a topless woman. They were both Western-looking, as were all the other lewd images in magazines and on condom packets; it was as if Chinese people were incapable of nudity.

A small door at the back of the hall opened; a man stepped out, closed the door quickly, then looked around furtively. I went over and opened the door. Inside seven or eight people sat around what looked to be a giant fruit machine embedded in a table. The air was thick with smoke; money lay on the table. They looked up at me and for a moment the only sound was the spinning of reels. Then they returned to the blur of bells and fruit. I went back to Rukiye who was busy racking up.

'I think they're gambling in there.'

He raised his eyebrows. I wasn't sure he understood. His snooker vocabulary was very good ('This is spider, yes?') but the rest was pretty thin.

'You know, they play a game for money.'

'Ah, yes, for money. Very good!'

'Isn't it that illegal? Aren't they worried about the police?'

'No. Chinese love to play for money.'

I broke off. Rukiye potted a red then the pink. His next red got caught in the jaws of the middle pocket. I swooped on it, potted the blue, missed my next red by a foot. As he was cuing up he said, 'Last week special police came to see me.'

'Why are they special?' I asked as nonchalantly as I could.

'Because they can do anything.' His voice lowered. 'Even kill.'

'We'd call them 'secret' police. So, uh, what did they want?'

'They ask about my students. And you.'

'What? Why?'

'About politics. And religion. But is OK. I tell them many, many boring things but is all nothing.'

I tried to remember if I had said anything suspect in class. The problem was that my conception of suspect probably differed from the authorities'. I knew better than to talk about anything political directly, but because these were the kinds of subjects I was interested in (as opposed to how to give directions to the supermarket, or whether love is more important than money), I often found myself giving the conversation a nudge in that direction. It was the kind of thing only a native speaker would notice, and I was the only one of those in the room, unless of course the room was bugged and they then got some willing foreigner to listen. I knew this was all incredibly unlikely, but it still bothered me. I tried to focus on

the more immediate difficulty of Rukiye's 20-point lead. Unfortunately there was little chance of solving either problem.

Afterwards a buoyant Rukiye and I went to his sister's house,
where our *isip* was being prepared.

'So what is it?'

'It is meat.'

'Anything else?'

'And some rice.'

Finally, the feted dish arrived. Amorphous cream-coloured
lumps bobbed in a reddish broth. Whatever it was, I was hungry.

'This is sheep meat.'

'Oh, good, I like lamb.'

'It is this part.'

He pointed at his chest.

'What is this called? You use to breathe.'

'Lung. It is the lung.'

'Leng?'

'Lung.'

I'd seen it for sale in the markets, big chunks of sheep's lung,
stuffed with flour. I always enjoyed seeing it as I felt sure I would
never have to eat it, because it was very time-consuming to prepare.
But Rukiye's sister had been exceptionally kind.

I kept putting it into my mouth but the bowl refused to empty.
It tasted all right, almost creamy, not a problem as long as I didn't
think about what I was eating. But Rukiye was intent on perfecting
his pronunciation.

'Lung.'

One mouthful then another.

'Lung.'

It's just turnip. You can do this.

'Lung lung lung.'

47

YINING IS THE CAPITAL of the Yili Kazakh Autonomous Region. I knew this, I heard or read it constantly, but it refused to sink in. In the same way that Urumqi didn't feel especially Uighur, Yining lacked any particular quality identifying it as Kazakh. Yes, there were plenty of Kazakhs, and yes, you could hear plenty of people speaking Kazakh, and yes, there were more than a few restaurants that specialised in Kazakh dishes (in particular, horse meat). But none of this seemed to cohere in the way that it did for the Han and Uighur. This apparent lack of distinctiveness may have been due to the fact that most Kazakhs in Yining didn't strive for the same kind of separation as the Han and Uighur. Many Kazakhs seemed happy to spend time with either, whereas I had never seen Han and Uighurs socialising.

In one way it was surprising that so many Kazakhs chose to associate with Han. I had naively imagined they would be more likely to connect with Hui or Uighur, due to their shared experience as minorities. But it appeared any such notion was as idiotic as the Chinese government's attempts to pretend that the whole country was one hyper-extended family: quite a few Uighurs didn't seem too keen on the Hui, and there was clearly some resentment towards Kazakhs, albeit nothing like that directed towards the Han. The main grudge against Kazakhs was that it was thought to be easier for them to get good jobs: in a nominally Kazakh region, there needed to be plenty of Kazakhs in positions of power, even if their presence was mainly token. It was a nice piece of divide and rule: it made Uighurs jealous of the Kazakhs, who for their part would be unwilling to start or support dissent for fear of jeopardising their position.

Yusuf – the fan of bin Laden – didn't have a particularly high opinion of them.

'Oh, those Kazakhs! They haven't been the same since they got their own country. Before we were much closer, but now maybe they think they do not need us.'

'So don't you have any Kazakh friends?'

'Maybe one or two. But when I was a boy it was unusual to see Kazakhs in the city. They were mostly in countryside. We would point at them and shout "Hello Kazakh!" and then they would get angry.'

'Why do you think they got angry?'

'I don't know!'

'Perhaps they felt you were laughing at them. Were you?'

'No, but maybe they felt inferior as their education was so poor. This is why they can accept Chinese things, like drinking and smoking, because they don't have many ideas. They are an empty space. But...'

'What?'

'But they're not too bad.'

'Why?'

He laughed.

'Because they're not Chinese!'

48

I FINISHED MY last book. Admittedly, it wasn't quite my last, I still had a few history books, works you might consult but not actually *read*. There was also a pile of old *Reader's Digests*. A brief glance at their contents pages ('Song of Survival', 'Help to Fat-Proof Your Child', 'Tea, the Cup That Cures') saw them returned to the cupboard. The only English books for sale in the town were simplified versions of Victorian classics: *Pride and Prejudice* in forty pages; *Vanity Fair* in sixty.

The only other source of English books in town was the library in the English department. Technically, this was supposed to be for the whole department, though in practice it was mostly used by Colin's students. It was locked, and only he and I had a key. There was nothing stopping me from using it, except the foolish feeling that it was *his* library. In many senses this was true: he was the one who set the library up and did the work of maintaining it. Everything was neatly labelled and arranged just so. I'd skimmed the shelves a few times before but never properly browsed.

There were plenty of choices: *The Godfather*; *Robinson Crusoe*; *The Diary of Anne Frank*. There was also book called *Heroes of the Faith*. I flicked open to a page headed 'Martin finds out the truth.'

> Why had he never read the Bible before? Why had he thought it would be dull? Every page he read was exciting! Suddenly Jesus seemed to be a real person, and the words He had said came to life. Suddenly all the misery of the years was swept away. God was *not* angry with him; God *loved* him.

I wasn't sure what this was doing in the library but I figured that Colin couldn't afford to be picky. I browsed on, mostly finding the same simplified classics available in town. But one title caught my eye: *The Greatest Miracle in the World*. The cover blurb promised that the book contained the 'amazing Memorandum from God... to you'. And there were others like it: *Two from Galilee- The Story of Mary and Joseph*; *A Swedish Gospel Singer*; *Our Lord, The Little Lamb*. Some of these contained address labels for Colin and Susan. On their own, each would have seemed innocuous; considered as a whole, they were decidedly strange, not the kind of books you might expect to find in a small library in a remote part of China. But perhaps a case could be made that many of these books were not solely religious in content, and after all, they were in English.

The clincher was a colourful storybook with lavish illustrations of shepherds, wise men, fishes, loaves and resurrection. It was not even in English. It was in Chinese.

49

THE FIRST SNOW fell in large, thick flakes that settled. White lines grew on windowsills; tracks formed in the snow. The caretaker panicked and had the workmen shovel too much coal in the furnace; black smoke curved out the chimney; the radiators grew so hot that people had to open their windows.

Traditionally, the first snow brings with it opportunities for mischief. Men start leaving verses (in Uighur, *qar xät*) for each other, usually when visiting. These consist of verbal challenges to provide hospitality. The great Swedish anthropologist, Gunnar Jarring, cites an example:

> God may he be exalted, through his mercy, gave us the snow,
> For this reason, let us meet brothers and friends,
> If, with some excuse, they catch the one who brought the snow [letter]
> He has to put cups and pots and sweets on a tray.

What did a man do if he found that a visitor had left such a poem? He ran after the challenger. If he caught him before he reached his own home, then the challenger would be made up, dressed as a woman and paraded through the streets. The challenger would then have to send out invitations within a week; if he did not his door would be barricaded. However, if he failed to catch the challenger, he would have to provide the party himself.

It all sounded great fun but I wasn't sure that people in Yining did such things; much of Jarring's work focused on south Xinjiang. I asked a few people who said yes, people still played such tricks, especially the young. They looked at me blankly when I mentioned the barricade and strangely when I mentioned the women's clothes. They also said that you could never tell who might leave you a *qar xät*.

For the next few days I watched every visitor to my house closely, half hoping, half fearing that they would produce some verse when my back was turned. Every bag was suspect. I even avoided going to the toilet. All this was rather wearing, and I soon gave up. A white week passed and then it was time for KU English Corner. Sometimes these occasions dragged; people would stare at their feet and wait for me to say something. That day was better than most. A chance remark about Thailand sparked off a vigorous debate about ladyboys. One woman said she found them disgusting; another said she pitied them as they all had a disease that caused them to die prematurely. Yusuf took no part in the debate, except to say they were silly.

Afterwards they thanked me, put their shoes on and left. I was tidying up when I found the paper: a small sheet with six lines of Uighur writing. I dashed out of my flat and ran down the stairs. Yusuf and Rukiye were just getting on their bikes. They looked up in surprise. I waved the paper in triumph, imagining them both in drag, perhaps with a wig and lipstick.

'Whose is this? Is it yours Rukiye?'

Yusuf said that it was his.

'Well, when's the party then?'

'What?'

'The party. I found your poem. That means you have to give a party.'

'Poem?'

'Your *qar xät*.'

Yusuf took the paper and grinned impishly. Then he began to read.

'Washing powder, biscuits, apples…'

He could go on no further. I swore quietly as they convulsed with laughter.

50

THE SNOW DIDN'T stop the war: the fighting moved inside. The faces were the same, but they were now sunk in thick coats and hats. The combatants moved with even more speed than before. Their hands shot out to slam down a piece, then retracted to the warmth of their sleeves. If women played a part in the conflict, it was an unseen one. For my part, I was purely a spectator. I hadn't played chess in years, and didn't feel like getting beaten in front of 20 Uighur strangers. But I couldn't help covet their boards, all of which were handmade. Most were carved from softwoods, stained brown or black, with white squares painted on. The pieces were made from harder woods, or even sometimes metal. My favourite set was a battered one that folded into a box. Its squares were scarred and stained, its 'whites' a nicotine yellow, its blacks a cloudy grey. The c4 square had a hole in it, presumably the result of some piece slammed down in triumph. The pieces were made of rough pewter, with no two pawns the same and the queen taller than the king.

The owner of the board was a middle-aged man who never lost. I didn't realise that he spoke English until he asked me to play. There weren't many other people around so I agreed. His name was Tursun and, like Murat, he ran an English course in the evenings.

'I really like your board. Where'd you get it?'

'My brother made it.'

'When did he make it?'

'Perhaps 20 years ago.'

Our pawns squared off; our cavalry massed. His queen swept regally out.

'Now I am beginning my attack.'

I couldn't see much danger; my pieces seemed protected. I moved my bishop into the centre. His queen smashed a pawn in reply.

'And now I show you my fist.'

My knight hurried over. She withdrew from the breach.

'But perhaps my fist is empty.'

He kept up this commentary throughout the game. On the one occasion that I managed to threaten him, he pursed his lips and considered the board.

'Is it a problem? No, it is not. Your fist is empty.'

And it was. After 15 minutes of play my king was cowering in a corner. I shook his hand and thanked him for the game. Tursun invited me to visit his English class. I said I would, then complimented him on his English. He thanked me then said,

'I remember the first English film I saw. I remember two lines.'

'What are they?'

'Simba, have you forgotten me? No father, how could I?'

'What's that from?'

'*The Lion King.*'

On the way home I ran into Gabe. He asked what I'd been doing. When I told him he got excited.

'No way! You played with Tursun? Did you win?'

'Nah, he thrashed me, he's really good.'

'I'll say. He's been the city champion for the last three years. Didn't he mention that?'

51

THE STREETS GREW a skin of ice. Before there had been patches; now every road was covered. If anything, this made the Uighur neighbourhoods passable; their usual state – mud churned by hooves – was now a firm, albeit slippery, surface. These streets called for a special gait, a kind of sliding shuffle. Those who tried to walk normally ended up on their back.

The Uighur children took advantage of the change. They made slides to whizz away the days. Gangs of boys hung about the back streets, stopping cars, then tailgating them. Han children stood and watched, sulking underneath their many layers. Gutters groaned with paused waterfalls; roofs brandished icicles. The Russian buildings were especially deadly; their long eaves bristled with daggers.

There was a particularly grand edifice not far from the square. A five-pointed red star hung over a frieze of forward-looking workers. Age and weather had caused the red star to leak on the workers below, which was symbolic, albeit unsubtle. The building itself was all but derelict; only a few rooms on the ground floor were being used as offices. A sleeper bus dozed in front of the building, resting before it began the 36 hour journey south to Kashgar. I knew the route that it would take: through mountains in the dark.

I went over to what I thought was a restaurant. It turned out to be a small cinema, its walls plastered with faded posters that advertised such art house fare as 'Korean Killer' and 'Death Ninja 2'. But I was feeling frostbitten, so I went in. I gave one yuan to a crumpled man who said hello in Russian. Then he gestured at the packs of chocolate and tissues that he had on the counter. I refused then pulled aside the thick blanket that hung in the cinema entrance.

Inside was completely black. A mean light sulked from a stove.

I could barely find the sections of sofa that served as seats, and certainly couldn't see anyone's face, something I was quickly glad of.

Onscreen a woman lay naked on a bed, her thighs spread apart, a man's head between them. A large black circle covered most of her groin, blocking his features like a black halo. He moved on top, and she made noises, more of pain than enjoyment.

The scene shifted to a man on a train. A young woman walked up to him and said something. He answered. Around me the audience yawned. After more dialogue, the sex resumed. I heard the sounds of men shifting to get comfortable. As the man began to finger the girl through her white panties I realised that the film was Japanese, and looked to be from the 1970s.

After a few minutes of penetration, the film cut to an outside view of a hospital. Then there was more sex, this time between a doctor and a nurse. Just as their climax approached, the telephone rang. The doctor picked it up. His face fell and he sank back limply. The nurse tried to rouse him but to no avail. She shrugged and used the receiver to bring herself off. The scene shifted to a girl in a phone box, listening to squelching sounds and looking bemused. The man next to me murmured, 'This is the best film I've ever seen.'

I agreed with him. It seemed only polite.

52

THERE WAS STILL a month of term left, but Eleanor wanted to leave so she could be home for Xmas. The college tried to persuade her not to but in the end could not stop her. Her students showered her with farewell gifts: a cushion embroidered with kittens; a plastic heart that dispensed perfume; a pencil sharpener in the shape of a dog (the pencil went into the dog's mouth; one twisted the tail to sharpen); a miniature alpine house that played *Twinkle Twinkle Little Star*. I found space in my cupboards for all these.

One of the more promising presents was a VCD (a poor cousin of the DVD) of 'lovely Uighur music', a gift from one of her first-year students. We sat back to enjoy.

A young Uighur man danced into view. He spotted a Uighur girl, veiled but coy, her eyelashes fluttering, her eyes downcast one moment, then flashing up to his. He pursued her, she fled. He searched for her, she hid. All this clowning took place to the accompaniment of a song in *Chinese* about how wonderful Urumqi was. The rest of the songs were the same.

One of her classes threw a party for her, of the sunflower-seeds and chatting variety. The token minority student, a Kazakh boy, was inveigled to perform for her, which he did along with some Uighur students from another department. The crowning moment of this rapture came at the party's end, when Eleanor was presented with a *doppa* which they begged her to wear, despite the fact that women never wear a *doppa* (although young girls sometimes do). When she did put it on, albeit reluctantly, there was much hilarity. But neither the Kazakh boy nor his Uighur friends seemed to mind. Perhaps it was only oversensitive foreigners who worried about such things. I asked the KU class what they thought about their singing and dancing stereotype. One of them wrote:

> Uighur people like to dance and sing, it's true. We have a saying: 'The Uighur child can dance when it can walk and sing when they can speak.' But this is not true. Not all Uighur people can dance and sing. We love these things but our own life isn't all about singing and dancing. If this was true, it would be terrible.

There didn't seem to be many roles for Uighur people in Han culture: terrorist or minstrel. However, one of the girls at the party later wrote:

> This afternoon we held a party with a Uighurs! We were singing, dancing and played many games. The Uighurs also gave many wonderful performances. We had a good time together. Through it I knew some Uighurs. They are all very kind and humorous. The Uighur's dance is a symbol of their colourful life. I hope I could form friendship with them and know more about them in future.

Yes, it was patronising and naïve, but at least it was a positive stereotype. It was certainly preferable to this kind of thing:

> The minorities are very fierce. You may feel uneasy and upset when you face their crude behaviour and vulgar language. I think there are more thieves and robbers here than any other city in Xinjiang. To be frank with you, I don't like this place very much.

One of my favourite students wrote this. He was bright, friendly, and bigoted. His prejudice refused to fit, which if nothing else at least proved he was a person rather than a character.

53

RUKIYE'S REMARK ABOUT the police had lodged itself in my brain. I didn't think that I was doing anything illegal but there were certainly a few grey areas, such as the KU class and some of my friends. Maybe I had asked too many questions. I knew I wasn't the only one that the police were interested in. Gabe told me all of his teachers had been instructed by the police to pass on anything suspect he said. I guessed the same was true of the other foreigners but that didn't make me feel any easier. I began to have absurd and frightening dreams where my students interrogated me. They threatened to implant devices into my nipples unless I gave them good grades.

The police, secret or otherwise, were not alone in their vigilance. The college (perhaps not unreasonably) demanded to know whenever I left the city, even if it was at the weekend. The post office opened every parcel that was sent to me; all books were thumbed, all tapes were listened to (I knew because they didn't bother to rewind them), something that had never happened when I lived in Hunan. Legally, they were supposed to open it in my presence, a regulation that their zeal caused them to forget.

Eleanor's remark that our phones were tapped also came back to me. I started censoring myself on the phone, trying to sound as innocuous as possible. But I didn't give much thought to where I went on the internet. I browsed through the news sites that weren't blocked, and tried to get round the barriers of those that were (such as the BBC) by using proxy servers. Then one day, whilst trying to open a site called 'Citizens against Chinese Propaganda', my connection suddenly went. I tried my phone. It was dead. I sat there a while, waiting for a heavy knock at the door.

Eventually I got on my knees and checked the telephone cable. A five-centimetre length of plastic had been stripped, exposing the wire; a circle of small black droppings lay around the scene. Even the mice were against me.

54

YOU DO NOT KNOW the joy of bread. Yours isn't made by an old woman who lives in a shed and rises before sunrise to pummel and shape dough. Each morning she presses it against a stone then pinches it to make a rim of crust. She stokes the clay oven's fire, then swiftly reaches in to slap the dough against the side. Thirty minutes later it is caramel brown and firm, a perfect disc of nan.

There were at least ten such bakeries near the college, each with a slight variation on this theme: some put onion in their nan, others added sesame seeds or spring onions. But I was usually content with the plain one, the kind that people in Central Asia have been eating for over a thousand years. For many Uighurs, a nan is a sacred thing. In Uighur, one of the most powerful ways to affirm the truth of something is to say, 'I'd rather step on a nan'. nan also mustn't be thrown away. To do so shows ingratitude to Allah, a scorning of His gifts. Anyone who sees a nan lying on the ground must pick it up and put it elsewhere, so it won't be stepped on. I was told that a few years ago, a person wasn't supposed to *choose* a nan in a shop; instead, you went and took the first one that came to hand, as every nan is good.

I could well understand this veneration but it raised problems with the issue of disposal: there are no preservatives in nan, which means that one that is soft and hot in the morning is forbiddingly hard by dinner. Some said they fed them to their animals (which was no good for me, as the last thing I wanted to do was encourage the mice), others that they threw them into the river so the fish could eat them. But I think most people used their leftover nan at breakfast, when they dunked it in their milk tea, thus making it edible. But I had no sheep, lived too far from the river and hated milk tea. At first I tried smuggling small pieces of it out in my rubbish, but quickly found myself ashamed to face my neighbours. A tower of nan began to grow in my kitchen. Mould made me desperate: I cut them into little pieces then shoved them down the toilet.

When I confessed my problem to Gabe, he was sympathetic.

'Yep, that's a tricky one. I had to hide mine in the bushes before I started using the tree.'

'The tree?'

'Yeah, if you hang some bread on it at night, it'll be gone by morning.'

He was right. Any bread hung from its bark or branches mysteriously vanished in the night. Who took it, and why, remained a mystery I had no desire to solve.

55

THIS WAS NOT the only magic tree. When I took the road south from Yining, towards the mountains and Kashgar, after 20km I found an old elm growing in the middle of the road. That this was hazardous, possibly deadly, was evident from the ring of broken glass that surrounded its base. Given this was one of the major roads south, constantly used by buses and trucks, yet without lighting at night, it was hard to see why the tree was allowed to remain there.

The other puzzling thing was the red sash that encircled its trunk. When I looked up I saw small red ribbons tied to the lowest branches, about fifty of them. Each of them was tightly knotted, obviously fastened with care.

When I mentioned this to the KU class, they told me that these ribbons were hung by women that have trouble conceiving a child. They constitute a prayer and an offering to the saint associated with the place. I was also told that the tree was full of blood and that anyone who tried to harm it would be paralysed, or die. Although no one could think of an actual incident in which someone was harmed, the ability of the tree to defend itself was still beyond doubt.

Many other places in Xinjiang have these shrines (*mazar*). In Turpan small pouches – wrapped in coloured thread, with sticks pushed through their middles – are hung from branches in order to ward off evil spirits. Jars of medicine or paper are burnt on top of tombs for a similar purpose.

Such ideas fall outside orthodox Islam. They are better thought of as folk traditions, the result of the eclectic mix of influences that have swept the region. These include shamanism (from Mongolia), Zoroastrianism (Persia) and Manichaeism (Iraq), belief systems almost dead yet still surviving in a custom here and there. Some Uighurs

THE TREE THAT BLEEDS

that I knew denounced such practices as superstition, or even heresy. I even heard tales of local *imams* working with the police to get such shrines closed down. They were not short of allies in the Yining city government, who in January 2002 announced their desire to remove 'feudal, superstitious and backward ideas'. But there were some who thought otherwise.

56

TURSUN WAS SO busy that the only time that we could meet was breakfast. In addition to his English course, he also ran a business that sold goods imported from Kazakhstan and Turkey, which meant he was forever shuttling back and forth between Yining and the border. He wasn't rich, but was getting there. His English course was more of a hobby, a way to stay in practice. He had learnt most of his English in Shanghai, where he had studied foreign trade.

There was a gentility to him, a softness untouched by wealth or education. You couldn't imagine he would ever offend you, a quality that brought out the same grace in others. He was incredibly courteous, genuinely nice, except for when he played chess. Then he was Genghis Khan.

That morning the restaurant was quiet. The only other customers were a party of three drunken Kazakhs, a Han women and her son. I watched her spooning sticky soup into his bird-like mouth. Most of it went onto his clothes but still she kept spooning; perhaps to try was enough. After a few minutes one of the Kazakhs came over to us, shook our hands, and said in Chinese, 'It's wonderful to see you.' He tried to sit down at our table but missed the chair and fell on the floor. His friends scooped him up and took him back to their table. Tursun and I looked at each other, then burst into laughter.

'Perhaps he's not Muslim!'

Tursun laughed even harder.

'What's so funny?'

'Maybe in Ghulja there are only 15 Muslims.'

'I think I know a lot more than that!'

'Maybe, it depends. You know, this is not Kashgar. People believe many things, maybe not all from Islam.'

'What about in the countryside? Maybe their faith is stronger.'

'Yes, they have a strong belief. But some things they do are different to what the *imams* say, like when they wear white for mourning.'

'What do you think about that?'

'It is different but what matters is that inside they have a strong feeling about God.'

'What about in the city? I see lots of people going to pray in the mosques. And lots of people say they are fasting, some of them in secret. Surely they're Muslim.'

'Oh yes, yes! Many say they are! I say that I am! But many people still eat. When I went home yesterday my mother made me eat some *ulgre*.'

'Couldn't you say no?'

'No, she is my mother.'

Peter Fleming was similarly unconvinced about the devoutness of some Muslims:

> There is a proverb about Chinese Muslims which gives a good idea of their attitude to Qur'anic law. Three Moslems are one Moslem. Two Moslems are one Moslem. One Moslem is no Moslem. In other words, the eyes of man matter more than the eyes of God.

'Islam' means 'surrender'. It appeared that some Uighurs weren't quite ready to do so, at least not unconditionally. But when I asked Tursun if he thought of himself as Muslim he became very serious.

'Yes, I am a Muslim. I am Uighur and Uighurs are a Muslim people. We are not like the Chinese. We have belief. Maybe some have more belief, some have less, but they are still Muslim.'

This was a world away from the pieties of Murat and Erkin. This was not Islam as religion, this was Islam as ethnic marker, as a badge of identity. It was a good illustration of the fact that people use religious beliefs for many different purposes. For Murat, Islam was one thing, for Tursun another, and it was not for an unbeliever like myself to say which was better.

57

THE LAST THREE DAYS of Ramadan are the most important, especially the 27th day, known as the 'Night of Power'. This is when the Qur'an was said to have been revealed to the Prophet Muhammad. To fast and pray in this period is said to be worth more than a thousand other days, which is handy for those unwilling or unable to fast during the rest of Ramadan.

The end of Ramadan is marked by a festival known in Uighur as *Ruza Eid*, which involves several days of feasts, gifts and charitable acts. People pay visits to the homes of friends and relatives, often only staying for the time it takes to peel a pear or drink a bowl of tea. Invitations are unnecessary, which means that for these three days a host (which in practice usually means his wife) can only relax when out of their home.

I expected *Ruza Eid* to be subject to the same restrictions as Ramadan but it turned out to be an instance where the authorities opted for benevolence over consistency. All the minority students, including those in the '99 class, were allowed several days' holiday. This led to an awkward moment where I had to divide the class according to ethnicity. The Han students had one week to prepare a presentation; the minority students had two.

Although *Ruza Eid* falls at the end of Ramadan, it is a mostly secular festival, not dissimilar to Chinese Spring Festival (New Year), in that it requires families to gather. However, whereas Spring Festival is a national holiday, *Ruza Eid* is only a holiday for minorities, which means they get an extra holiday. I asked one of the Kazakh students what his Han classmates thought about that.

'Many of them think it is unfair.'

'Is it?'

'No, because they get to have Spring Festival.'

'Yes, but so do you. You have an extra holiday.'

He sighed, and then whispered, 'You know, in China, we have some discrimination.'

58

IT WAS EASY TO forget about the Hui. They didn't look or sound different to the Han. Only religion seemed to distinguish them, usually in the form of a white skullcap that only middle-aged and elderly men wore. So I was surprised when Yang Mei, a tall and somewhat voluptuous girl, who looked older than her classmates, asked me to her house for *Ruza Eid*.

'I didn't think Chinese people celebrated *Ruza Eid*.'

'No, they don't.'

'But you do.'

'Yes, Hui people do.'

'Ah.'

Another thing I didn't know was that she was married (which is usually forbidden for college students). She was training to be a kindergarten teacher (unlike her classmates, who were mostly bound for secondary schools) and didn't have to attend all the political classes that her classmates did.

I turned up at her house just after one o'clock. I took off my shoes and put on the fluffy slippers offered. The lounge was tiled and chilly, the furniture hard and shiny. A sideboard stood against the wall, crammed with fake flowers and kitsch. A hulking karaoke rig brooded next to the TV. In all these respects it was indistinguishable from a thousand Han houses.

But there was also a long coffee table spread with fruit and cakes, with pride of place taken by a mound of *san zhi*, a twisted coil of dough that oozed cholesterol. Yang Mei's husband sat in the corner looking brittle. Like Tilawaldi, he was a civil servant, though in another department. His Chinese boss had insisted on taking him out and plying him with drink, surely in ignorance of the fact it was a Muslim festival. I complimented Yang Mei on her *san zhi*.

'Do you like it? It is supposed to be like the family.'

'It looks like a chain.'

'And it is very hard to make.'

Her husband roused himself. His name was Dai Ming and he spoke Kazakh, Chinese, Russian and Uighur.

'But none of these languages are mine,' he said in Chinese. 'The Hui language died 300 years ago. Sometimes I feel sad about this.'

'What was it like?'

'Similar to Arabic.'

'Doesn't anyone speak it?'

'At the mosque the *imam* reads the Qur'an in Arabic, but no-one understands it.'

The 12th *sura* (chapter) of the Qur'an states, 'We have sent it down an Arabic Qur'an', which many interpret to mean that a translated Qur'an is not truly the Qur'an. This presents a potential quandary for most non-Arabic speaking Muslims. If the Qur'an is recited in its proper Arabic, it won't be understood. If it is read in their own language (e.g. Chinese or Uighur) then they won't be listening to the Qur'an. The orthodox response is for these people to learn Arabic, a pious if unrealistic answer.

I had just refused my third cup of tea when the noise began, the same humming I'd been hearing for weeks. I asked if they knew what it was, expecting the same blank looks.

'Birds,' said Dai Ming.

Then he said something in Chinese I didn't understand. Yang Mei translated.

'Pigeons.'

'How do they make that noise?'

'They have something on their wings. Like a whistle.'

I knew there were lots of pigeon fanciers but had never made the connection. They weren't the vulgar grey kind common to European cities. Their plumage was brown or snow coloured, which coupled

THE TREE THAT BLEEDS

with their cooing made them seem like graceless doves. One of my Uighur neighbours kept about 20 of them in a shed opposite our building. On sunny days they could be seen roosting or squabbling over corn. At twilight the children would be sent out to call them home, which they did by shouting, stamping, clapping and emitting the most piercing whistle I have ever heard. I asked Dai Ming if he had any pigeons himself.

'No, but my brother has a lot. He lets them roost freely; all he does is give them some maize.'

Yang Mei translated the rest.

'He said his brother doesn't put whistles on their wings as it hurts them. And he says that when they swim it is so lovely.'

She suddenly remembered something.

'Do you eat pigeons in your country?'

'Not often.'

'You know, they are good for you. If you have some mental disease it can help. It has many vitamins.'

'Any mental disease?'

'If it is little and not serious.'

They were a nice couple and I regretted wanting to seduce his wife.

59

THE HEATING OF THE college depended on an old rusty wagon that travelled between the coal cellar and furnace. In the depth of winter, when it was sometimes −35C at night, this wagon visited the furnace every ten minutes. Gangs of workers shovelled coal into the cellar maw, feeding it so it could feed the wagon which would fuel the furnace.

Modern technology was out of vogue elsewhere. Instead of using their fridges, people hung their food outside. Carpets were brought out to be pummelled; their beating left a square of dirt on the snow. And on every street there was the sight of people attacking the snow and ice with shovels, hammers and pickaxes. In the college the students had to shovel snow during their lunch break.

I had given up on Beijing time. By the time of the winter equinox it had become farcical: no one could be expected to accept that the sun rose at half past nine. I converted to Xinjiang time, which made my mornings painful, but the evenings longer.

60

THE MAIN STREETS in Yining seemed prosperous enough. The shops on Liberation Road – the street that ran between the college and the square – sold bikes, TVs and washing machines, a prime example of the much-touted 'free market with socialist characteristics'. The pavement was made up of the same white tiles that coated the buildings. An artery of dusty trees flowed down each side of the road. Traffic lights informed every intersection, telling pedestrians and vehicles how long they had to move or wait.

After you crossed the square it was a different story. Grubby kids roamed around, offering to shine shoes; pavement stalls offered inner soles, key rings, hairbrushes, plastic combs and lighters. There were men with strips of sticking plaster dripping from their arms; girls selling individual bottles of shampoo; older women with stockings and tights that ran down their arms like wings. There was also a form of hoopla, where you could pay to throw wooden rings around cartons of fruit juice.

But there were many with nothing to sell. Men and women, kneeling in the snow and ice, their eyes glued to the floor. They had strips of carpet or rubber bound around their shins. A stream of pleading words dropped constantly from their mouths.

Almost everyone begging was Uighur. Although there were probably other reasons for their poverty (mental illness, domestic abuse, disability), I guessed that unemployment was principally to blame, not least because so many Uighurs bemoaned the widespread jobless-ness. In China, little or no unemployment benefit is available, which makes the poor dependent on the sympathy of others. I wasn't sure if this was in great supply.

I asked my Han students if they ever gave to beggars. Two girls said they always did, a statement that was greeted with incredulous laughter, and several begging gestures. The rest said never or rarely. Their reasons were that they had too little money themselves and that 'many beggars try to cheat'. They said that many were able to work but were just too lazy and that there were 'rich beggars'.

To my surprise, most of the KU class were in agreement. I had expected them to blame the Chinese government, either indirectly, through general economic policy, or as a result of deliberate discrimination against Uighurs. But they showed no inclination to do so. It could have been a religious matter – *zakat* is not supposed to be paid to such people. Or it could have been the same indifference people feel all over the world.

61

WHILST I DIMLY knew there were these young Americans studying Uighur, it was still a surprise to bump into them. They had come as a four, two boys and two girls, though not, I am sure, as two couples. The two guys were called Brad and Jamie. At six foot four, Brad was probably the tallest person in the city. He always looked as if he had just woken up. Jamie was short and gingery and very seldom spoke. The girls were called Lisa and Michelle; they were both so banal that I could scarcely remember which was which. All four were teetotal and Christian. This was all I knew about them after four months.

I knew why I was in Yining; my motives were innocent enough, just a healthy interest in learning about riots and ethnic discrimination. But what were they, and Gabe for that matter, doing in a small city on the edge of China? Ostensibly, they were learning Uighur, but this only posed a further why. People do not learn obscure Central Asian languages on a whim. We might learn French or German for fun; Uighur is the kind of language only learnt by ethno-graphers and -linguists, and they didn't seem like either. They were also paying a considerable amount for the privilege. But given that we never spent more than 30 seconds together, it seemed unlikely that I would gain any insight into their motives.

But one polar night I wandered into a restaurant and there were Brad and Jamie. They saw me and stopped eating. Convention demanded they ask me to join them. I said I'd be glad to. When I ordered they looked at me incredulously.

'You eat pork?' said Brad.

'Sure, don't you?'

'No, we don't.'

'Why not?'

'Well, we have a lot of Uighur friends.'

'Me too. That's why I don't eat pork in my house. But I don't see why I can't eat it in a Chinese restaurant. *I'm* not Muslim. Or Jewish.'

'Sure,' said Brad, and Jamie nodded, as if they agreed.

We spoke about the weather till my food arrived.

'So guys, I'm just curious, what made you want to come and study Uighur?'

They stared into their rice. Brad broke the silence.

'Oh, well, you know, I think Uighur culture is very interesting and I wanted to know more.'

Jamie didn't look like he was going to say anything. I gave him a verbal prod.

'Um, well, I studied business, and, er, when you study business it's real useful to speak a foreign language.'

It was a truly pitiful performance, half platitude, and half just utter rubbish: Uighur, the well-known international business language, surely preferable to French, Spanish or Chinese. It should have been abundantly clear to me what kind of people they were, but some part of me continued to resist the obvious deduction. All these Christians in this remote town, surely they were…

62

BUT THIS WAS WHAT did it.

> Today Colin invited eight of us to go to his house. We have already
> go to Colin's house several times. Firstly Colin prepare some
> delicious food for us like coffee, biscuit, pastry. Secondly Colin shown
> us a film about Jesus. And he explain something that happened at
> that time so we can understand the film. After I saw that film, I
> knew God loves people. Today we have a good time!

One of Colin's students wrote this in her English diary (an assign-
ment he knew nothing of). The fact remained: every other foreigner
in Yining was a missionary.

It explained a lot: Xiao Mei's remark about Colin trying to
make them believe; the attentions of the 'secret' police; those sickly
books in the library.

Chinese law is clear on this matter. Article 8 of 'Regulations on the
Supervision of the Religious Activities of Foreigners in China' states

> Foreigners within China's borders who conduct religious activities
> must observe Chinese laws and regulations; they are not allowed
> to establish religious organisations, set up religious offices, open
> places for religious activities or run religious institutes, nor *may*
> *they develop followers, appoint religious personnel or conduct*
> *missionary activities among Chinese citizens'* (italics mine).

There were a number of similar clauses in our contracts, not that
I imagined this mattered to them. To my mind, they were trying to
take advantage of people's desperation, to offer a false hope. It
wasn't as if Uighurs lacked their own religious traditions, however
patchy their observance. And then there was the basic dishonesty
of it all. However, I fancied that there was one person I might get
a straight answer from.

* * *

'Gabe, do you fancy dinner?'

There were many things to admire about Gabe. His Chinese and Japanese were as good as his Uighur. He was cheerful, widely read, and prepared to help anyone who asked. Such people are a magnet for the crazed and desperate. Gabe had his share of these, in particular a middle-aged Uighur woman whose son was in prison for stealing bicycles. She was convinced that Gabe could secure his release, and spent many of her waking hours trying to cajole him into doing what she believed was easy for him. I often saw her outside his door, laden down with cakes and fruit. Most people would have ended up snapping at her but I never saw him to be anything but patient. I also felt I knew him a bit, that we were almost friends. However, that didn't make it any easier to broach a subject I knew he would not welcome.

I didn't manage to bring it up on our way to the restaurant, nor while we were waiting to order. I resigned myself to my usual tactic of just blundering in.

'So, Gabe, I was wondering, you know, you've learnt all these languages, where is it going, do you have some goal?'

He gave me a sharp look and I felt bad for being so disingenuous. But then he began.

'Well, have you ever read the Bible?'

'Some of it. Mostly the New Testament.'

'Do you know the good news? That Christ died and was risen? This is *news*, he was the message, and this is news that everyone must know.'

He proceeded to elaborate. He said that this good news was best told to people in their own tongue, hence the fact that he studied language.

'Do you have tell people directly? Isn't it sufficient to lead a virtuous life, and teach people by example?'

'That's important but not enough. You can't *show* the good news; it must be *told*.'

'How do you choose the people that you tell? Have you chosen to talk specifically to Uighurs?'

'The people I meet are chosen by God, although I think it would be good for Uighurs to be united under Christ. But I still have many Chinese Christian friends, and when I speak to them I try to emphasise those parts of the Bible that preach tolerance of those who are different.'

'Some might say that it's unethical to bring these ideas into a culture that has its own equally valid beliefs. What do you say to that?'

'We are all agents of change here, Nick. No culture is unchanging and static. The status quo isn't always the best way.'

So much for cultural relativism. I asked him if he'd had any problems with the police, and he said no, though he wished they'd come to see him, rather than hassling his teachers. At the end of our conversation, I still disagreed with what he was doing, but found that it didn't bother me as much, perhaps because of his honesty. The others were another matter.

63

THERE HAVE BEEN Christian missionaries in China since the seventh century. Some of the first were Nestorian Christian, a sect based on the teachings of Nestorius, patriarch of Constantinople, who maintained that Christ's divine and human aspects were separate. They consecrated their first church in Ch'ang-an (present-day Xian) in 638AD. But the Jesuits, Methodists, Protestants, Baptists, Anglicans and Catholics were close behind. The degree of welcome for these *chuan jiao shi* (Chinese for 'missionary') has waxed and waned; but despite their persecution, imprisonment, and murder, they have continued to come.

Some of the earliest missionaries in Xinjiang were Swedes, who were mostly based in Kashgar. The Bible, or at least sections of it, were available in Uighur from 1898 onwards. The Swedes estimated that from the late 19th century until 'Liberation' in 1949, 60–70,000 religious books or pamphlets were sold or given away. However, it would be rash to assume this figure reflected the degree of interest in Christian ideas. George Hunter, a Scottish missionary in the 1920s, related how Uighurs would sometimes 'buy gospels and tracts specially to tear up in one's presence or burn publicly on the main street'. It must have been the spirit of forgiveness which moved him to say that Uighur people were 'as a whole, extremely bigoted and ignorant'.

The remoteness of the region, coupled with frequent periods of war and instability, has meant that Xinjiang has been all but closed to foreigners, whatever their ilk, for most of the last century. The Joshua Project, an evangelical web site, includes Uighurs in its list of 'unreached peoples'. Another site puts the 'percentage of Uighurs LOST' at 99.9 per cent.

Such palpable luck of success (and the small matter of the law) has not deterred the missionaries. The extent of their presence in Yining was proof of that, and nothing compared to the number of them in other cities in Xinjiang. Some teachers from Kashgar told me that they knew of at least 30 in the city; in Urumqi there were far more. Most were 'students' or teachers, one of the easiest ways for foreigners to get residential visas, and surely an answer to one website's prayers for 'creative access strategies' to the LOST Uighurs.

Given the illegal nature of what they were doing, I expected few to guess the true motives of all these Uighur-learning foreigners. I soon realised I was far from the first to suspect.

One of the students in the KU class, a bear-like man named Dolkun, had been absent for a few weeks. He was a cardiologist in one of the smaller hospitals who also did the odd circumcision. One day he came in halfway through a lesson, grinning sheepishly. After class he came and apologised for not coming to class. I asked if everything was all right.

'Yes, but my boss at the hospital, he does not want me to come.'

'Why not? Do you have a lot of patients?'

'The patients are no problem. My boss says this college full of Christians. Maybe they try to change me.'

'Maybe your boss is right.'

'Why do they try? I think they waste their time. Uighur people are Muslim. It is impossible.'

'I guess they don't think so.'

'Maybe some people will take their money and help. But only this.'

'Do some people pretend to be Christian?'

'No, they cannot do this. It is an impossible. If a Muslim says he is a Christian, he is not a Muslim. It is finished.'

He was quiet for a moment then grinned.

'Maybe some people pretend. If they are not serious Muslims. But most people do not like these kind of Christian. Last month I was in Kashgar. There were two men on the bus, they were very drunk. A young foreign man, maybe American, he tries to give them a little book. It was about the religion. The men look at it, then they start to beat the American. He says sorry, they keep hitting him. He got off the bus very quick.'

Dolkun was not the only one with such stories. Both Rukiye and Tursun told me stories of how some missionaries offered to pay poor students' tuition fees and living expenses, as a means of ensuring their attention when they came to talk about less earthly concerns. Such 'converts' are known as 'rice-bowl Christians', whose faith depends on their stomachs. However, neither Tursun nor Rukiye, nor any other Uighur I spoke to, seemed especially concerned about all these missionaries trying to supplant their faith. They just thought it was silly: to be Uighur was to be Muslim.

It was one thing for Uighurs to be so blasé. But if it was such common knowledge, why didn't the police put a stop to it? One possibility was that they hoped it would undermine belief in Islam, which was at least one possible source of Uighur unity. Another idea was put forward by an anonymous writer in the *Eastern Turkestan Information Bulletin*:

> They [the government] are playing a dirty game. The aim is to provoke Eastern Turkestanis against the missionaries. If Eastern Turkestanis are provoked the Chinese use the missionaries to stamp Eastern Turkestanis as fundamentalists. The Chinese know very well that Western countries fear fundamentalism and every peaceful demonstration in this country is presented by the Chinese as a fundamentalist provocation. The aim is to justify the persecution of our people. At present, we are in a very difficult situation. Can you help us find a solution to this problem? We would be very grateful if the missionaries would try to make the world aware of our plight instead of trying to convert us to Christianity by offering material benefits. What good does it do Christianity if some are converted merely because of material gains?

Why didn't the college put a stop to it? One reason might have been that it was hard to find foreign teachers who wanted to work in a remote region for less money than they could have made in Beijing, Shanghai or any other major city in the east of the country.

Another was the not inconsiderable amount of money that the college made from the foreign students. There was also the tricky matter of proof. Short of catching them conducting a service or handing out pamphlets, there was likely to be little evidence. Most of their work would be done one-to-one, in quiet get-togethers at somebody's house. The only way to prove such meetings would be to bug their houses or their guests, and even I wasn't paranoid enough to believe they were doing that. And whatever I thought I knew, it would only be my word against theirs. Any accusation from me would also invite a certain scrutiny that I did not relish, what with the 'secret' KU class.

64

THE WAITRESS ASKED me to sit then said, 'Your friends were here earlier.'

'Which ones?'

'Those Americans. The students.'

'They're not my friends.'

'But you're all foreigners.'

'Yes, but they are missionaries.'

'No!'

'Yes.'

She looked genuinely appalled for a second; then went and gave the cook my order.

In the weeks that followed I found myself repeating this exchange, not just to waitresses but to anyone that would listen: students, teachers, fruit sellers, the slightly retarded man who emptied the bins; everyone needed to know. I was sure this would get back to them, and wondered if they would then confront me.

Just for good measure, I slipped out one night and quietly purged the library. I wasn't sure what to do with the books so just threw them in a cupboard. It occurred to me that perhaps it was none of my business, and that maybe these people were harmless. But I nonetheless carried on telling people. The books kept appearing.

65

WHATEVER WAS SAID in private, on the surface Yining was calm. Although the Han and Uighur strived to exist as separately as possible – eating in different restaurants, going to different shops, living in different neighbourhoods – it was impossible for them not to have to share the same space sometimes. Public buildings like the post office and hospital enforced such proximity. The staff and clients of such places represented the whole ethnic range. A Uighur man could serve or treat a Hui or Han without visible rancour, perhaps because it was an impersonal situation where the roles were clear.

The buses were another place where Han and Uighur had to mix. There were two kinds of buses in Yining: long single-decker ones with designated stops, where all the fares went into a perspex box and you had to have the right change, and smaller minibuses with fixed routes but flexible stops. The latter were operated on a franchise system, whereby a conductor and driver hired the bus from the depot but were allowed to keep the fares. The combination of these two types meant you never had to wait more than five minutes for a bus. Despite this, there never seemed to be enough of them, the result of which was that the buses were always packed, especially in winter. Twenty people would be crammed into a space meant for ten, Han and Uighur squashed together. But again, this seemed to pose no problem. The only hostility I witnessed was between a man and a thief who'd tried to steal his phone. The thief got a punch in the face.

If there was a hierarchy on the buses, it was structured by gender rather than ethnicity. Most of the conductors were female, their voices honed to a bark by years of shouting ('Move to the back, get off, quickly, quickly, quickly!'). But the real matriarchs were the

'Learning science to build and safeguard the motherland'

Traditional Uighur house, Yining

Back street market, Urumqi

Bishek in a village near Turpan

Cock fight, Yining

Fortune telling

Gravel bathers

Hui shepherd

Meat market, Yining

Miss Cai at her desk

Photo studio, Turpan

Spectators at horse event

Tomb of Tughluq
Timur

Traditional medicine stall

Street market, Yining

The tree that bleeds

middle-aged and elderly Uighur women. As soon as they got on, men stood and offered them a seat, no matter how full the bus. These were the women that seemed invisible in their own homes, at least when I visited. They would bring food and then disappear, reappearing only to remove the dishes. Most of my male Uighur friends said they were married, but I only had their word for this. No one brought their wife to any of our meetings.

In south Xinjiang it was common to see women wearing veils or *hijabs*, but in Yining few women even covered their heads with a scarf. Married women mostly wore long, loose-fitting dresses, in theory to avoid drawing attention to their bodies, thus preserving their modesty. However, the colours of such dresses were usually so vivid that they attracted the eye as much as their voluminous fit discouraged it. Emerald, magenta, cyan, turquoise: they were chunky birds of paradise, spreading and resplendent.

However dutiful and docile they acted in the home, when they were out with their peers it was another story. Most gathered together with their colleagues or neighbours in a restaurant for *chay* (tea) several times a month. The tables were spread with enough food for a wedding, as if the women had decided to reject their husbands and remarry each other. These occasions usually lasted between two and three hours. Men were never present. When I asked some of the women in the KU class what they talked about at their *chay*, their only reply was to smile. I wondered what their husbands thought about these gatherings.

66

TURSUN WAS UNHAPPY. The chief cause was that a large consignment of blackcurrant juice had been sent back at the border, owing to the fact that its best-before date had passed. I watched him trying to eat off his anger, his teeth stripping the meat from the kebabs as if it were still attached to the bones of the customs men. After 15 such attacks he wiped his mouth and sat back. For a moment he seemed resigned, almost calm. Then he blurted:

'Why must they send it back?'

'I thought you said it was because they were out of date.'

'The date on the labels is always wrong! And what does it matter if they are a little over anyway, yes?'

'When was the best before date?'

'1998.'

The other reason for his displeasure was the shrieks coming from the main dining room. We and several other men were eating in a small side room, as the main room was being used by an especially vocal *chay*. Tursun kept scowling in their direction, the frustration over his impounded goods feeding his irritation with the sounds of merriment. Another outburst followed.

'Don't they have work at home? What kind of husbands do they have?'

He muttered several other things in Uighur.

'And do you know what they are talking about? Rubbish. *Vot vot.*'

'What's that?'

'It is RUBBISH! Nothing! Foolish things!'

'Do they gossip?'

'Gossip?'

'You know, talk about their husbands, about their neighbours, anyone that has done or said something recently.'

'Yes! Do women in England do this?'

'Of course. But men do too. Don't the men here have *chay* or something similar?'

'No, we have *mäshräp*, but that is very different. There we talk of important things.'

I asked what kind of things they talked about but Tursun suddenly went quiet. All he would say was that they were like a club where men gathered to eat and make speeches. It was not like him to be so reticent.

67

A *MÄSHRÄP* IS MANY things. It is a means of regulating social behaviour and transmitting cultural and religious practices from one generation to another. It is above all a male ritual. Sean Roberts, an anthropologist, described his first *mäshräp* thus:

> I quietly sat unnoticed in a corner as I looked around at the many young Uighur men who sat crossed-legged around the perimeter of the cold damp room that was poorly lit by two bare light bulbs... A young man in a fur hat stood up and said 'I have an *azru* [complaint]—do I have permission?'
>
> [He] explained how he had seen his friend Abdull drinking vodka at a birthday party last week... The young Abdull looked visibly embarrassed as he tried vainly to get sympathy with excuses about peer pressure. The *qazibäg* [judge] explained that drinking alcohol was harmful to one's health and was a waste of the money that was needed to feed and clothe one's family. Furthermore, it was *haram* [forbidden] and partaking in such activity was contrary to a Muslim's act of submission to God.

For all the apparent formality of a *mäshräp*, the ritual has no legal status, which is reflected in the type of sentences passed. This was Abdull's 'punishment' for drinking vodka:

> The *qazibäg* proclaimed that he would have to 'go fishing in the lake'... The *saqchi* [guard] left the room and returned with a basin of water, a towel and three pieces of hard candy. The candies were placed in the water and [Abdull] was forced to get the candy out of the basin with his mouth. Several times, he fell face first into the water, and all the men in the room erupted into laughter. Each time, the *saqchi* would wipe his face off with the towel and taunt Abdull, asking him if he would like a drink of vodka now.

The aim of such embarrassment is to make the 'guilty' renounce their transgression and promise to behave better (which Abdull did). It is also supposed to dissuade others from committing similar 'crimes'. But in keeping with the light-hearted nature of the 'punishments', a *mäshräp* is also often a forum for riddles, joke-telling and music.

Mäshräps are thus potentially a means by which a sense of community can be fostered among Uighur men, as the ritual provides an opportunity to define and transmit a unified set of values, primarily of a religious nature, though with a cultural dimension too.

The origins of the *mäshräp* ritual are unclear, although many Uighurs claim it is a 'very, very old thing'. But after the Communists took control of Xinjiang, the ritual was seldom practised, as such traditional customs were thought to be 'backward'. However, the *mäshräp* ritual was revived in the early 1990s, in response to the general climate of despondency that had resulted from the unemployment and poverty brought by the economic reforms.

The first of these new *mäshräps* were held in Yining in 1994, and then later spread as far as Urumqi. Initially, the *mäshräps* met with the agreement of the city authorities. They were supported by several cultural institutions in the city, who donated materials for a library in Kepekyuzi, one of the villages surrounding Yining. The *mäshräps* were organised regularly in villages for a period of months. By the spring of 1995, it was estimated that there were up to 10,000 young men participating.

The popularity of the *mäshräps* may have been their undoing: the authorities must have been alarmed by the level of participation. When in April 1995, the *mäshräps* in the Yili region elected a leader – Abdulhelil, a 28-year-old businessman with three children – they decided to act. The police reportedly summoned Abdulhelil and other participants for questioning but took no further action at that time. He was detained again in August, again for no apparent reason. This provoked a demonstration by young Uighur men in Yining the next day. Soon after, the authorities banned the *mäshräps*, denouncing them as havens of separatist ideas. However, the *mäshräps* continued secretly. Their illegality may have strengthened their appeal, since to participate had become an act of opposition. It was thus not the kind of thing to shout about in a crowded restaurant.

68

THE TERM APPROACHED its end. Christmas loomed, and with it the realisation that I had no one to celebrate it with except the missionaries. I chose instead to teach and ended up giving an exam on Christmas Day. It didn't matter. All I wanted was to get out of Yining and go somewhere warm. I was tired of the prejudice and paranoia, of pretending to be interested in the future perfect tense. But I did feel somewhat closer to understanding what had happened in 1997, and how it related to the problems of the present.

I was particularly indebted to my students in the KU class, who had had to put up with the many varieties of my ignorance. To thank them I invited them out to dinner at the King of Kebabs. But I had a hard time trying to book a private room. The manager was suspicious.

'This is a Muslim restaurant,' he said. 'There must be no drinking or smoking.'

'Yes, I know, I've been here before.'

'No drinking! No smoking!'

'Yes, yes, of course.'

'And if anyone does, you'll have to leave.'

'There's no problem, no one will.'

He still looked unconvinced.

'What kind of people have you invited?'

'Uighurs.'

He laughed and brought his hands together.

'Oh, that's fine! How about seven o'clock?'

We assembled outside just before seven, said hurried hellos, then went in. We were ushered to a small room in the back and seated at a large round table. Tea was drunk and hands were warmed but there was little talk. It occurred to me what an unlikely group they were, the doctor next to the bridle-maker, the farmer next to the gynaecologist, the devout and the uninitiated, with one thing in common: the desire to learn English. There were cogent professional reasons for the doctors and teachers to do so, but it was less obvious why Yusuf (the horse-equipment seller) and some of the others were prepared to wrestle with the mysteries of English grammar. The same could be said of the hundred or so other people who attended evening courses like those run by Murat or Tursun. Yining didn't have the steady tourist flow of old Silk Route cities like Kashgar and Turpan, so there was little need for interpreters or guides. It was also hard to imagine that being able to speak English would be much of an asset in the depressed job market of Yining. There was one other possibility though.

'Yusuf, your English has really improved.'

He beamed.

'But what are you going to do with it?'

'Oh, well, maybe I will go abroad.'

'Where?'

'Maybe America. Maybe Egypt.'

'Egypt?'

'Yes, I'd like to study there. They have good *madrasas*.'

'What about the rest of you? Does anyone else plan to go abroad?'

Fifteen heads bobbed up and down. Dolkun raised a finger and looked as if he had a point of order.

'But at the moment this is very difficult. Especially for Uighur people. The government try to stop us. For young man it is very hard. Old man, no problem, Chinese man, no problem.'

Fourteen mouths tutted. I asked Dolkun if it was difficult for people to come back once they had left.

'It is easy, if you left... if the government said you could, but if you did not have permission, and then you left, maybe it is impossible.'

I asked how many people actually came back and stayed, thinking that I hadn't met anyone who'd been further than Uzbekistan.

'Not many.'

'But would you?'

Dolkun's yes was lost in a chorus of affirmatives. He looked around, gratified by the support.

'Of course. This is our home. We will come back to help our people.'

I wondered how many of the unreturned had said the same thing. Yusuf's voice interrupted this thought.

'Maybe some of us will go to England. If we do, can we visit you?'

'You bet.'

'Bet? What is this?'

'It means for certain. It's also what you do when you gamble.'

He frowned.

'Good Muslims do not do it. But the Chinese love to, they always do this.'

A thought struck me.

'Yusuf, do you know Murat?'

'Yes, of course, he is my good friend. Why?'

'Oh, no reason.'

Cut to a restaurant, from the outside and by night, somewhere on the barren plain between Urumqi and Yining. Trucks and buses are parked in a line in front. Ice crunches underfoot as you head for the door, wanting sleep rather than food but settling for less. The door is blocked by frozen strips of carpet that slap your face as you enter. Electro-karaoke booms from speakers with flashing lights. There's no need to order, they only make one thing. The waitress brings your food, her thumb in your noodles. You search for meat amidst the fat, find a single piece.

A young Uighur man enters. He walks to the centre of the room, claps his hands, reaches into his pocket for a tea towel that he lays on the floor. He shouts for attention. You are glad to ignore your food. The man produces three cards from his top pocket and lays them face up on the towel: a three of hearts and two queens. He flips them over then starts switching them around. He speaks words heard many times in every place and language.

'Come on come on, it's easy, just try and find the three.'

The room pauses. The music is turned off. Then a man bets 20 yuan. He stoops and picks up a card. A three.

Another man tries. He also wins, then after a pause, people start to bet 100s. Two men win and then a Chinese woman says, 'A thousand.'

The man with the tea towel smiles. 'Are you sure?' he says.

'Of course,' she snaps. Her boyfriend puts his hand on her arm, then murmurs in her ear. She shoves him away.

The man with the cards asks to see her money. She produces a wad from her purse and shakes it at him. He shrugs, and then it is her turn to ask. He produces a thicker wad of notes than hers, but she does not look worried.

The cards are placed on the tea towel. They blur across its surface, the man's hands switching back and forth, lifting cards, sometimes moving them, sometimes putting them back where they were. The room is quiet while he does this. When the cards are still, he straightens. His eyes flick up to hers.

She picks the card on the right without hesitation. Just for emphasis (and perhaps to make sure), she places her boot on it. Her adversary nods and stands back. She peels the card from her sole; she drops it; it is a queen.

She pays the man; returns to her noodles; quickly, the man leaves.

69

THE BUS BUMPS towards Urumqi. Out the window, all is white. You seek solace in your book but the sound spitting from the television will have none of it. The film still looks (and sounds) to be the one put on five hours ago, a kung fu film whose plot consists of a Chinese woman punching Japanese men.

No one else seems interested; they slump, feign sleep or stare into the bleaching void, willing time forwards or back. Snow falls with the intentness of rain, eager to settle and transform the terrain; for everything to be smooth.

The bus pulls into a yard with restaurants on three sides: an L-shape of Hui places, a brief stroke of Han. You head for the latter, thinking it will be quieter. The atmosphere inside is funereal and you are halfway through turning to leave when a man shouts at you. He tells you to sit; you do. He asks what you want; you say noodles. He stomps into the kitchen, screams the order, and is met by the shrill cry that there are none. The volume increases, and the pitch, and suddenly there are emphatic thumps. You make your exit and head for one of the Hui restaurants. Your shoes seek purchase on the ice but fail. As you lie on the ground, you stare at the ice, beneath which playing cards are frozen. You see a queen of hearts, a ten of spades. You do not see a three. Then a man helps you up and leads you into his restaurant.

Inside the air is thick with steam and breath. A woman brings you a bowl of caramel-coloured tea. The air smells of mutton and smoke. You rub the window into visibility. A flock of sheep surround the bus. They scratch themselves on the exhaust, nibble at the wheels.

Your *laghman* arrives, first at your table, then your lower intestine. But there is no time to digest. When the bus driver sounds his horn, everyone bolts for the toilets.

Each stall consists of two planks over a hole, underneath which lurks the cesspit. In summer the stench would be awful, but on this winter day it's almost beautiful: faeces glisten in weak light; the ice is yellowed and smooth. The only thing that spoils the mood is the man squatting next to you. He strains and grunts, then sighs, relieved, his difficult task complete.

From Urumqi, you fly south to Kunming ('city of eternal spring'), and from there to Bangkok. All the foreign men you meet there seem intent on taking you to as many strip bars as possible. You flee to Cambodia, where the men instead try to make you accompany them to the $3 brothels. One evening you find yourself in a grubby one street town 11km north of Phnom Penh. Limbless children wave their stumps in your face while diseased dogs fight. Two fat American men feed a teenage girl ice cream. At the end of the street the spire of a Catholic church rises above it all.

Your companions disappear inside one of the brothels. You play noughts and crosses with the girls while you wait for them. Young men wander in and out, offering cocaine, speed and other 'make you happy' substances. You know there's more to Cambodia than this, but all you can do in these few weeks is impact on the surface.

It's early March when you return to Yining. You dig your flat out from its dust, start to prepare your lessons. After your first week of teaching, you have forgotten about Cambodia and its problems. You teach, you eat, you play chess. You cycle out to the tree that bleeds whose branches are bright with new ribbons. The skies are clear, the weather warmer; optimism is easy.

Spring

70

ONE MORNING, on the way to class, I stopped upon the stairs. A syringe lay at my feet. Its needle was a few steps down, broken, brown with dried blood. I went to pick it up then stopped. I returned to my flat and got a yoghurt pot. I nudged the syringe, then the needle into the pot with my shoe. A door opened behind me. My neighbour mumbled a hello to me, then stopped when he saw the contents of the pot. He shook his head and swore. He mimed injection, his thumb twitching as he pushed the plunger.

'Heroin,' he said.

71

IT WAS NO SURPRISE that there were drugs available in town; whenever I went to the bazaar a man would sidle up to me and mutter '*hashish?*' Then he would launch into a mime routine that consisted of inhaling and crossing his eyes. But being offered hash is not the same as finding needles outside one's door. It made a certain depressing sense: unemployment produces poverty, leading to depression, hopelessness and the search for release.

Such issues were of course not unique to Yining. Cotton production had been affected throughout Xinjiang in the early 1990s, which led to widespread economic hardship, a situation aggravated by the closure of many state-owned enterprises. By the late 1990s, there were an estimated 30,000 drug users in Xinjiang. But where did the drugs come from, and who took them?

72

IT'S NOT DIFFICULT to teach, only to teach well. I tried to speak as little as possible when teaching my Han students, so as to give them plenty of chances to practice their spoken English, which in most cases was somewhere between average and poor. A simple question like 'What makes a good neighbour?' could kill a third of a lesson, what with pair work, group work, and some blackboard writing. In the KU class this took even longer. The 15 of them could generate more language than a Han class of 45. I asked a short and usually silent woman named Madina to tell the class about her neighbours.

'My neighbours they are very kind and good.'

Finally, a safe topic. I asked if anyone had bad neighbours. Dolkun's hand shot up.

'OK, Dolkun, why are your neighbours so bad?'

'My neighbours they are very bad, they gossip, make trouble, are unfriendly and also sell drugs.'

The man next to him laughed.

'Oh, so your neighbours are Hui?'

There was much laughter and agreement. The speaker's name was Abdullah; he was a clerk in the local government offices.

'The Hui will do anything. They will hunt protected animals, sell drugs or smuggle weapons. Sometimes the Hui *imam* will sell drugs in the mosque. The law is nothing to them. They are without fear, unlike the Chinese, who are always afraid.'

His tone was almost admiring. I asked where the drugs came from.

'Maybe from Vietnam and Laos, via Guangzhou or Hong Kong, and perhaps also a small amount from Afghanistan.'

He was surprisingly knowledgeable about the international

narcotics trade. But there did seem to be a high degree of consensus that the Hui were responsible for supplying drugs to the area, and while this didn't make the accusation any truer, it was interesting to find such consistency to people's prejudices. There was even a shred of plausibility to the idea, as the hashish sellers in the market were usually Hui.

However, for all Abdullah's familiarity with the drugs scene, he could not tell me who the main users were. This was a question that made the class go quiet.

73

IF THERE WAS one restaurant that needed knocking down, it was the *Old Hui*. Every time it rained the ceiling sagged a little further. Flakes of plaster fell into the food; on wet days there were puddles on the floor. But the place was seldom empty, perhaps because the decay was so awe-inspiring, more likely because the food was so good. My favourite was a dish called *ding ding xihongshi jidan xiao mian*, a grand name for a dish that was macaroni with egg and tomato.

The *Old Hui* was run by a young Hui man called Yunis. He spoke Russian and Arabic, as well as Chinese and Uighur. How he had come to run this shell of restaurant was a subject about which he was somewhat evasive. But he was quite chatty about other subjects.

One day I was flicking through *News from Tartary*, Peter Fleming's account of his trip from Beijing to India, via Xinjiang and Tibet. Yunis came over to have a look. He flicked through it till he came across a photo of some Hui soldiers. He nodded and handed the book back.

'My grandfather went to Hami in 1930 to fight. There was a lot of trouble.'

This was something of an understatement. The early 1930s were marked by almost continual conflict, as Chinese Republican forces fought with various Uighur factions, particularly in the south of the province. Most of the Republican forces were Hui, who were thus responsible for putting down various secessionist rebellions.

I suggested that this might have coloured some Uighurs' view of the Hui.

Yunis mimed the action of aiming.

'Yes. But the Hui are very good with a rifle.'

'What about now? You seem to have lots of Uighur customers.'

'Yes, Uighurs and Kazakhs like to come here.'

Hui restaurants were neutral territory. They were *halal*, and thus free from pork, which meant that Uighurs could eat there. There were usually a few Han customers too, which was quite heartening, as it suggested that whatever differences there were between them, they could at least be in the same room with each other, even if, as in the snooker halls, it was usually at separate tables. The fact that many Uighurs regarded the Hui as drug dealers clearly didn't stop them from patronising their restaurants.

'Um, some Uighurs say things about the Hui selling drugs. Is there any truth to that?'

He paused to consider my question, his reply or both.

'Yes, *some* Hui do. Some. There's a lot of money to be made.' He laughed and spread his hands, then said, 'Yining is a poor city with many millionaires.'

'Who do you think buys most of the drugs?'

He shrugged and smiled, said he didn't know.

74

I LEARNT MUCH of my Chinese from taxi drivers. A taxi is the ideal practice environment. You have a captive language partner and an endless succession of conversation topics streaming past the window. There are certain drawbacks, though. You get asked about a fairly restricted set of topics: your job, your country, what you think of China, if you like its food and people. If you want to progress beyond these topics, you need to take control of the conversation. My usual strategy was to ask the driver equally nosy questions.

I was already 20 minutes late for my meeting with Rukiye when I got into a red cab waiting outside the college gate.

'Where to?' asked the driver, who was Han, and had a very thick neck.

'The square.'

He nodded, lit a cigarette. As we turned onto Liberation Road he said,

'You're foreign.'

'Yes. I'm English.'

'English people are good at football. Like Beckham, Owen...'

'Yes they're good but most people aren't.'

He grunted doubtfully. The conversation was already half way down an over-trodden path. I attempted a diversion.

'Are you from Yining?'

'No, I'm from Henan. Pindingshan is my hometown. I'm only here to work. I'll go back next year.'

'Don't you like it here?'

'No, there are too many bad people.'

'Who do you mean?'

'The minorities. Especially the Uighurs.'

'What's wrong with them?'

'You can't trust them. Yesterday I had some in my cab. When we arrived they started arguing about the fare, saying it was too much. I said no, it's not! The fare is what the meter says! It was ten yuan but they wouldn't give more than eight. They're always causing trouble, fighting or taking drugs. They're all criminals.'

'What?'

'Drugs. They all take drugs. Even some of the children. I hate them.'

'How do you know?'

'Everyone knows. I always see them waiting to buy drugs. If they have no money, they will steal. Don't you know about the trouble in 1997?'

'No, what happened?'

'A lot of Uighur criminals went crazy. They stole and killed people. They set an old woman on fire. But the police stopped them. Now those people are dead.'

At the time I dismissed this as just more bigotry. Later I remembered that this was one of the official explanations put forward soon afterwards, the notion that there was no political or religious motivation behind the riots. They were said to have been no more than a crime spree perpetrated by drug addicts and other 'social garbage'. It was an appealingly simple explanation, one that placed the blame on individuals rather than society.

75

THE OTHER DOCTOR in the KU class was called Hamit. He was thin and softly spoken, with a particularly good ear for the quirks of British English. He was married with one young daughter, who lived with his wife in a small town about 30km from Yining. Hamit usually went back every other weekend, and one Thursday invited me to go with him.

'What's the name of your town?'

'It is no. 56 *tuan*.'

'*Tuan*? As in *bingtuan*?'

'Yes, it is now a *bingtuan*. Some people ask why we choose to live in a *bingtuan*, but we were there first. My grandfather came from Kazakhstan to escape the Russians. In the 1960s most people in the village were Uighur or Kazakh, but then many went to Kazakhstan because of problems. After they closed the border our family was separated.'

'But your father didn't go?'

'No, he thought that because we came from there it would be going backwards to return. But the Communists took a lot of his land and animals as a result. He was quite rich before. At least they did not hurt him.' He sighed. 'Now he is very sick.'

I hadn't been to a *bingtuan* before, and found myself imagining some vast plantation, part labour-camp, part-garden centre. It turned out to be not dissimilar to many other Chinese towns, in that it looked to be constructed from grubby white Lego. Its streets were wide enough for tanks and all the trees looked artificial.

One added feature was the large police checkpoint. The policeman spent five minutes looking at my residence permit, then still had to phone his superior. He asked if I had a camera, first in Chinese, then in Uighur, and on both occasions I smiled and shook my head like a dumb foreigner. We also had to pay to enter the area. Although it wasn't much, only two yuan, having to pay to enter his hometown bothered Hamit. Once we were past the checkpoint he exploded.

'Money, they always want money! We have the lowest wages in Xinjiang! But the highest cost of living! Most of our goods come from other provinces. Our cotton and metals go to inner China, and come back as expensive things. And the government, they know this!'

It was hard to disagree. There was certainly a lot of investment in the area, all part of the Chinese government's much trumpeted initiative to *Xibu Da Kaifa* ('develop the west'). But it was difficult to say how much of the profits would be reinvested in the province.

Hamit's house lay on a side street that a small stream ran across. His daughter heard his voice and ran out to meet him. He picked her up and kissed her. When he put her down she started showing him a dance she had just learnt, then stopped when she saw me. She looked at me for a moment, trying to decide whether I was someone to be shy of. I said hello. She laughed and got on with her routine, a cute mixture of skips and hops.

Hamit's father was sat inside, next to the fire. His knees were drawn up to his chest; he looked shrunken and pale. Hamit went in and spoke to him. I stood outside and felt uncomfortable. After ten minutes he came out.

'It is OK, he is sleeping now. Do you want to go for a walk?'

We squelched down the road, still muddy from the melted snow, passing a number of other small houses, some of which had the Chinese characters for 'fortune' and 'double happiness' pasted on their gates. The Han and Uighur seemed to live in much closer proximity than in Yining. I asked Hamit about this.

'Here there are now many Chinese, they come from inner China. They say they only come for a year to work but they do not go back. They make things difficult.'

'How do you mean?'

'There are not enough jobs and there isn't enough good land. The *bingtuan* workers take it all. Many are very rude. My neighbours are Chinese, you know. Last year, one of them break one of our walls. My brother was very angry.'

'What did he do?'

'He hit him very hard.'

'Won't he get in trouble for that?'

'My neighbour?'

'No, your brother.'

'It is no problem. The neighbour knows he was wrong.'

The path wandered into an orchard. Fat birds sang in the trees and the air was scented with blossom.

Hamit started chuckling.

'What's so funny?'

'When I was a boy I used to steal apples from here. Now it is my orchard but I still feel I am thief.'

'Yours?'

'My brother and I rent it for three years. He does most of the work but I help him pick. But we have problems getting enough water. The Chinese take most of it.'

'Can't you complain to anyone?'

'There is no one. The *bingtuan* is the law.'

Hamit's complaints may have sounded like the well-worn refrain of 'they come over here and take our jobs', but that didn't make them any less true. After I learnt the Chinese characters for *bingtuan*, I realised they were all over the area. Even the petrol stations were part of their mandate. For those already impoverished by unemployment, the *bingtuans*, and the state they were part of, were obvious targets for resentment.

The wind started to bully the branches, bending their fingers back. Slate-coloured clouds built to the west. I wondered aloud if we should go back.

Hamit shook his head.

'No, the storm is far away, still in Kazakhstan. Let's go for a ride.'

We borrowed a motorbike from his brother, a small man with a moustache whose eyes disappeared when he smiled. Soon we were speeding down a road empty of traffic but the occasional tractor. The trees on either side of us seemed thicker in the dusk. I asked Hamit to turn on the lights; he laughed and said, 'This bike, no lights!'

The sky turned violet, then deepened to purple; the first drops of rain sizzled on the engine. Thunder rolled, then lightning flashed. We turned back for home.

As we pulled to a halt the rain was falling in thick sheets. We went in and took our shoes off. Hamit went out the room and returned with a small metal watering can and a bowl. 'For your hands,' he said, and put the bowl on the table. Then I put my hands above the bowl and he poured water onto them. After I did the same for him, his wife brought us two bowls of *laghman*, then did the usual disappearing trick. We ate and then talked for an hour about Britain, then Hamit made a bed for me on the floor, whose inch-thick carpet was as good as a mattress. I drifted into sleep to the drone of rain.

Next morning dawned clear and bright. Everything looked varnished. After a breakfast of milk tea, we zoomed off, this time to indulge my obsessive desire to see as many old things as possible. Many Han Chinese boast of their country's 5,000-year-old history, which is indeed splendid and rich. However, it is sometimes difficult to find tangible signs of this glorious past. In the 1960s and 70s, during the Cultural Revolution, the Red Guards did their best to destroy as much of this legacy as possible. Out of 8,000 sites and monuments in Beijing, only 78 were deemed worth keeping, many of which were still damaged. Those sites that survived have in general been restored to the point where they look as if they have just been built.

But the tomb I saw that day was a rare exception. It towered 40 feet above, its gate a swirling mass of Arabic that began at head height then soared up and over to form an archway of devotion. The surrounding tile work was a delicate dissection of the spectrum between blue and green, a subtle blend of cyan, turquoise and aquamarine. The adobe was poking through in places, and there were a few scorch marks (courtesy of the Red Guards) but otherwise it looked good for its six and a half centuries. The name of the man buried inside was Tughluq Timur. Timur was the last khan of the Chaghatayids, the Mongol clan that controlled much of central Asia during the 13th and 14th centuries. Timur ruled from 1347 to 1363 and is principally remembered for encouraging the spread of Islam throughout the region. He converted when he was only an army captain. It is said that one day he heard a sound coming from the mountains, a rich and resonant cry unlike any he had heard before. He asked his men what it was but no one knew. Finally, a Uighur told him that it was the call to prayer. He was so impressed he converted immediately, as did all the men under his command.

The caretaker was a wizened man whose spine was almost perpendicular to his legs. He shuffled over and unlocked the door. Hamit said that the man's family had been custodians of the tomb for the last five generations, but that the man had no son to take over from him. Inside was as austere as the outside was lavish, just whitewashed walls and an omega-shaped sarcophagus. I interpreted this minimalism as an expression of piety, of modesty before the divine and infinite, until Hamit informed me that during the Cultural Revolution the Red Guards had forced people to keep pigs inside.

We thanked the caretaker and went in search of an old mosque. After 20 minutes we stopped at the edge of a graveyard. We walked the bike through slowly. As we passed one small grave covered in blue flowers Hamit said, 'That's my mother's.'

I was glad for the narrowness of the path. He walked in front and neither of us spoke for the next few minutes.

The path fed into a larger track, its ice almost thawed. The poplars were their usual brilliant selves, stark and silver, their shadows stretching blue across the still-white fields. A single leaf rattled in the breeze; our footsteps seemed too loud.

The mosque was buried in the woods, busy with collapse. A

THE TREE THAT BLEEDS

sign warned us not to enter as the building was unsound. Inside were three large graves with sheets draped over them. We clearly weren't the only ones to disregard the sign, as the floor was well swept and there were stubs of burnt-down joss stick. But the prospect of dying in a small woodland mosque on the Kazakh border dissuaded me from a more thorough inspection.

I had to go back to Yining as I had class that afternoon. On the way to the bus station we stopped and checked on Hamit's father. He was sitting in the same position, only now his eyes were closed, his mouth open too wide. He looked too much like the picture by Munch. A week later, he passed.

76

THE LARGEST CONCENTRATION of Uighur shops and stalls was on a street named Han Ren Jie. This was the area that I had walked round with Murat and Ismail on my first day in Yining. I didn't give any thought to the etymology of the name until I drew a map of the town for a lesson on how to give directions. Then the oddness of the name struck me: Han People Street. It could not have been more of a misnomer. This was not a street where the Han went if they could help it.

Before class, I asked Dean Geng about the origin of this name.

'A hundred years ago there were not many Chinese here. Not many Han, only a few merchants. The street where they had all their shops came to be known as Han Ren Jie.'

This wasn't just an interesting historical snippet. It illustrated how radical the reversal had been, how the Han had gone from being a minority to being the largest ethnic group. I wanted to ask him more, but then the bell for class rang.

The lesson lurched from language point to point. Turn left then go straight. Then right at the junction. I put the students into pairs, then gave them a city map and told them to ask each other for directions. A hum of faulty English began. After five minutes, one boy put his hand up, and I sidled over.

'Nick, have you been there?'

He pointed towards Han Ren Jie.

'Yes. Have you?'

'No, but I want to.'

His neighbour dismissed the possibility.

'It's dirty and there are many thieves.'

'Maybe it's dangerous,' said the girl behind.

A free-for-all ensued.

'Some of the minorities are very fierce.'

'They like fighting, especially the young men.'

'They are wild and smell like sheep!'

To them, it was clearly the wrong side of the tracks. But it occurred to me later that the students weren't entirely to blame for their prejudice. They had grown up without much meaningful contact with Uighurs, a state of affairs perpetuated by the college. They had never been encouraged to think about what life was like for Uighur people, let alone that they might have some legitimate grievances without being terrorists. But they were my captive audience for 12 hours a week. Perhaps we could have a different kind of lesson.

77

THOUGH THIS WAS a nice idea in theory, the practice proved more difficult. It wasn't like teaching grammar, where there was little doubt about what the correct answers were. Students could acknowledge their mistake and accept correction. But I couldn't (nor did I have the right to) tell them that everything they thought they knew about Uighur people was wrong. All I could do was try to make them question some of their ideas.

I started by showing them *Pleasantville*, a Hollywood film about two teenagers who get stuck inside a television sitcom where nothing bad ever happens. However, there is also no creativity. The teenagers try to introduce rock music, painting and sex, but meet with fierce opposition from the town's moral guardians. There are soon two different types of people in the town, who look different, seldom mix and do not trust each other. The message of the film is that we should tolerate and accept those who are different from us. The students appeared to enjoy it, and laughed or expressed dismay in all the right places. Afterwards I asked them to write down any similarities between Yining and the town in the film. The first results were less than promising.

Everyone in Yining city loves each other.

In Yining, people are friendly and warm hearted. But their mind is not open enough. They have their own living way.

There are some minorities here. So people are not open minded and don't get along with each other well.

I wondered if the students saw themselves as agents of modernity, come to rescue the Uighurs from their backwardness. However, there were a few encouraging responses.

In the film, people must obey the law, and they can't do anything they want. So, they have something in common with people here.

In this film and here there are many people who do not understand each other well. This causes problems. But in the film they solve the problems.

After the film I got them to debate whether 'When in Rome, do as the Romans do' was sensible advice or not. I gave them a few minutes to think about it then asked one of the better students to begin.

'Oh yes, of course you must. You should do whatever the local people in a place do. That is what is right. You must imitate those Romans.'

He sat down looking rather pleased. A petite girl shot up.

'No! I don't agree with you. You say we should do what the local people do. But what about your own customs? Can you forget all of those?'

The boy stood up, almost livid.

'No! You can't forget them. But they must be the second thing. The second! Or there will be trouble. If you do something that the local people think is bad they may hate you and fight you.'

The girl was back up before he had sat down.

'If Uighurs went to a place where the only meat was pork, should they eat it? Of course not. This is an important custom for them.'

Her neighbour added, 'It's more than a custom. It is a belief.'

This was one of the days when I actually liked being a teacher.

78

I HADN'T SEEN Erkin since his wedding five months earlier. I ran into him and Ismail outside the King of Kebabs.

'Sorry, I haven't called you,' he said. 'I've been busy, working very hard.'

'Especially at night!' said Ismail.

Erkin tried to look angry but then laughed.

'Yes, it is true. My wife is pregnant.'

'Congratulations!'

'Yes, God has chosen to bless me. Shall we have ice cream?'

A television muttered to itself in a corner. A puffy-faced man crooned upon its screen. His face looked familiar, but at first I could not recall where I had seen him before. Then I remembered that I had a tape of his, a pleasant confection of synthesiser and accordion. Erkin pointed to the screen with his spoon.

'You see him? He uses drugs.'

Ismail corrected him. 'No, not now. He has stopped.'

'How do you know?'

'He gave a concert in Kashgar last year. He cried and asked the audience for their forgiveness.'

I asked Erkin if he thought that many people in Ghulja used drugs.

'Some, especially young men.'

'Chinese men?'

'No, Uighurs.'

Ismail shook his head, but Erkin continued.

'What? It's true isn't it? Why should we deny it? If we do, things will get worse, like before.'

'Before...?'

'In the past the problem was very bad.'

213

'When?'

'Seven or eight years ago. That's why we have the *mäshräps*.'

Erkin went on to say that they had hoped to reduce the growing use of drugs and alcohol by promoting a Muslim lifestyle. At the time there were no state programmes for helping drug addicts. The *mäshräps* were supposed to both encourage people to give up and provide a supportive atmosphere for those attempting to do so. He claimed that the *mäshräps* had managed to help a significant number of people and had consequently won the support of many parents. Their closure by the authorities was thus especially unpopular, given that they were trying to tackle a problem particular to Uighurs, a problem that the government was doing little about. The ban might not have been sufficient to provoke a riot, but it certainly would have contributed to the climate of discontent.

Yet something didn't make sense. If the *mäshräps* had been proscribed for the last seven years, and there was still so much unemployment and poverty, why hadn't drug use increased to pre-*mäshräp* levels? Had they really been so effective? Erkin had an answer for this.

'The war changed many people here.'

'What war?'

'In 1997. You know, February 5.'

In the wake of the September 11 attacks, this was apparently now the trendy way to refer to the riots.

'It made people think. People became more serious. Afterwards they were better Muslims. More women covered their heads. Many men gave up drinking and smoking. Perhaps the war was a good thing.'

This was the first time anyone had suggested that the riots had made things *better*. But it did coincide with what Tilawaldi and others had said about being less devout in the past. And if being Muslim was a mark of difference from the Han, then the more that some Uighurs hated the Han, perhaps the more they would embrace Islam. Certainly, the likes of Murat, Erkin and Yusuf, the self proclaimed 'good Muslims', tended to be more outspoken in their dislike of the Han. And the more that hate fed faith, the more the Chinese government would try to suppress it, leading to further hate and who knows what extreme of religiosity. There was a vicious logic to it, one that seemed to promise further bombs on buses. Ismail cleared his throat.

'My uncle used to use the drugs. We asked him to stop many times but he did not. One day I said to him, 'I hope you will die soon. You give our family so much pain. Hurry up and die.'

'What happened to him?'

'One day he was in the house and we thought he would take the drugs. We called the special hospital and they came and took him away. After eight months they let him out. We sent him to his aunt in Urumqi, so he would be away from some bad friends. Now he is married with a daughter.'

Whatever effect the renewal of faith had had on the drug problem, it clearly hadn't been the sole agency. The 'special hospital' that Ismail had referred to was one of many claiming to offer rehabilitation. The road between Urumqi and Yining was lined with advertisements for such clinics. However, the high prices charged by such clinics, and their essentially cold-turkey methods (methadone only recently became available in China) probably deterred many from enrolling in such programmes. An added deterrent was that such clinics often have to provide the police with a list of their patients. Whilst this does not automatically lead to criminal charges, there is still the risk of ending up on the *zhongdian renkou* ('special population') register – whose members include criminals, prostitutes, and dissidents – essentially a list of anyone that the government feels it necessary to keep a special eye on. Once on this list, a person may find difficulty in finding employment or housing and have their freedom of movement curtailed.

Given the scale of the drug problem in Yining, there was clearly a need for some other support mechanism, preferably independent from the state. However, starting a local *shetuan* ('social organisation') is far from easy. Any attempt to do so may be taken as a criticism of the local authorities, the inference being that said authorities are incapable of handling the problem by themselves. In order to register, a group needs to have 30,000 yuan and fixed office premises, as well as the approval of the relevant government department, who may not fancy the extra responsibility, even in the absence of a political or religious dimension to the group. Given such restrictions, it was astonishing that the authorities had taken so long to crack down on an unregistered (and thus illegal) quasi-religious organisation such as the *mäshräps*. I asked Ismail how the organisers had imagined they would get away with it.

He replied, in a tone of pride and sorrow, 'Many thought that we would fail. But we wanted to try. Did we have a choice? Should we have watched our young men die? No, we could not.'

79

ONLY THE BRAVE or foolish generalise about China. Customs, cuisine and language, not to mention climate and geography, vary widely from north to south, let alone east to west. The collection of rubbish is one exception; prostitution is another.

In virtually every town and city, from Beijing to Urumqi, the sight is the same. As soon as it gets dark, the pink bulbs flick on. Girls begin to lounge in earnest. Men start to straggle in. Technically these places purport to be 'beauty parlours', places where one might go for a haircut or massage. During the day, it can be difficult to tell the difference between the brothels and the hairdressers, but at night there's little chance of confusion: it doesn't take six girls to cut hair after midnight.

Yining certainly had its fair share of pink-lit 'hairdressers'. In general they obeyed the same rules of distribution as the other businesses. Rather than disperse themselves throughout the city, they chose to aggregate along a few streets. So in addition to the streets of ironmongers, shoe shops or wedding outfitters, there were also roads that glowed pink. The fact that prostitution is illegal in China didn't seem to matter. Everybody knew what went on in those places, even my students. They laughed nervously, tried to change the subject, but made no attempt to deny it.

Cases of HIV infection have been reported in every major Chinese city. The modes of HIV transmission appear to vary with geography: in the central province of Henan – rural China *par excellence* – a large number of villagers were found to have been infected by contaminated blood. In the south-western province of Yunnan, intravenous drug use is thought to have been the major route of infection. Yunnan has the highest number of recorded HIV cases in China; Xinjiang has the second.

85 per cent of all those diagnosed with HIV in Xinjiang are Uighur; Yining has the highest rates of infection of any city in Xinjiang, even more than Urumqi. In 2000 a UNAIDS study reported that 85 per cent of intravenous drug users tested in Yining were HIV-positive, compared to 40 per cent of users tested in Urumqi. Intravenous drug use is certainly not the only route of HIV transmission in Yining; the same study reported that almost a quarter of all prostitutes tested HIV-positive.

This is likely to be an underestimate for two reasons: first, the majority of their clients do not use condoms, and second, prostitutes are only subject to medical checks if they are arrested. As with drug users, anyone who tests HIV-positive is likely to end up on the *zhong-dian renkou*: legally, HIV is a notifiable disease, which means that the relevant municipal or provincial authorities must be informed.

So in addition to the unemployment, ethnic tension, drug use and prostitution, Yining had an AIDS epidemic waiting to happen. But something was being done. There were posters here and there, instructing people on how they could and could not get HIV or featuring a large photo of a television presenter with the caption 'MEN MAKE A DIFFERENCE!'

This might not sound like much. But in China, there is still little sex education, with the exception of some of the most prosperous cities. One explanation for this is a general social conservatism: previous attempts to show advertisements for condoms were vetoed for being contrary to 'traditional' values. My Han students were all terminally coy about anything to do with love, let alone sex. Any mention of boy or girlfriends would reduce them to embarrassed giggles. Some even denied that they had a boy- or girlfriend, despite the fact that they had been holding hands with them a second ago. In such an atmosphere, even the posters had to be considered a success.

My students were a low-risk group: I couldn't imagine many of them taking drugs – even beer seemed hopelessly illicit to most of them – or going to prostitutes. But they still needed to know something about HIV and AIDS, if only to reduce some of the general ignorance. It occurred to me that if I didn't teach them about this, no one else would. The only problem was that I had absolutely no experience in sex education.

Initially, I planned to leave as little room for misunderstanding as possible by doing a demonstration with a banana and condom (I suppose there was in fact an even more explicit method available) but by the time I was due to give the class I was reduced to drawing a condom on the board. Even this was enough to reduce many of the students to quivering embarrassment, except for one girl who just stared and smiled. At the end, I gave them all a piece of paper and told them to write either a question or something they had learnt, so that it wouldn't be obvious who had asked a question. The responses were alternately sensible,

'What should we pay attention to the first time we have sex?'

'Is there any other sexually transmitted disease? Tell us more.'

worrying,

'If everyone leads a normal and healthy life, I think HIV and AIDS are far away from us. So it's none of my business but doctors.'

heartening,

'We have never had a lesson like this before. We are girls and feel shy. But thank you.'

'Although this lesson is shy, it is necessary for our daily life.'

and interesting.

'In the novel of 'Lady Chatterley's Lover' do you think Connie fell in love with that man because of sex or true love?'

Some of them may have learnt something about HIV, if only that it couldn't be caught from chopsticks or kissing. But the problem was that I had tried to talk about how to have safe sex without actually talking about the act. I had been infected with their reserve; I found myself embarrassed to say the word, let alone what it involved. In Britain, I could have safely assumed that the majority of a similar audience would have had some sexual experience, but in China pre-marital sex is still the exception, especially outside major cities. Traditionally, women are supposed to remain 'pure' until they marry.

Female virtue is also important in Uighur culture: traditionally girls should remain virgins until they are married. It is still the custom in some places in Xinjiang for the parents of the bride to display the nuptial sheets the morning after the wedding night. Even if they are not actually hung up, they are likely to be asked about. In the past, the absence of virginal blood would have been grounds for an immediate divorce. However, the decline of arranged marriages has meant that most husbands can no longer blame their parents if their spouse is less pure than they might like.

I asked some of the men in the KU class about this, and they said if the girl was known to be 'a shy girl', there wouldn't be much fuss. However, perhaps the greatest challenge to the survival of this custom is that private hospitals now offer relatively cheap (200–500 yuan) operations to reconstruct the hymen. But these factors notwith-standing, there are still some who take the idea of bridal purity very seriously. Hamit told me about one of his friends who woke to find his wedding sheets unblemished. He said nothing to his wife or parents, and instead went to the river and drowned himself.

It was interesting to find something that Uighurs and Han agreed on, even though they offered different justifications for the need for female purity. This was not the only thing they had in common. There was also the same shyness about relationships with the opposite sex: of the many young Uighur people that I knew, few spoke openly about their boy- or girlfriends. Often I would not even know they were going out with someone until they announced that they were getting married. Their reticence might also have been due to the fact that their own chastity might have been called into question if they were known to be going out with someone, especially if they ended up marrying someone else. I pointed out some of these simila-rities to the KU class, who looked doubtful but didn't actually disagree. I would have done the same with my Han friends, but for a small problem. I had none.

80

THERE WERE PLENTY of Han that I knew – Dean Geng, Miss Cai, the other teachers in the department, plus all of my students – but no one I saw socially. The other teachers ignored me unless they wanted some piece of grammar explained. I tried several times to invite them for a meal, but was always met with a nervous smile and an unconvincing excuse. I might have been forgiven for thinking that the Han were less friendly than the Uighur.

But I knew this was wrong; it had been different in Hunan. There my students had often come to my flat to talk or watch a film. I had known doctors, nurses, teachers and businessmen. In some respects, life in Yining was no different, in that I was friends with people from the same professions; what was different was that all of them were Uighur.

Another explanation was that the teachers in the department lacked the necessary confidence in their English to talk to a native speaker. In Hunan, this had made some teachers a little shy at first, but after a few months most were familiar enough with me for it not to matter. But after eight months in Yining the other teachers seemed no more at ease than when I had just arrived. I had virtually given up on them until I got a phone call from the dean, inviting me to a lecture by a visiting professor. Usually, I would have had 'something to do', only this time there was the promise of a meal afterwards. Maybe this would loosen people up a bit. Perhaps my colleagues would talk to me about something other than phrasal verbs.

The lecture was in English and Chinese, and far better in the latter, as it allowed me to make up most of what he was saying. Afterwards, my applause was loudest, which seemed to impress my colleagues. Dean Geng announced that the professor was due to leave for Urumqi next morning, so we would eat *jiaozi*: steamed dumplings full of meat or vegetables that have a mollusc-like appearance. There is an old custom that when a person leaves they should be given *jiaozi*; when they return they should be given noodles. *Jiaozi* are supposed to keep a person safe; noodles are supposed to bind a person to a place.

I arrived at the restaurant early. A waitress in a long red dress showed me to the room booked for our party, where I crunched sunflower seeds for the next 20 minutes. Then the dean arrived, followed by a young teacher called Liu Feng. He was tall, thin and looked like a bit like Leonard Nimoy. I often ran into him in the college, doing some shopping or taking his daughter to kindergarten. We would smile and swap hellos but seldom stop and chat. But that evening Liu Feng took the seat next to mine, even though all the other seats were empty. I asked him what he thought of the lecture.

'It's hard to say. What do you think?'

'Well, I was pretty bored because I couldn't understand most of it.'

'Really? People said you enjoyed it the most.'

'Oh, well, I was just being polite. He spoke too fast for me.'

He laughed and said, 'Maybe you were lucky.'

'Lucky? Why?'

'I understood all of it and I was *very* bored!'

The rest of the teachers arrived. They greeted me in a perfunctory fashion, then locked eyes onto their cups of tea. The waitresses started bringing in food, first a selection of cold vegetables, then the *jiaozi*, great steaming bowlfuls waiting to be dipped in chilli and vinegar. The dean stood up, thanked the professor for his fascinating talk, then toasted him with *baijiu* (a toxic rice wine drunk throughout China). The professor thanked him, they drank, then the professor toasted the rest of us, and we all drank, then Liu Feng toasted me and we drank, then I toasted the dean and we drank, and after another half an hour of this, oblivion seemed welcome. Both Liu Feng and the dean had red faces, something that happens to many Han when they drink. I was looking forward to passing out at home, but Liu Feng insisted the two of us continue drinking elsewhere.

We ended up in *The Big Dog Bar*, an orange-lit cellar off Liberation Road. If I had been less drunk, I might have questioned Liu Feng's sudden friendliness. Instead we ordered a large jug of beer, then toasted each other.

'To foreign friends!' he said.

I drained my glass, and he did the same, then we thanked each other for drinking. He filled my glass, then coughed and said, 'Now, Nick you're a man, I'm a man, maybe I can, ah, ask you something? You know, something private. Because we're men.'

I nodded drunkenly.

'How many times can you... do it? You know, the sexual intercourse.'

At the time it seemed a completely appropriate question, one which deserved an honest answer.

'In a night? Twice, sometimes three times. It depends.'

'Yes,' he said. 'But not four or five times?'

'Er, no.'

'Really? I've seen some sex films where the men can do it many times.'

'Yes, but those are *films*. None of it's real. Those men are acting.'

'Oh.'

He looked reassured, and then disappointed.

'How long can you do it for?'

'Um, well, that depends too.'

'The people in the films can do it for a long time. A very long time.'

'Yes. Well. Like I said, those are films. They're only pretending.'

'Sometimes I finish quickly, before my wife. In the films the man sometimes... he puts his mouth onto the woman's...her *bi*?'

'Her vagina.'

'Onto her vagina. I have never done this. I think Chinese men do not do this usually.'

'Maybe they should. It would make their wives happier.'

'Do you have some foreign *bi yun tao*, some… condoms, yes, that I could borrow?'

'Yeah, I think so. And you can have them, I don't want them back. But why do you need foreign ones?'

'Maybe they are thicker, so I will feel less and be able to do it for longer. This will make my wife happier. But maybe they are too big.'

My mind flashed to a vague recollection that in China condoms had initially been made in different sizes.

'Maybe Western penises are like Uighur penises.'

'In what way?'

'Maybe bigger. You know, Uighurs must have an operation when they are young because their penises are too big.'

'It's called circumcision. They have done it done for religious reasons.'

He looked doubtful. But he still had one more thing left to ask.

'You said you don't have a girlfriend. So what do you do? Do you use your hand?'

After I told him, he took another swig of beer, then sat back to mull over this fresh piece of intelligence. After this exchange, I felt I could ask him anything.

'Liu Feng, in my old college, I often went out with the other teachers. But tonight is the first time that I've been out with any teacher in our department. Why do you think that is?'

He drained the bottle and called for another.

'Ah. You see, well, Yining is a border town. There are special rules.'

'Yes, I've had this conversation with Miss Cai. But how does that explain the fact that all the other teachers avoid me?'

'There is a rule. Students can only go to the foreign teacher's house in groups of three or more. Teachers can only visit with one other person.'

'That's so fucking stupid. What do they think I'll do?'

'Maybe you don't know. It was several years before. There was a teacher from Norway. He talked a lot about Christ in his lessons. He tried to make his students believe. Finally the police sent him back to his country. It was very bad for our college.'

Perhaps it wasn't such a stupid rule. After all, the other foreigners *were* all missionaries of one kind or another. The college was ultimately responsible for us, given that they were the ones who had approved our visas and work permits.

We sat and peeled the labels from our bottles. Perhaps Liu Feng regretted some (or all) of the things he'd said. We drank up, argued over the bill, finally went Dutch and then left. Outside a light rain fell; the air was fresh enough to trick me into feeling sober. We weaved our way back to the college. When we reached my flat, I started to say goodbye but he interrupted.

'Nick, tonight you shouldn't use your hand!'

'What? Why?'

'Ha ha! Are you hard?'

He reached out and touched my groin. I was not.

'Well, goodnight!' he said and laughed.

I did not see him in the staff room for the next few days and when I did, it was business as usual. A smile, a quick hello, then on with our separate lives.

81

AVOID YINING IN APRIL. During the other months rain is so scarce as to be a wonder. But the deluge of that fourth month, a comparative monsoon, is enough to make a person glance upwards and curse. The knowledge that the downpour is integral to the success of the season's crops, to the livelihoods of over half the population, is no comfort at all.

One is wet, miserable and cold, sometimes even when indoors: all those pretty courtyard houses have flat roofs of mud, timber and straw. These can withstand several days of rain but not a week's worth. After the first few days of heavy rain the television news started showing pictures of homes that had collapsed, especially those near the river, which was running swollen and hungry. The remaining homes were soon sheathed in plastic. The KU class had to be cancelled; they were all fixing their roofs or a friend's. Meanwhile the Russian buildings looked on, their sloping eaves quite smug.

It took five days for the clouds to dry. Normal life poked its head from the window, held out its hand, and on feeling nothing, decided it was safe to continue. The sky was blue, I had no class. I brushed the dust from my bike.

The pavement was the sky's mirror, its scattered pools a shining copy of the blue and white. The houses had been unwrapped; their plastic lay to one side. The tiles of a mosque glittered green and white. Poplars passed on the backs of trucks, headed for the lumber yard. Unchained convicts ambled by, blue suited and friendly, on their way to their next piece of forced labour. I overtook their junior counterparts, a class of children with shovels strapped to the back of their bikes.

'Where are you going?' I asked.

'To plant trees.'

'Is that fun?'

The boy shook his head so hard he almost fell off his bike. The laughter of his friends receded.

I kept on the main road, looking for a possible turn off: the rains had made most of the streets impassable. A streak of grey signalled a road with an actual surface. It wasn't clear what the street had done to merit asphalt, but no doubt it went somewhere. I stopped a pregnant woman wearing a green hat.

'Excuse me, do you know where this road goes?'

'Yes, it goes to the hospital.'

My eyes travelled the road until it vanished amongst the hills. I knew there was no town out there.

'A hospital? Really? Have you been there?'

She laughed. 'Oh no, not yet. I'm not that old!' She frowned, seeing me to be less than convinced. 'Go see for yourself.'

The road ran on, and soon changed in colour from grey to black. Coal trucks thundered by, their load spilling in inverse proportion to the distance from the mine. As for the hills, they were spotted with sheep that drifted in Brownian motion. A small boy ran around in place of a sheepdog; any sheep that strayed was brought back by a high-pitched ululation.

I pumped the pedals harder as the gradient increased. The straight lines of a building detached themselves from a hill. White walls came into focus, atop them a red cross. So yes, there *was* a hospital on this hill in the middle of almost-nowhere.

A thick-jowled man sat behind a desk at the gate, leafing through a bird-fanciers' magazine. He reached for a book of tickets as I approached. He waved them at me and asked for eight yuan. I hesitated; treatment may not be free in Chinese hospitals, but you don't have to pay to *enter*. But he was emphatic, and I wasn't about to turn back having come so far. I paid and wandered in.

It didn't look much like a hospital. A few single-storey buildings stood around an old oak tree. Chickens clucked beneath a bush.

An old woman cranked water from a rusting pump, its groans mirroring the effort on her face. She saw me and paused. I said hello, she replied and then resumed her pumping. She straightened up, her bucket full, and saw me still standing there. She pointed to a flight of concrete steps descending the hill.

The steps wound down towards a row of stone huts. Blankets hung in the doorways, each bearing the character for 'double happiness'. A pungent smell entered my nose, the rotten egg scent of sulphur. An old Uighur man hobbled into view, his body buried under numerous coats, themselves partially hidden by a quilt draped over his shoulders. Sweat beaded his forehead; his beard needed to be wrung. He came over and asked where I was from, and nodded approvingly at my answer. I asked him what the matter was.

'It's my leg, always bad in spring. Too much rain. I have to come every year. But maybe I'd come anyway, this place is good for you even if you're not sick.'

'Is this place famous?'

'Yes, very. People come from Urumqi and Kashgar. Last year there was a man from Shanghai.'

Behind the blankets lay low-ceilinged rooms with benches along their walls. The air inside was thick, the temperature tropical. There were separate rooms for men and women to sweat out their sickness. In one a family huddled round a broken-looking boy, limp in every department bar his voice. He lay across his mother's lap, her wails accompanying his. In the next room, a man sat cross-legged before a small stove, frying an egg and muttering.

In addition to the saunas, there were also gravel pits, long troughs of sausage-pink people having grit shovelled on them. A sign painted on the wall instructed people not to eat or drink when using the pits. The ground fell sharply after that in a mass of scree. The rocks around were covered with names and dates; paeans and prayers had been spelt out, mostly in Arabic, in white pebbles on the opposite hillside. I was doing my best to read the ones in Chinese when I heard a girl say softly, in English, 'Hello, are you from London?'

I turned to see a Uighur girl in her late teens. She had long brown hair, large green eyes and an extremely cute nose. Her name was Edipim and she was accompanying her grandfather, the old man with the bad leg. She said had been studying in Urumqi but had returned to Yining to spend time with her grandparents. Then she made me an offer I couldn't refuse.

'Nick, would you like to see the tomb of the snake girl?'

'Very much.'

She told me about 'the snake girl' as we scrambled down the hill. Once there was a girl who was born mute. Her parents sent her to the hospital in hope of a cure. When she came to the entrance she found a large snake blocking her way. She was so frightened that she cried the first words of her life, 'Father, mother, save me!' Her father heard her call and ran to the gate. He drew his knife and killed the snake with one blow. But when he looked around, he saw that his daughter was also dead.

Edipim said that some people came to pray at the girl's tomb, and that the girl had become a folk saint. Strictly speaking, the worship of local saints is frowned upon by orthodox Muslims, for whom it smacks of pantheism. However, these *mazar* can be found through-out Central Asia, suggesting that for many, their observance of Islam is mediated through local folk traditions.

After several near-death moments later we reached the bottom of the hill.

'So, where is it?'

'Look, there.'

I stared at a piece of rusted metal propped above white gravel. Clearly the snake girl still had some way to go before she became a bona fide local saint. Out of the corner of my eye I saw Edipim lift her hands in prayer. She muttered something then saw me looking at her.

'I don't really believe the story. But if it's true, maybe she will hear my prayers. And if not, it doesn't matter.'

'Maybe Allah won't like you praying to some other being. I

thought the whole point of being a Muslim was that there is no God but Allah.'

'It will be OK. Allah knows what's in my heart.'

She paused, then asked if I believed in Allah. My atheism didn't trouble her much, although she did say, 'We all do bad things. If there is no next world, when do we pay for them?'

We climbed back up the hill. Edipim went to check on her grandfather. We swapped phone numbers then I cycled off. It was ten km downhill, a smooth speed through the late-day sun; a gentle breeze blew from the east. Maybe I was too focused on the riots. Perhaps it was sufficient to explore this interesting place, to just cruise around. I told myself that I would do the same tomorrow, that I would get up early and spend the day just cycling round the countryside. And I probably would have, had it not rained for the next week.

82

CHINA IS THE world's most populous country. At present its official population stands at approximately 1.4 billion. Traditionally, it was thought that the larger the family, the better. There were sound reasons for this: many hands were needed for farming, especially those of sons; it also ensured there would be someone to look after the parents when they were old.

However, whilst this might be good for the family, it presents a logistical nightmare for any state attempting to feed and educate such a large number of people. In order to put a brake on population growth, the Chinese government introduced its one-child policy in the early 1980s. There are, however, a number of exceptions: rural parents are allowed to have a second child if their first is female; minorities are allowed two children if urban residents, or three (and sometimes more) if from the countryside. Any parents that have more their quota face a large fine, or if from the countryside, the confiscation of land. There have also been reports of forced sterilisations and people losing their jobs.

Whilst this probably sounds somewhat draconian, it is undeniable that there are too many people in China. Five minutes in any train or bus station will tell you that. Although the authorities have had some success in enforcing the law in cities, it has been more difficult in the countryside. People have also found plenty of ways around the law, such as bribing an official, going to a different province to have a child, or sending it to a distant relative once born.

Uighurs had plenty of legitimate reasons to resent the government, but at least they were exempt from the one-child policy, being allowed to have two or three children compared to the Han's one. If anyone should have objected to this piece of positive discrimination, it was the Han, and there were a number of occasions when I heard people complaining in rather colourful terms about 'the Uighurs being able to fuck as much as they liked.' Surely the Uighurs had nothing to grumble about.

83

'LAST YEAR THEY took a pregnant woman to the hospital. They killed her baby then she died. Some say they killed her too.'

I was talking to a young woman named Mikray, in a small restaurant by the river. She had been a good friend of Eleanor and sometimes the three of us had met for lunch, though never just Mikray and I. This was the first time we had met since Eleanor's departure, and it felt very awkward. For want of anything else to say, I asked whether she liked her job. She said no, and when I asked why, she told me about the pregnant woman.

'Who made her have an abortion?'

'The police and some doctors.'

'How many months pregnant was she?'

'Eight.'

The woman had been forced to have an abortion because she already had two children. Mikray said that although this wasn't very common, it still happened sometimes. Her department wasn't actually responsible, being primarily concerned with trying to educate people about the benefits of family planning. Her job consisted of going around Uighur neighbourhoods, trying to promote the spread of contraception. However, in many people's minds this was similarly objectionable.

'Many people say that it is not their choice. They say that they do not decide. It is only Allah who decides whether a couple have a child.'

'What do you think about that? You're Muslim aren't you?'

'In the end, yes, it is up to Allah. But there are laws too. And there are also some reasons why a smaller family is better. There is more money for the education of children.'

There are further costs for Uighurs that have too many

children. Mikray told me that they usually lose their *ji hua shengyu guangrong zheng*: a family-planning honour certificate that entitles parents to a ten-yuan monthly subsidy.

The conflict between pragmatism and religion made Mikray's job difficult enough; the heavy-handed methods used to enforce the regulations made things even worse. Finally, there was the blatant contradiction between the number of Han migrant workers who came from other provinces to work on the *bingtuans* and the official line on the need to restrict population growth. One could be forgiven for thinking the government wanted to control Xinjiang by sheer force of numbers.

But the fact remained that the Uighurs were allowed to have more children than the Han – despite the fact that both groups wished for large families – even if it wasn't as many as some would have liked. The fact that people resented a piece of legislation that was biased in their favour was indicative of how badly the local authorities had mismanaged its application.

84

YINING NEVER FELT like a city, despite its half a million people. There was no bustle and throng; it was neither vast nor impersonal. It was more like a small town: you couldn't help but run into people you knew in the market or bookstore, given that there was only one of each. Yet what did most to give Yining its provincial air was rumour and gossip. The Uighur grapevine snaked its way through every street and district, disseminating stories and jokes about the latest piece of Han mendacity. One week they were said to be putting pork fat in the water, the next they were accused of killing babies to make *jiaozi*. Even jokes could become rumours. Tursun told me one about George Bush visiting Urumqi and being disappointed to find no beautiful, long-haired Uighur girls, only girls with fashionably short hair. After he complained to the provincial leaders, they decided to make it a rule that students would only be accepted if they had long hair. A few weeks later Hamit told me the same unlikely story in ultra-serious tones.

The most ludicrous example of this was a joke about the origin of *djinns*, the spirits sent by Allah to watch and report on the deeds of people. In the joke, the first *djinn* (*bur djinn*) is said to have come from Cain, who went to Beijing to die. The joke relies on the similarity between *Bur djinn* and Beijing, an appalling pun that no one would be expected to mistake for truth. Yet this story was trotted out as the definitive article whenever the subject of *djinns* came up.

What made people so gullible? If you had asked Liu Feng or Miss Cai, they probably would have said it was due to the Uighurs' low level of education, or because Yining was so remote and backward. However, there were less pejorative explanations. One was to do with a general willingness to believe the worst of the government.

Allied to this was the problem of restricted access to information. In China, and especially in sensitive areas like Xinjiang or Tibet, all media are state-controlled; no newspapers, books or magazines can be published without official permission. Politically sensitive acts – such as violence against hospital staff for their role in enforced family planning – generally go unreported. Though the internet is harder to police, there are still many restrictions on which sites can be accessed, and content is heavily monitored.

Most people in Western countries possess some degree of scepticism about the information they receive from the mass media. However, one reason why people continue to buy newspapers and watch TV is that questions can be asked of a free press. Bias exists, but there is at least a choice of bias. But imagine if you only had one source of information, and that you knew it to be selective at best, and controlled by those you despised and blamed for your current ills. In that situation you might put more stock in what your friends and neighbours told you, particularly if there was no reliable independent source of information against which to verify it. And then there is the fact that gossiping is fun.

85

AN ALMOST-FORGOTTEN voice leapt from my telephone.

'Hello! Hello!'

'Hello.'

'It is me! Murat! Yes! When can we meet? Now? I have many important things to tell you.'

Half an hour later we were eating kebabs in a restaurant by the river. He didn't look to have changed much, except that his hair had been cut so short that it was bristles. He was wearing a green T-shirt emblazoned with the single word 'Spain!' Murat asked what I had been doing. I started telling him that I had been on holiday, to Thailand and Cambodia, but he interrupted.

'What about those nancy boys?'

He had clearly learnt some new words since last we met.

'You know, those… things. Men like women. Most Thai people are.'

'Some, yes. But not most.'

'They should be killed.'

'What? Why?'

'They always make some trouble, and they are bad.'

The world was either a very difficult place for Murat or a very easy one. So many of the people in it were bad or wrong, not just the Chinese, but other Uighurs, in short anyone who wasn't like him. When I told him there were transsexuals in Britain he was very surprised but got over it quickly, especially once I had reminded him that most English people did not believe in God. In fact, he became quite jolly, perhaps at the thought that we were damned already.

'What did you want to tell me?'

'Our house has been repaired. The roof is stronger now. It is better.'

'Oh, right. Anything else?'
'Yes, I have a surprise for you!'
'Is it a good surprise?'
'Yes, of course! Very good.'
'When will you tell me?'
'I will tell you now!'
'Yes?'
'I have a new class! All new students! And they want to meet you!'

They did. They had only been learning for a few months but their English wasn't bad. After an initial shyness they were asking me a series of thrilling questions.

'Do you like coffee?'
'Do you like dancing?'
'Do you like pretty girl?'

I said 'yes' to all three. Meanwhile Murat sat behind his desk and tried to look benevolent. All he managed was pride, perhaps at his students, perhaps at his ability to provide them with native speakers.

To emphasise our renewed friendship, he invited me to his house. When we entered the courtyard I saw his two-and-a-half-year-old daughter sitting on a red plastic stool. She was gnawing on a carrot with quiet determination. Next to her was a bucket containing a sheep's hooves and head. The face wore a stumped expression; the eyes were crossed, the tongue stuck-out. For a moment it seemed to wink; then the fly buzzed off.

Murat's wife emerged from the kitchen long enough to ask what he wished her to prepare. Then he beckoned me into the living room.

'We have a long time before the food is ready. But this is good. There is something you must see.'

He turned on the television and put a disc into the VCD machine. An Arabic word floated golden into view. Murat turned to me and said solemnly, 'This is the *Hadj*.'

Shots of Mecca filled the screen. Thousands of men rotated

around a black cube. There were moments of prayer. People squatted upon cliffs. Stones were thrown at several posts pretending to be Satan. A man received a haircut. A *muezzin* gave the call to prayer from a crumbling minaret (something not permitted in Yining). And with that, the screen faded to black. There was then a respectful silence. Murat was the first to speak.

'Again?'

'Yes please.'

'The more you watch it, the more you will understand.'

Was he trying to convert me? Possibly. I began to fear he would insist upon a third viewing. My eyes searched the room for some other entertainment. I offered up a secular prayer of thanks when I saw the squares of a chessboard. He saw the object of my gaze and asked if I wanted to play.

Our pawns advanced, our knights rode out. Fifteen moves later his bishop began to panic, as it found itself in a pincer movement from my queen and rook. Murat suddenly got confused about the rules, and tried to argue that as a male, the king was the most powerful piece and could thus move any number of squares, in any direction (and possibly in time and space as well). An argument was only averted by the arrival of Ismail.

Ismail was abnormally happy. He laughed at everything we said, clapping us on the back and generally acting as if he were high. Murat acted as if nothing were amiss. When Ismail went to wash his hands, I shot him an enquiring glance.

'A man becomes like this before he is married. I was the same.'

'Married? I didn't even know he had a girlfriend.'

'Oh, yes. For more than a year.'

In the eight months I had known him, Ismail had never once mentioned that he had a girlfriend, let alone introduced us. He came back in the room, still smiling.

'What's all this about you getting married?'

'Yes, I am going to.' His grin broadened. 'Then I will have sex.'

Murat slapped him on the back.

'There will be no more jumping over Satan!'

'What's that?'

'You know, when you have a sex dream.'

'Oh. So, who's your girlfriend?'

'A good Muslim women.'

'I think all men like Muslim women,' ventured Murat.

'Really?'

'Yes, the Muslim woman is free and modest.'

'Free?'

'Yes, she doesn't have to work. She can stay in the home.'

'Perhaps it's just Muslim men who like Muslim women.'

'Yes, because they are very good.'

I wasn't sure if he meant the men or women. Then Ismail started talking about 'the naked' people in the West.

'What?'

'Yes, like in the films. There are many girls who are naked. They show their... their breasts. And there is so much sex, especially kissing.'

'There's a big gap between the films and reality. I don't see many women's breasts in England.' I suppressed a vision of *The Sun*. 'And kissing isn't the same as sex.'

'But the people are not married.'

'It's only kissing. Haven't you ever kissed a girl?'

'No, I won't until I'm married. What about you?'

I hesitated. Even the small number seemed impossibly large.

'Yeah. A few times. But what about young Uighur people now? Some of them don't care either.'

'Yes, perhaps they are not so intelligent,' said Murat.

'That's right, they are not careful.'

'Do you mean when they have sex?'

He frowned.

'No, they do not take care with what they eat and drink. Maybe you do not know. The Chinese put chemicals in the food and drink. If you eat a lot of this you can't make children. And when you get married you must go to the doctor who will give you medicine that also stops you having children for the next five years. But I will be safe. I am careful and I know good doctors.'

There was no arguing with this. It was just more paranoia. However, there were rumours that had more substance.

86

EVERYONE HAD MEETINGS. Not the usual weekly affairs – the manda-
tory ones that could be read or slept through – whose topic was
usually the most recent speech by Jiang Zemin. These new, additional meetings took place almost every day, sometimes at the weekend, not just in the college, but in all the schools, hospitals and public
institutions of the city. People were expected to actively participate,
to write articles and even take exams on the topics discussed.

I tried asking some of the KU class what the meetings were
about but got nowhere. They were worried enough not to gossip.
All I could gather was that Tursunjan Amat, a Uighur poet, had read
out a poem at a New Year's performance in Urumqi. There was
subsequently a police investigation and Tursunjan was arrested.
Whether it was the poem or the performance that the authorities
objected to was unclear. But there was one person from whom I
could be sure of getting the official line.

'Miss Cai, can I ask you something?'

'Of course!'

'Has something happened?'

'What do you mean?'

'I've heard there was a problem in Urumqi.'

'Who told you?'

'Oh, you know, people talk. Does it matter?'

She gave me a look that suggested it did. Then she said,

'Someone read a poem that had a bad meaning. It encouraged
people to cause trouble, to try and split our country.'

'Have you heard the poem?'

'No, but it was bad.'

Exactly why was unclear. Some claimed that the poem was an innocent celebration of Uighur tradition and customs, and that any overt ideological content was the result of errors when it had been translated from Uighur into Chinese. But from the government's perspective, promoting a sense of cultural pride was perhaps a step towards the wish for independence, albeit not an especially short one. Several weeks after the reading of the poem, the chairman of the regional government emphasised the need to 'strengthen the anti-separatism struggle in the ideological field'. He claimed there were 'a very small number of people making use of the literary and art stage to peddle their anti-people works that spread ideas of ethnic separation'.

The number of such people might have been 'very small', but this did not deter the authorities from launching a series of study classes, similar to those that religious personnel had been forced to attend, only this time for key personnel in literature, art and the media. The aim of the classes was to 'extensively educate them in opposing ethnic separatism and safeguarding the unity of the motherland'.

The meetings were not the only result of the poem. On 31 January 2002, the Xinjiang Communist Party Committee held a mobilization rally for the struggle against separatism in the ideological field in Urumqi. During the rally, Wang Lequan listed the means used by 'ethnic separatist forces inside and outside the region' for 'penetration and sabotage'. These included 'illegally printing and publishing reactionary books and journals, mailing, posting up and distributing reactionary pamphlets, letters and posters, spreading rumours to cheat the public, and creating separatist public opinion'. He called for further intensification of 'face-to-face propaganda and education for the cadres and masses of all ethnic groups'. He also pointed out the danger of separatism's influence in schools, and called on media and cultural units in the region to 'step up education for young people of all ethnic groups'.

Three months after the poem had been read, the meetings were still going on. Several of the younger teachers in the English department had even started to moan about it to me, illustrating just how fed up people were, Han and Uighur alike.

Whether it was an overreaction or not, the authorities' response suggested that they took the threat of further unrest seriously. However, there had been no reported act of 'terrorism' within the province for over a year. Wang Lequan had an answer for this:

> The anti-separatist struggle in the ideological field had always been a major battleground without the smoke of gunpowder.

But there was soon smoke from other sources.

87

'THEY ARE BURNING BOOKS, so many, a big fire.'

'Slow down Hamit. Who's burning books? Where?'

'In Kashgar, the police. Many history and culture books. They were all right before but now they are not.'

It made an awful kind of sense. Now the lines had been redrawn, anything which emphasised the cultural and ethnic distinctiveness of Uighurs (apart from singing and dancing) was potentially 'subversive'. The war against separatism was a convenient excuse for the government to attempt to edit Uighur culture, to remove anything they disapproved of. I told Hamit I thought it was cultural violence, that it was arrogant, and a form of intellectual cowardice, and as I did my face grew hot. I felt a sense of outrage I knew he would share.

But he only shrugged and said, 'It is bad news but is also good news.'

'How is it good?'

'Because more people outside China will know what the Chinese government is like. And then maybe things will improve here.'

'Perhaps,' I said whilst doubting it would even be reported.

Several months later Tursunjan was released; afterwards the authorities denied he had even been held.

88

ANYONE WISHING TO launch a cultural pogrom in Yining would have been hampered by the shortage of targets. There were no theatres, museums, galleries, or cinemas (except the porn one). The only bookshop was the state-run *Xinhua* one. The only performances given were those within the college: garish extravagances at which minority students were enjoined to sing and dance.

This dearth of cultural entertainment could have been due to the poverty in the city, the increasingly tight restrictions on the media or a general preoccupation with other issues. When some cultural event did happen it was therefore very exciting. The only problem was finding it. The absence of any official venue meant that shows were forced to take place in whatever space happened to be available: gymnasiums, playgrounds, unrented office space. When Abdullah, Dolkun and Hamit invited me to an exhibition of photos by a local photographer, it took us two hours to find its location, a draughty space with a wet concrete floor above a jewellery shop. But the glossy blowups pasted to the walls and pillars confirmed it as the right place. The pictures were of people from south Xinjiang, mostly Kashgar and Hotan. Many depicted traditional customs and crafts, such as weaving, metalwork and bee keeping.

The most interesting photo showed a group of men sat round a boy lying on his back. He was propped up on cushions, arms behind his head, naked from the waist down. All eyes were focussed on his penis. In the boy's eyes there was fear; in the adults', there was pride. A man knelt at the boy's feet, knife in hand, ready to perform the procedure that would make him a man.

'It is a good thing, yes?' said Dolkun.

'I don't know. I think it is a *painful* thing.'

'It is very necessary because of the cancer. In Israel and Muslim countries most people have this and they have very little of this cancer.'

For some reason, I felt I had to defend the right to be uncircumcised. 'Some say that it means that circumcision reduces the pleasure of the man during sex. Perhaps the woman's too.'

'No, she likes it,' said Dolkun.

He went on to say that sometimes he did five or six circumcisions in a day, and that he was glad to do it.

We moved onto the next picture.

'Ah, this is *bishek*,' said Dolkun.

A baby lay asleep on an open-sided crib; a rooster stood guard to one side. Closer inspection revealed a set of straps tying the child the frame. I had seen similar cribs for sale in the market, painted in primary colours, with a hole in the bottom for the child to urinate through.

'*Bishek* is traditional way to look after baby. If you must go out to work, especially in countryside, you must put baby into it. It will keep baby safe.'

'When do you stop using it?'

'When the child is six months or one year old.'

Hamit came over to look at the photo. He tutted.

'This is an old thing. We don't do this in the city. Now many think it is not good. Our ideas have changed.'

Dolkun replied, 'But in countryside, many people do. It is still useful.'

They switched to Uighur and began to argue. I wasn't sure that it was good to tie up children for their first few months, but if there was no one else to look after the child, maybe there was no choice. Hamit and Dolkun began to grow heated, and I was on the verge of interceding when Hamit laughed and said, 'I only think the baby should be active.'

'You! You're just too lazy to clean the child,' replied Dolkun.

89

IT WAS THE season to fly kites, even out of windows. The children in the opposite flat took turns to hold the frayed string of their home-made effort, an ingenuous construction of old shirts and balsa wood. Pigeons whistled round the black trapezoid, fighting both the wind and their confusion at this strange new kind of bird. The sound of slamming windows echoed through the college, occasionally punctuated by the protest of a breaking pane. The pipes belched and sighed, undecided whether to give water. Taps were turned on in vain and then forgotten. I returned home from class to find my kitchen flooded.

At such times, my usual course of action was to go out on my bike and cycle furiously. The majority of cyclists in Yining were content to crawl along at little faster than a walking pace. On a bad day I derived a perverse enjoyment from swerving round these dismayed snails.

I was thinking of yellow jerseys, land speed records, when another bike whipped by. Its rider slowed to come level with me, a Uighur man with a chest like a tree stump, dressed entirely in black. Some words in English flew at me.

'Hey boy! You go so fast. That's great you know! I like to go fast too.'

'So I see.'

'You know, there are the wolves and the dogs, and if you put the wolf into the house for long enough it becomes like the dog.'

'What?'

'What I say is this, that the wolf can be tamed, some people think.'

'Yes, but what does that have to do with bicycles?'

We swerved around a street cleaner's cart.

'What I mean is, now there are many Chinese here. They want to make us quiet. Like dogs. Like them.'

I told him that as far as I had seen, the Han didn't have a monopoly on cycling slowly. He shrugged, swerved round a woman walking a white dog, then said,

'Do you like fighting?'

'No. Do you?'

'A little bit sometimes. I like boxing. You know Tyson?'

'Yeah.'

'I want to be like him. He is the iron man.'

His name was Kuresh and he taught yet another English evening class, the seventh I knew of. The quality of teaching in these classes varied enormously, and in many cases the qualifications of the teacher extended no further than ownership of a textbook and an elementary grasp of the language. However, there was something impressive about this wish to learn a language otherwise denied them.

We cycled over the-bridge-that-must-not-be-crossed then stopped to rest by the bank. Kuresh asked if I had a girlfriend. I told him I didn't, then asked if he did.

'Yes, and we want to be married but it is difficult. She has a problem with her leg, she can't run but can walk. My parents can't accept her. They say I cannot marry a girl who is not healthy.'

He went on to explain that his parents were worried that she would give birth to disabled children, an opinion shared by most of his relatives.

'But I don't care. I love her, she is my darling.'

The cloud was too thick for a sunset. Kuresh scratched at the mud with a stick and started talking about how much he hated criticism of something or someone simply because it was different. And he didn't just mean his girlfriend.

'When I was riding, I wear the short pants, people laugh and point, this is rubbish! Who cares?'

Kuresh seemed different from the other Uighur men I'd met.

There was an immediate openness, a need to talk about things that mattered to him. We had only just met yet he had already started talking about his personal life and what he saw as the inadequacies of a very traditional society, one where to be conventional was the same as being good.

The strains of a stringed instrument came from the other bank, a breathless succession of chords cajoled in scales that kept switching direction. There was also a roughness to it, as if the instrument were resisting its player. We cycled over to investigate.

We found a Uighur family sitting on rugs spread along the shore, picking through the scraps of a picnic. Sunflower seeds and peanut shells littered the centre; some small hotpot dishes bubbled on a fire. They asked us to join them. We made feeble protests, then did. They were having a farewell party for their eldest son, who was going back to Urumqi to resume his studies at college. It was he who had played the music we had heard. His father was a policeman, his uncle a businessman. There were six or seven other children drifting around, playing badminton and a curious form of tag that involved hopping. The boy's old music teacher was also there, a narrow man whose greying beard was resting on his knees.

Our host poured me a cup of wine, a thin liquid smelling of raspberries. He went to do the same for Kuresh, who put his hand over his bowl and made protestations of faith. The man made as if to pour, but the bluff didn't work; Kuresh's hand was firm. But when the offer was repeated, ten minutes later, Kuresh capitulated, perhaps deferring to a present host over a distant God. The old teacher picked up the *dutar* and began to play; the policeman danced with his wife while we clapped and shouted. He thanked us for our applause then passed the instrument to the boy. The teacher asked his former pupil what he was going to play. The boy smirked and said the name of a song. His teacher looked surprised, then began to lecture him that this song (which contained a good deal of toilet humour) might be acceptable to boys, but an older man could not sing (and perhaps did not wish to listen to) such a song. The boy shrugged and began to play. I couldn't understand the words, only their effect upon his former teacher. His face registered surprise, almost shock. The others signalled their appreciation with great whooping cheers. The boy kept his eyes on his teacher the whole time, his expression proud, almost insolent. His teacher looked grave and afterwards was quiet. He reached for a cigarette, lit it, exhaled, then said to the boy that he was very satisfied with his playing. Something passed between them, a respect free of bitterness.

Then I felt moisture on the back of my neck, the beginning of rain that was soon falling fast. Kuresh and I prepared to leave but our host pointed to a small pavilion underneath the trees. Five minutes later we sat sipping mutton broth. The rain fell in broken lines. Candles appeared; the *dutar* resumed. People got up to dance. The river struggled to keep pace with the song. The warmth and hospitality, the laughter and smiles: it was almost enough to make me feel I belonged.

90

THE PROSTITUTE PUT her arm around me. I shifted with unease but made no other response. A drunken voice bellowed,

'Are you enjoying yourself?'

'Yes Mr Geng,' I said. 'Very much. Thank you.'

'Good! But you must enjoy yourself MORE!'

I should have been delighted to be out with Dean Geng, Liu Feng and several other teachers from the English department. It suggested that they were beginning to accept me. And the evening had begun enjoyably enough. We had gone to a *jiaozi* restaurant, had a few drinks, swapped jokes about George Bush. But then the *baijiu* came out and soon the rest of the table was doing its best to get me drunk, pressuring me with comments like 'If you do not drink, we are not friends' and 'Drinking is what friends do together.' Once their faces were red from drink, the karaoke machine got powered up. Each member of our party stood up and sang in turn, their performances making up in volume what they lacked in harmony. When it came to my turn, I tried to plead fatigue, nausea, then a throat infection, none of which persuaded. The dean began to boom, ordering me to sing, a cry soon chorused by the equally drunken others. That I might not wish to was clearly of little concern to them. But I sang their song, as I had drunk their drink, not wishing to offend.

Eventually the dean deemed that enough had been sung and drunk; we were allowed to pour ourselves into taxis. I asked the driver to take us back to the college, a request refused by the dean, who told him to go to the *Red Flower Hotel* instead. The car sped down unlit, deserted streets, filling with cigarette smoke. We pulled up outside a building flooded in pink neon. The manager came to greet Dean Geng. They shook hands and swapped cigarettes; then we were ushered inside.

'There are girls from many places here,' said Liu Feng. 'Uighur, Han, Kazakh, Hui, Kirghiz and Uzbek, maybe even some French or English!'

He laughed at his joke.

We were brought into a small room lined with sofas. Drinks appeared, then girls. They squeezed themselves between us. The girl next to me was Uighur. She wore tight brown leather trousers and a black t-shirt. Her lipstick was purple and thickly applied. The dean pulled the girl beside him to her feet. They began to slow dance, his hands smoothing down her hips. Liu Feng and the others sat and watched, their hands on the girls beside them, all playing follow the leader. What amazed me about this was not that these men were all married but that they showed no embarrassment at being unfaithful to their wives in front of each other (and to the minor extent that I mattered, me). This was not the first night out of this kind for them. They were too at ease.

The girl with the painted lips nestled against me. I realised that no one would hold it against me if I took her home. The dean had made it clear that this was his 'treat'. The only people that would know would be those who had done the same themselves. But something in my socialisation would not allow me to convince myself that it was all right. I stood and made my excuses. The dean sighed and said, 'You are a naughty boy!'

91

LIFE IN THE teachers' college followed a strict timetable. There was a time to wake (when the peddlers arrived with milk, gas, and meat), a time to have class, a time to have lunch, a time to sleep in the afternoon. It was easy to be lulled by these rhythms. Weeks and months went by in this fashion. Then something would happen to remind us what was actually going on.

It began when a student in the computer department wrote, 'Increase national separatism!' on one of the desks, possibly in jest. This was a joke no one got. The students had to undergo handwriting tests, as a result of which one Uighur boy was expelled. It was probably scant consolation for the boy that he didn't have to attend the series of mind-numbing meetings and speeches to which the rest of the students were subjected.

The next incident came a few days later, when two Kazakh students got into a drunken fight. They were both from the same village, both in the PE department, both in love with the same girl. The fight was somewhat one-sided. One stabbed the other 18 times. The injured boy dithered for a few days between death and life, finally choosing the latter. Everyone agreed that this had been enough excitement for the week. Thursday slouched into Friday; the bells rang; the students surged within the triangle of dormitory, classroom, and canteen; the hawkers cries jostled for auditory space; everywhere the sight and sound of patterns trying to return.

92

ALL NEW STUDENTS at the college, Han and Uighur alike, spent their first month pretending to be soldiers, wheeling in formation like the good citizens that they were supposed to be. From first light until well after dark, the stamps and shouts of boots and voices sounded throughout campus. I expected my Han students to enjoy it about as much as they had cotton-picking, but instead of the *mei ban fa* response, they were uniformly positive:

'It is interesting and good for us to learn this discipline.'

'Before this I was a weak girl but now I am strong and healthy.'

'Now I know I can do anything. I hope that in future I can be a soldier and fight but not die for my motherland.'

Some of this zeal was probably fake; the students knew the right answers. The sight of these green pillars of obedience inspired a kind of bewildered fascination in me. I was unable to pass the parade ground without stopping to gawk at their antics. It was easy to imagine how a group of 19-year-old British undergraduates would react to such a drill.

One day I sat under a pine tree by the edge of the parade ground. I was reading a book Gabe had lent me. It was called *True Humanism*, and its main argument was that liberal humanism was just another form of evil. He had underlined this passage, either for his own benefit or mine:

We shall not say more about secular humanism as a point of view. Clearly, it is not in the same league when it comes to what used to be called 'soul making'. It hides from us our eternal destiny, drops God out of our minds, encourages egotism and self worship, undercuts morality by its relativism and permissiveness, undermines compassion for the weak and useless who are not socially useful, encourages social programmes to manage people as we manage animals... If individual humanists are not brash, bossy, arrogant and insensitive, it will be despite their doctrine, not because of it; it will in fact be because they still bear the impress of the Christianity they reject.

Strong stuff. I flicked forward to see what else was underlined. This was next:

How is Christianity's mission as a generator of culture to be fulfilled today? The short answer is: by letting loose the biblical message to assess, critique, purge, and remodel the manifold forms of culture that surround us... [There is] a fascinating variety of local, ethnic cultures, which Christians should not seek not to sweep away but to appreciate...Though they are marked by the evil of man's rebellion, the first thing to say about them is that in and through them the creativity of God himself bubbles up like a great fountain.

My internal reply of scorn was stopped by a shout. I looked up to see the drill instructor, a bald and burly Han, giving a dressing down to a short Kazakh girl. She kept her head down, mutely accepting the reprimand. Once he was satisfied by her obedience, he nodded and barked for them to continue marching. I continued reading to the thump of their boots.

Cultural relativists who censure Christianity for undervaluing and sweeping away the marvellous artifacts and traditions of pre-Christian cultures show their unbelieving bias at this point. Ethnic and pagan cultures always bear the marks of human sin and are closely bound up with what Christians cannot but call idolatry.

There was another shout: the girl was out of step. The instructor called her an idiot, a claim he kept repeating as he strode toward her, his vitriol increasing with each step, until he was virtually spitting in her face. She began to cry but the heaving of her shoulders only infuriated him further. He began shouting something else, a word I didn't know but clearly something bad, judging from the aghast expressions of the other students. A tall thin Kazakh boy stepped forward and asked the instructor not to say such things. The drill sergeant found a new level of rage. He spun around and started shoving the boy. When the boy yelled something back, the instructor slapped him in the face. The whole troop of students seemed to take a step back. When four of the larger boys rushed at the instructor, the first got punched in the face. He fell back, his nose bleeding. The second dived at the legs of the instructor, who kicked him away. The third and fourth tried to wrestle him to the ground. The girls stood to one side, khaki cheerleaders shouting encouragement. The other boys circled around, angry but uncertain.

The instructor pushed the two boys away. He looked ready to pummel the rest of the squad, and perhaps would have, had it not been for a moment so miraculous it verged on cinematic. A camera pan to the left would have revealed a stream of schoolchildren hurtling towards the instructor, crisp and cute in uniform, the eldest no more than twelve. All of them were Uighur. They launched themselves at the instructor, grabbing his clothing, trying to pull him down. He faltered with shock and disbelief, giving his older assailants the chance to get him on the ground. The cheerleaders approached frenzy. Feet and hands set to work, striking, punching kicking, until he was thoroughly beaten. But a chorus of shouts announced reinforcements: the police and some other soldiers sprinted into focus. The crowd scattered from the bloody ball of the instructor, knees drawn to his chest, tensed for the next blow.

93

'NICK DID YOU hear what happened?' said Liu Feng. We were in the staffroom.

'What?'

'Some Uighur children attacked a soldier. He was hurt very badly.'

'Why did they do that?' I asked.

'I think they have no good reason. They are just wild. It is also a problem when they are older. This is why the college tries to keep them busy. If we do not do this, then in two weeks there will be no one here. They will all have gone away, or be in prison.'

'Really?'

'Oh yes. It is a fact.'

94

THE BOY'S NAME was Ahmed. I knew this because a circle of people were shouting it. The other thing I knew was that he wanted to hurt someone. The knife in his hand said so.

I had been on my way home from the market when I heard the shouts. By the time I arrived on the scene Ahmed was gesturing with the knife and making threats. He had a narcotic eloquence, a series of halting syllables that broke into fluid speech. But after a few minutes of screaming and air slashing, his ire began to fade. The knife lowered; he staggered. A boy wearing a green *doppa* took this as his cue. He walked towards Ahmed, slowly, arms outstretched. When he was still a few paces away, Ahmed told him to stop. The boy took an extra step but then thought better of it. I heard him ask Ahmed to put the knife down. Ahmed nodded but did not move. The boy went to put his hand on Ahmed's shoulder, perhaps hoping to reassure him. The knife wrote an arc through the air via the boy's forehead. He fell back bleeding, his hand stuck to his temple. Ahmed's audience grew.

For the next few minutes he shouted and cut the air. Then the peacemaker returned, crudely bandaged and escorted by a larger boy who seemed to think he could shout Ahmed into submission. More knife-brandishing ensued. Whether it was due to the boy's bellowing or the effects of the drug, Ahmed was starting to wilt. His flourishes became less pronounced. He lurched and almost fell. His eyes strafed the semicircle of his audience. Our eyes met briefly and I briefly worried that he would suddenly spring to stab the nosy foreigner. But his gaze swept on, in desperation, till he turned and fled into a bar that was beneath street level.

A police van drew up. Two Uighur policemen got out. The crowd gestured to the bar. A few minutes later the boy was led meekly out. The two policemen were joined by a third man, the owner of the bar. He slapped the boy several times, then punched him in the stomach. The police said nothing until they bundled the boy into the back of the van; then they told us to go home. A dull thud came from inside.

95

ONE NIGHT, when I opened my door, Kuresh was on the stairs. He had not knocked; I had only opened the door to put some rubbish outside. He seemed to have been there a while.

He said hello then tried to look past me.

'Are there any other persons in your house?'

I gestured to an empty room.

He turned, and spoke a few soft words. Then he said, 'This is my girlfriend.'

A woman's face came out of the dark. How nice, I thought, he wants to introduce her. They came in and as soon as they had sat, Kuresh said, 'I can't go home tonight.' I looked at him blankly. He rolled up his sleeve to reveal a blood-soaked bandage, and suddenly I noticed that there were bloodspots all over his shirt. He said he'd been to the hospital and pulled up his sleeve. A row of stitches ran up his arm, ugly but efficient. I wanted to know what had happened, but didn't want to ask, which made things difficult. All he ventured was that it had been 'an accident', but without any real attempt to convince me that this was true.

'Is there any danger?' I asked.

'No, no danger.'

'Was it glass or metal?'

'Metal.'

Kuresh said he didn't want to go home because his parents would fuss too much and it wouldn't be good for their blood pressure. He said that his girlfriend was worried and wanted to stay with him. His parents would not allow them to spend the night together, even if they had approved of her.

He gave me his shirt to wash. He was a hairy man. I made up

THE TREE THAT BLEEDS

a bed for him on the sofa, then one for her in the spare room. She smiled weakly then went to lie down.

'Nick, please don't tell other persons about this.'

'Of course.'

'I don't want to disappear.'

I looked at him quizzically.

'That's what happens to young men who fight. Or pray too much.'

I bit back curiosity. He was tired and still partly in shock.

96

HUIYUAN LIES 50KM from Yining, one of the many small towns that ring the city. Most of these have substantial military bases, often with People's Liberation Army troops in addition to those of the *bingtuans*. In some ways this is a policy of encirclement: any trouble in Yining or on the border can be snuffed out quickly. Huiyuan itself had been the site of a major rebellion several hundred years ago, led by a Uighur named Sadur. One of my students, who came from there, said she would show me round if I visited.

The bus dumped me at a crossroads built around a gaudily restored tower from the Qing period. The streets straggled from the tower, lined at first with shops and stores, then blank adobe walls. The largest structure was the big military base, which still had an old gate and sections of wall from pre-Liberation times. There were also a few old Russian buildings, their eaves emblazoned with blocky Cyrillic letters under the Chinese. When I rang my student, she was predictably not in.

I killed time at a refreshment stall that consisted of a shallow cabinet on wheels, its insides plastered with garish wedding invitations, scenes of brides and grooms trapped within montages of mountains, valleys and Ferraris. It contained a large block of ice swathed in insulation blanket, some bowls, a hammer and chisel and a large container of yoghurt. It was owned by a middle-aged Hui woman wearing pink trousers and a green sweater. I watched her attack the ice, splintering offshavings with minute judders of her chisel. She swept them into a cracked enamel bowl, then spooned yoghurt on. She paused and held up a bottle of liquid that caught the sun. I nodded and watched its golden swirl across the white of the yoghurt. She handed it to me and I slurped the sweetness through the melting ice.

I wondered what else to do. There looked to be plenty of Hui and Uighur around, so I figured there had to be a mosque I could visit. The yoghurt lady didn't know but said the baker might. I wandered over to ask. He was busy slapping loaves onto the sides of the clay oven and didn't look up at first. He was surprised to see a foreigner but recovered quickly. He pointed into a yard piled with rusted metal.

'There?'

'Yes, there.'

'A mosque?'

He nodded, grinned, then made a squatting motion. I gave him a black look.

'No. Not the toilet. The mosque, all right?'

He threw up his hands, and pulled a face which I took to mean 'How can I be expected to understand a foreigner?' Luckily, a passing boy told him what I wanted.

'He wants the *qing zhen si*.'

'Oh, why didn't he say?'

He laughed and pointed down the road, then went back to the bread. I grumbled my thanks. I'd been walking for about 20 minutes and was starting to wonder if he'd given me the wrong directions. I asked a passing cyclist if the mosque was much farther.

'Just down there. You want a lift?'

I squeezed onto his rack and we wobbled off. Five bottom-numbing minutes later we stopped in front of a large brick and tile gate, not quite to the standard of Timur's tomb, but more elaborate than those in Yining. Blue and red lozenges glinted from their sand-coloured bed. A pair of minarets stood proud on either side, their very shape a call to prayer. As if in answer, young and old men began to stream inside. My camera and I were all set to loiter in our official capacity as paparazzi of the devout; my ride had other ideas. He beckoned me in. When I hesitated, he said, 'You're a Muslim, aren't you?'

And there were many acceptable answers to choose from: that I was just curious; that I found worship fascinating; that I thought mosques were beautiful buildings.

Instead I nodded and said, 'Yes.' Because it seemed the *best* answer, the one I thought he wanted to hear. It did not occur to me that this reply might have consequences.

'Come on then,' he said. 'It's time for prayer.'

Immediately, I was afraid. I didn't know how to pray. It seemed inevitable that my lie would be uncovered, that I would be punished.

I hung back, and raised a hand in objection. I told him I hadn't been a Muslim long, only a few months.

'Don't worry,' he said, and took my arm. We walked up the steps, and were almost inside, when I had an idea.

'I don't have a hat,' I said, and felt sure this would get me out of it.

'No problem,' he said, then pointed to a shelf above the shoe racks. 'We have some extra ones.'

I put on a skullcap, slipped off my shoes, then entered the prayer hall. It was a long, low ceilinged room, with a thick, red wall-to-wall carpet and a pulpit at the front. It was the main Friday prayer, so the hall was almost full, between two and three hundred men. There were hats of all kinds, white skullcaps, green and red *doppas*, a few turbans up front, some Nike baseball caps. I headed for a space at the back, but my new friend was insistent. He brought me to a spot four rows from the front.

I searched for a safe place to rest my eyes. The walls and ceiling were decorated with flourishes, but to gawk around too much might have led people to think I'd barely set foot in a mosque before. Straight ahead was no good, the *imam* was already limbering up his tongue. The side was no good, I couldn't meet my neighbour's eye. I settled on my breast, hoping this would pass for pious introspection.

We knelt and the *imam* began reading from a large book I took to be the Qur'an. I did my best impression of devotion: head cocked, face earnest, eyes shining with spiritual rapture. My neighbour yawned and from behind there came a burp. After a few minutes I realised that he was saying *Ruski* and *Amerika*, and that these had just been opening remarks.

The *imam* went out to deliver a final call to prayer. It was a rich cry that swelled and echoed; the stragglers entered and knelt. When the *imam* came back in, everyone stood up. He began reading again, this time in Arabic. At first people just listened, then they began the prayer sequence. First the hands behind the neck, as if straining to hear something. Then the hands were brought down to the knees, and held there a few seconds. After this, they knelt and prostrated themselves three times, then stood and started the sequence again.

All this I copied, with a two second delay I hoped nobody noticed. Then an ululation began, behind and in front, a swelling rising sound impossible in English. It did not inspire devotion in me, just a terrified wonder. Still we knelt, prostrated and straightened. The *imam* was now holding a stick, still talking. They prostrated, and I followed, imagining how much the stick would hurt. A brief intermission followed, during which some people left, leaving the devout and me. I hung on for a few minutes, then tiptoed away.

97

'HI THERE NICK. How's it going, mate?'

'Colin.'

'We called you yesterday to ask you round for Monopoly.'

'I was out.'

'Out with some mates? Good, good. Listen, I'm just calling to ask if any of your students have been borrowing books from the library. There seem to be a lot missing.'

'Any in particular?'

'No, I don't think so. I guess I'll have to chase mine some more for the books. And if any of your students want to borrow books, that's great, but please, please, ask them to write their names in the lending book.'

'I'll be sure to tell them.'

98

THE DAYS BEGAN to lengthen. The syrup that was winter's light changed colour as it stretched: it faded from gold to mustard; by summer, when it was light for 19 hours, it would be elongated to white. The Uighur children seemed to do nothing but play, kicking balls, shouting, whistling, making mischief from dawn to well after dusk. The morning skies seemed swept, the mountains vivid and close.

Class usually began with some kind of student presentation. The advanced pedagogical rationale for this was that it gave me time to wake up. Commonly this took the form of a Show and Tell exercise, which was often less than riveting ('This is my pencil box it is very lovely don't you think so?' Or: 'What is this do you know yes you are right it is a special pen'). There was the occasional surprise, as when one boy brought a bullet in. He held it up and said, 'This is to remind me of the day I shot a gun for the first time. That was my happy day.'

When one girl said she'd brought her holiday snaps in, I actually yawned. But I was wrong (as well as rude), for instead of the expected pictures of the Yili river or Urumqi, there was shots of soaring mountains, yaks and women with giant blue earrings.

'This is Tibet. *Xizang.*'

In my brain, the word wandered around. Soon it bumped into another word I'd stored and then forgotten. *Xizang* gave it a nudge and there was a shock of recognition. Nomo – the man who lived in the riverside burrow – was Tibetan. My next thought was to wonder if he was still there after six months of snow and flood.

That afternoon I threaded my way along the cliff top. The rains had worn away large sections that made going difficult, if not dangerous. But after a nervous hour I finally spied the telltale hulk of his armchair. The sound of metal on metal came from below. I scrambled down and round the corner and there he was, a little more stooped but otherwise unchanged. He was trying to scrape the rust off a pair of shears. I said hi, he said hi, and then he went back to what he was doing. I wasn't sure he remembered me until he came over and asked if I had any sweets. I handed him the tin. He straightened up and smiled, showing a mouth with considerably less teeth than before.

'What happened?'

He pointed up.

'I fell.'

If anything it was even harder than before to understand him, as the air rushed out of his mouth in all the wrong places. He gestured to a log; we sat sucking in silence.

'You're from Tibet, aren't you?'

'That's right.'

'How did you end up here?'

'I was sent here in 1970. I made some mistakes. They put me to work in the coal mines. I've lived in here since 1972 because I don't have the money to live in town. It was hard at first but now I like it. It's quiet.'

'Are you married? Do you have any children?'

'Six. They live in Kashgar.'

He got up and went to the burrow. After a few moments of rummaging he produced a black and white photo, grubby and worn with love. Three girls and boys sat cross-legged before a screen painted with pagodas and pandas. Their father stood behind them, arms at his side, almost at attention, as if he were a drill instructor and they his cadets.

'When did you last see them?'

'1990 or maybe 1991.'

'Don't you miss them?'

'Yes, but I have this photo.'

His finger traced the outline of their faces.

99

A GIRL'S VOICE peeped from the phone.

'Hello Nick, how are you, this is Edipim. My grandfather has become much better. He had an operation. So I have some free time. Would you like to come to my village?'

'Sure. How do I get there?'

'Take the No. 3 bus from the square and get off at Yarkiki Togruk.'

The bus was brand new – its plastic seats just moulded, its hand-rails still gleaming – and wasted on a road that went from cratered dust to rubble. It sneered at the bus's newness, issuing jolting rebukes whenever the bus forgot itself and attempted to move faster than ten miles an hour. Its disdain increased until finally it grabbed hold of an axle and twisted. There was a shearing sound and we lurched to a halt. We filed off and clustered round the buckled wheel. The next bus was due in half an hour, enough time for a quick reconnoitre of the area. I saw fallow fields; blue houses; a tidy cemetery. Its graves were earth mounds covered by large stones. They had small headstones and faced towards Mecca. A small round building stood to one side, its base circled by shattered green tiles. Its roof rose to a flattened dome, like a squashed oast house. I squinted through a slit of window. The dim interior was dominated by a tarpaulin-covered mound. Formless paintings could be seen. Books mouldered on a shelf.

A replacement bus tried to sneak past; I ran back to the road and got on. We picked up speed, and as the fields blurred by, I remembered this was the route towards the Tree That Bleeds. When it came into view, its branches were green with new leaves, against which the ribbons seemed like blossom. It was larger, stronger looking than I recalled, and as we got closer, there was that sense of inevitability that precedes a collision. The tree blocked the road ahead; the bus was too wide to pass. The tree loomed, filling the windshield; I braced myself for impact.

Then we were past it, whether by inches or feet. We crossed over a churning river and arrived in Yarkiki Togruk.

I caught sight of Edipim. She sat under a tree, nibbling at something. Her nose looked even cuter than before. I fought the urge to kiss her and instead shook hands. We set off towards her grandparents' house. Poplars repeated in perspective. Chickens scratched at the earth. A burly woman shooed geese through a gate while a tractor coughed for attention. It was the usual busy day in the countryside.

I asked Edipim if there were any Chinese in the village.

'No, this is a clean place. You would be able to smell them.'

'What do they smell of?'

'Spices, mostly chilli.'

'What do they say you smell of?'

'Lamb. Many Chinese, they can't stand this smell. When they come here for the first time, they will –' (she mimed retching) 'when they smell this.'

Edipim greeted everyone we met. Some asked who I was; others were unconcerned. We stopped at a vine-covered house.

'Do you mind if we go in?'

'Is this your grandparents'?'

'No, it's my uncle's.'

She went into the courtyard and called to him. He appeared after a few minutes, evidently pleased to see her. He was stout and slightly hunchbacked, his black hair streaked with grey. We were ushered in and pressed to drink and eat. The usual gauntlet of fruit and sweets was followed by *goosh* nan, the closest thing to pie in Uighur cuisine. Minced lamb oozed between soft slabs of bread.

'Do you like this Nick?'

'It's great.'

'Usually it is hard to find *goosh* nan like this in restaurants. But I will sell it in mine. Then lots of people will come.'

'You're opening a restaurant?'

'Yes, in the square, next to the King of Kebabs.'

My face must have shown surprise.

'Do you think that is strange?'

'No, it's just I can't don't know many 18-year-olds who have their own restaurants. Where did you get the money from?'

'I have another uncle who sent me some money. He is in Arabia.'

I was beginning to realise that Edipim was far from typical. She had not only the drive but also the means to achieve what she wanted. Her English was good and she was well connected. She could easily have been a spoilt little rich girl but if anything she was almost demure. Her faith seemed real and deep seated, and she had never had a boyfriend. Yet her clothes were ultra-fashionable, her nails always painted. She seemed quite capable of having it both ways.

Outside a group of boys were driving sheep towards a cloud convention. They floated by, serene and smelly; twilight dropped on the fields.

An old voice called Edipim's name. It belonged to her grandfather, who had come to look for us. I asked about his health in Chinese, but he didn't understand. Edipim translated into Uighur, then his reply into English.

'He thanks you for asking. He says he is much better but he is still old.'

'How old is he?'

'Ninety-one.'

Dinner was waiting for us when we arrived: a massive platter of *p*olo garnished with hardboiled eggs. My stomach forgot it had just been filled.

Edipim thanked Allah for the food, then said, 'Nick do you want to go to a wedding? It will be very traditional.'

'Who's getting married?'

'Our neighbour's eldest son. He is very handsome. But his wife is not very beautiful. Oh! Maybe I should not say that. I should say sorry to her.'

'It's probably better if you don't.'

The reception was held in the village square. Several hundred people stood round its sides, while music pumped from a keyboard. Everyone was waiting for the bride and groom.

The crowd hushed when they stepped forward. The bride's dress had so many delicate layers it was like an inverted rose. The groom wore a double-breasted black suit with a red carnation. They walked into the centre and started to dance. The sound of shaken aerosols was heard; then the couple were attacked. Within seconds they were covered in silly string, their clothes streaked pink and green. At the end of the song we cheered. Young men went up to girls they had been eyeing all evening. Dances were requested and in most cases, given. People twirled, spinning slowly or fast, according to age and skill. The best dancer was a young boy named Tashmimet. People shouted his name in encouragement; he seemed not to hear them as he moved flawlessly.

The excitement of the occasion kept causing the crowd to surge forward. The organisers had foreseen this problem and placed a man with a big stick at the edge of the dance floor. Anyone who didn't move back got a tap from it.

It was a long way from Erkin's sober affair, with its no dancing and gender segregation. This was a wholly different tradition, where the only surrender needed was to enjoyment. It was in this spirit that I asked Edipim to dance. She blushed and tried to refuse but I was already leading her forward. We danced beneath the stars for the next few hours.

100

THERE WAS SOMETHING wrong with Abdul. For weeks he had been
distant. On a bright morning in early May, he slipped his moorings
and began to drift.

It happened at work, a small sewing firm run with a staff of three
relations. His mother started up her machine, preparing to run a seam
up some nylon slacks. Abdul twitched. When his sister kick-started
her machine, Abdul burst into a ballet of tics. He grabbed a pair of
scissors and began to spin. The women started in horror. He leered
at them and wiggled his tongue, all the time still whirling. They
stepped back from their busy Singers which lapsed into muteness,
taking Abdul with them. His eyes rolled up into his head, showing
milky white as he slid to the floor.

For the next two days his family tried everything to revive him.
His mother put his favourite food in his mouth; his brother slapped
him hard; his wife kissed him tenderly, all with no result. They carried
him to Old Verina, who looked in his ears and mouth, rubbed sugar
on his hands, and asked his wife a series of questions that made her
blush. Finally, she threw up her hands, took ten yuan for spiritual
expenses and admitted defeat.

The village elders called a meeting. They agreed that something
must be done. One of them knew of a man in the next village who
was said to have knowledge of such afflictions. A messenger was sent.
He returned with the news that the man would come the day after
next.

When the healer arrived they were sceptical. He did not appear
to be anything other than he looked, a short man in a long coat with
a pointy chin. But he gave his orders in a commanding tone and
appeared to know what he was doing. The villagers assembled in

the square at the designated hour, the men in their best felt hats and stripy coats, the women in the striped dresses usually reserved for weddings. A drum and tambourine ensemble began to thump out a tune. Abdul was led into the square, mute and otherworldly.

The healer began by tying Abdul down using a rope decorated with strips of white cloth. Next he wound a green sash around Abdul's waist. He struck his bottom with a stick of ash three times. The tempo of the drums increased. The healer signalled to Abdul's brothers. They rolled him up into a blanket so tight that he could not move. Then his wife lit some incense which she placed first in his mouth, then round the rim of a nan, like a birthday cake. The ash from this was blown into his face. A chicken was killed and Abdul anointed with its blood. The ceremony went on for another hour; the healer used every remedy known to him (including several he made up) but at the end Abdul was as absent as he had been before.

Did Abdul recover? I don't know; I had to go and teach. I turned the TV off and left.

IOI

THEY WERE THERE each morning, bundled up, in front of the employment bureau. Seldom more than 50 people, never less than 20. As soon as they saw the officials, they began to shout. But this was no daily riot: the officials appeared unruffled; the complainers' ire was measured. Both parties seemed accustomed to their roles.

The protestors had been laid off from one of the largest factories in town, a state-run textile mill that had fallen victim to the economic reforms needed for World Trade Organisation membership. That the factory had been badly managed and inefficient was not in dispute. The problem was that the mostly Uighur workforce had been laid off without proper compensation. In ten months of unemployment they had only received one small payment, the result of a special tax on the employed.

Tursun's youngest brother was among the protestors. He had two children to support, one of whom had weak lungs that required regular (and expensive) treatment. He hadn't worked since the factory closed and was completely dependent on Tursun. I never heard the latter complain about this; he looked on it as the duty of an elder brother. But the injustice of it was another matter. That filled him with rage.

'What kind of men are these? What? How do they treat other men like this? They say one thing, they do different, their words are nothing. Dogs! This is what they are. Not even! Do you know how many years my brother worked at that factory? Six years. *Six*. Six years working for *animals*. It makes me sick. They would not do this if we were not Uighur. No one can do such things to their own people.'

His anger was understandable, but he was wrong. Far away, on the other side of the country, tens of thousands of workers were facing the same problems. In March 2002, 50,000 retired oil workers protested in the north-eastern town of Daqing; in nearby Liaoyang, 30,000 other workers staged similar protests. Their complaints were the same as in Yining: unpaid pensions, wages and redundancies.

China has no national social security system; the current welfare system places these responsibilities on employers. A factory can end up paying unemployment benefit to the same workers that it has made redundant. Such payments are often beyond the ability of businesses struggling in the new market-based economy.

Corruption is another factor. The government has been making a lot of noise for the last few years about the need for honesty and fairness in business. The newspapers have run prolonged campaigns on the evils of excess. There have also been numerous high-profile trials of public officials (including several mayors and lesser Party leaders) for smuggling and embezzlement; death sentences had been handed out. The official acknowledgement of what virtually any Chinese person will tell you in private (that corruption permeates almost every major social and economic institution) has meant that people can now point the finger, so long as they don't point it too high.

So in this respect, Yining was nothing special. The unemployment in the city was not necessarily the result of ethnic discrimination. But perhaps the difference between ethnicity and state had blurred in many Uighur minds. It was undeniable that the majority of those in power were ethnically Han. How were Uighurs in Yining supposed to know that there was equal, if not worse, poverty and deprivation in the provinces of central and north-east China? They knew few people there and had little reason to visit. All they heard of such places were media stories of hope and prosperity, which, with nothing to contradict them, couldn't help but seep in. And if Han elsewhere were doing fine, how else could the difficulties of Uighurs be explained other than by the idea that the (Han) government were against them?

There was plenty of evidence to support such a conclusion: the crackdown on religion, the ongoing campaign against 'separatism', the forced abortions and public sentencing rallies. Their enemy needed a face, preferably a different one, and no one fit the bill better than the Han.

102

IT SEEMED TO violate the laws of matter. There I was, sitting in the courtyard of my friend Madina – one of the women in the KU class – sipping black tea under the shade of an apple tree, when a Han woman appeared. She paused in the doorway, peering through the gloom of her sunglasses, a camera bouncing on her hip. She looked like a lost tourist.

Madina called to her in English. 'Hello, Luo Hong!'

I stared in amazement.

Luo Hong introduced herself and all became clear. She taught journalism to the students in Madina's department. That they were colleagues was probably less important than the fact that Luo Hong wasn't from Yining. She was a postgraduate at Nanjing University who had only come to Yining for a term. Luo Hong was thus less aware of the history of problems between the Han and Uighur She may have been Han but in some ways was almost as much an outsider as I was.

Madina disappeared into the kitchen, leaving me with Luo Hong. I asked her if she liked Yining. She said it was very beautiful, and that she loved the weather. As she talked her hands darted to the hanging berries on a nearby bush. Within a few minutes she had stripped one side of the bush completely, and probably would have worked her way round to the other side, had Madina not appeared to announce that the food was ready.

When Madina started serving the food, Luo Hong got her camera out. She didn't ask Madina if she minded, just started taking pictures. When Madina did something that she missed, Luo Hong asked her to repeat it. The tea had to be poured twice, my hands washed three times. She made me feel like scenery, something to be arranged for her convenience. If Madina felt the same, she was too polite to show it. But I had no such qualms; the *polo* was getting cold. I interrupted her picture-taking by asking if it was difficult teaching journalism, given the limitations the government put on what journalists could write.

'Yes,' she said, and lowered her camera. 'My students complain about this, the difference between theory and practice. But there's no other way.'

It was a reasonable answer, and most importantly, it gave Madina the chance to finish serving. We filled our stomachs, then sat back. Madina chose this moment of bliss to ask if I was Christian.

'No,' I said several times.

'Then what do you believe?'

'Nothing, I suppose.'

She looked perturbed but didn't ask why. When she asked Luo Hong the same question, she replied 'Marxism.' I saw the chance for a petty bit of point scoring.

'Can I ask you something?'

'OK.'

'Do you think China has a socialist economy or a capitalist one?'

'Well, there is the system, but it is only a tool. Like Deng Xiaoping said, "It doesn't matter whether the cat is black or white, only whether it catches the mouse".'

'Yes, but is it socialist or not?'

'It's a free-market economy.'

'So that means it's capitalist.'

'Yes.'

'Didn't Marx say that the fundamental nature of a society is determined by its economy?'

'Ideology is what matters; it is the system the economy serves.'

'But if the economy is capitalist, so must be the system.'

She fell silent and I felt like a bully. But then she replied.

'Yes, we can see there is also a gap between our idea and reality.

There are contradictions. My students and I often talk about this. When we were young we learned about socialism, but now things are not like that. Sometimes we feel confused. But what matters is that we help our country to develop. This is first.'

I admired her for not taking refuge in dogma. When Luo Hong apologised and said she had to go, I worried that my bad manners had driven her away. As it turned out, she had a meeting to go to.

'It will probably be very boring,' she said. 'The leaders will just talk and talk. But if don't go I will be criticised.'

Madina laughed in agreement then thanked her for coming. Luo Hong smiled and apologised again for having to go early. She waved and left and I wondered (perhaps naively) why things couldn't always be thus.

We sat in silence for a few moments. Then I asked Madina if was the first time that she had had a Han person in her home.

'Yes, and it was a little strange. It was all right, she is nice. But many Chinese people here are not good. You know, there are so many problems.'

'Don't you think that the main problem here is the economy? Maybe if more people had jobs things would be all right.'

'No, that is what the government might say. I have a job, I have this house but it is not enough. The problem is that the Chinese do not respect us. They think we are not as good. But not everything is their fault. Many of our *imams* are to blame. They only want to keep the old ways. We cannot develop. Some *imams* do not understand what is the real Islam.'

'Like in Saudi Arabia?'

'Yes, that is the real Islam.'

'So would you want to wear the *burqa*?

'No!' she said then laughed. 'I would not need to. This is only their local custom. Not Muslim. An Arab custom. They do this because it is a hot place.'

I backtracked a little.

'So you don't think the real problem is unemployment?'

'No, the problem is the Chinese people. They always think they are the best, their character is this.'

'All Chinese people?'

'Yes.'

'What about Luo Hong?'

'She is OK. Maybe there are some Chinese who understand a little. I used to think the same as you, that it was because of jobs. But I do not believe this anymore. If you lived here longer, your mind would change.'

'I don't think the Han people are the real problem, although they could learn to respect Uighur people more. I think it is the government that needs to be changed. But this may take a long time. Maybe 50 years.'

'Fifty years? We cannot wait this long. Maybe then there won't be many of us.'

103

THINGS WERE GOING well for Kuresh. His arm had healed and he had opened a new class. Best of all, his parents had finally given their permission for him to marry. We sat by the river in a sunset haze, neither of us saying much as the sun slipped from view.

'I very appreciate what you did,' he said.

'Don't mention it.'

'No, I mean it. If you have some problem I will try to help you.'

Swallows skimmed the river's surface. A donkey brayed in a field. Lights began to prick on up and down the bank. Although I hadn't known Kuresh as long as Murat or Tursun, I felt he trusted me more than they ever would. In hindsight, it seems strange that it took me so long to ask someone what I most wanted to know, especially given how blunt I could be about other questions. Perhaps he was the first person that I thought would give me a straight answer.

I picked up a stone, tried to skim it, failed. Kuresh's went half-way across the river. I said, 'A few weeks ago you talked about young men disappearing. What did you mean by that?'

He didn't seem to have heard, just kept staring into the gloom. It was almost dark when he replied.

'After they stopped the *mäshräps* a lot of people were angry. Some *imams* said we needed to protect our beliefs. They told the young men they should fight if necessary. A lot of young men believe very strongly. Some people said angry things and then were betrayed. If the police heard you say something they did not like, they would come at night and take you. Many did not come back. Some bodies were found in the countryside; some were not found.'

'How many men do you think were taken?'

'I don't know. Maybe one hundred. Maybe more.'

The moon had yet to rise. A bird croaked on the shore.

'How did people react to all these young men disappearing?'

'They were scared but also angry. Some very brave people complained.'

'Who to?'

'The police, leaders in Urumqi, some even wrote to the government in Beijing. But it made no difference.'

'What happened after that?'

'Some fathers of the missing went to the square. They took their clothes off and shouted. They demanded to know where their sons were. The police came and arrested them.'

'When did this happen?'

'In January. At the end of January.'

It was the right time to ask; I hoped he was the right person.

'So was this why the trouble started in February? The protests?'

'Many people were worried that the fathers would not come back, that the same thing that happened to their sons would happen to them. Some of their relatives went to the police station and asked to see them. The police refused. Many more people came. A young soldier became scared. He used his gun. A woman was killed. When people heard this they were very angry. People came from many places to complain. There were more than a thousand. But not all of them came because of that woman. Some came because they hated the Chinese or the government, some because they were angry about not having jobs, some because their *imams* told them to, some because they like fighting.'

'What about you?'

'I don't like people telling me what I can do. But I think those who fought were wrong. This should not be our way.'

Finally, some kind of answer. It made sense which didn't mean that it was true. It could have been just another rumour. In the absence of a time machine, there was no way to know for sure. But the more thoughtful Uighurs that I knew concurred with this explanation. Hamit said he had seen the men in their underwear, as did

Ismail, who also added, somewhat mystifyingly, 'They had the wrong idea then but now they know'. The closest thing to official confirmation was a comment from Ma Shiqiang, director of the Yining police department's administrative office, who had alleged that the initial set of protestors had taken off all their clothes and shouted, 'Don't sleep. Don't eat. Don't work'.

The riots were thus perhaps best viewed as the result of numerous grievances: unemployment, religious repression, draconian birth control practices, the wish for real autonomy. Five years on, the same grievances remained, and in some cases, most notably religious freedom, the situation of Uighurs appeared to have got worse.

Summer

104

Even in the best circumstances the position of a minority is uneasy.

Albert Hourani, *A History of the Arab Peoples*

WOULD THERE BE more riots in Yining? Perhaps. The causes of dissatisfaction were unlikely to disappear. But at the time it seemed unlikely that anything would happen on the scale of the 1997 riots. Then the authorities had been taken by surprise. Since then the number of soldiers in and around town had massively increased. There were three large-sized garrisons stationed within the city centre, plus all the bases in outlying towns like Huiyuan, not forgetting the numerous *bingtuans* dotted round the countryside. Any protest or revolt could be quickly suppressed.

It was the same throughout the province. In addition to the military presence, the ever-increasing number of Han migrants from other provinces meant that the Uighurs were no longer the largest ethnic group in the province. Even if they had not been outnumbered and outgunned, there appeared to be no party or leader around which they could coalesce. This was partly due to the instant suppression of anything or anyone that smelt of 'separatism', as well as the general lack of unity amongst Uighurs in Xinjiang. The only chance of them gaining independence was if the Chinese government miraculously imploded, which, though not impossible, was extremely unlikely. The Uighurs had to accept that the Han would not go away.

There appeared to be two choices open to Uighurs: they could embrace victim status, sink into despondency and hate, let the Han marginalise them until they became as assimilated as the Hui. Or they could struggle to maintain their culture and identity, whilst engaging more with the Han. However, this second option depended greatly on the attitude of the government, whether they would allow the Uighurs any real autonomy.

105

THE EDICT CAME from on high: Uighur would cease to be a language. Though these were not the actual words, the meaning was clear. Starting from September 2003, Uighur would no longer be used within Xinjiang University (in Urumqi) except for teaching Uighur literature. Previously, students had been offered the choice of learning in Chinese or Uighur; in future, all first- and second-year courses would be taught exclusively in Chinese. The official rationale for this was that it would raise the level of education of local Uighur students who, it was claimed, often fell far behind their Han class-mates. The new measures would improve their prospects of finding a job after graduation.

There was some truth to this. The education system was already slanted towards Chinese speakers. Many of the exams had to be taken in Chinese, and in subjects like computing or science, the majority of books or journals were only available in Chinese. A better command of Chinese would, in theory, allow Uighur students to compete with their Han counterparts.

However, the fact that the system was already biased towards Chinese was no reason to make it more so. While this would un-doubtedly help some students, it would also exclude all those with poor Chinese. There was also the implicit judgement that in some way Chinese was a better language than Uighur. It seemed like a direct attack on their culture and identity, a clear case of 'big brother' Han deciding what was best for the backward minorities.

It almost wasn't worth bothering to ask people what they thought about the new law. The Han would be in favour of it, the Uighurs bitterly opposed. I had, after all, been living in Yining for almost a year, time enough to acquire an understanding of people's problems, how they thought. When I did ask Hamit's opinion, I was confident about his reply.

'Oh yes,' he said. 'It is a very good thing. Very good. It will help us very much.'

I blinked my disbelief.

'Our children will have more chances to succeed. You need good Chinese to get a good job. So it is very good.'

'Aren't you worried that they won't be able to speak their own language very well?'

'The children will still learn Uighur.'

'Where? At school?'

'No, they will also stop using it in the schools.'

'When?'

'Maybe in two or three years.'

'So Uighurs will not be able to learn in their own language at all?'

'That's right.'

He did not seem bothered by this. I asked him where they would learn.

'At home. We will teach them.'

I had my doubts. I'd met a lot of *Min Kao Han* students who spoke Chinese to each other, even when out of the classroom, some of whom couldn't read or write Uighur at all. There were clearly many parents who lacked Hamit's pedagogic zeal.

Hamit was not alone in his approval for the new regulations; most Uighur parents that I spoke to seemed to welcome them. When I tried to tell them what had happened in Wales, they thanked me, then asked where it was. They were quietly unconcerned. Perhaps such worries were a luxury. Their immediate worry was for their children's economic future. I seemed to be the only one that cared.

106

'PEOPLE SHOULD BE able to learn in their own language. This is a good thing. It is their mother tongue. Would you like it if someone did not let you learn in Chinese? I do not think you would.'

Wang Dong sat down to a ripple of applause. Those not applauding shook their heads or stared into the middle distance, dreaming of lunch or the bell. I had asked the class to discuss whether people should always be able to learn in their first language, having first given them an article about the similar debate occurring within the US education system. In effect, I was asking them to evaluate their own government's policy towards the minorities. Looking back, I'm surprised that I dared be so direct. I can only put it down to impatience. My time in Yining was running out and I felt short of answers.

It was a strange irony that this 18-year-old Han boy should be defending a right that some Uighurs seemed indifferent to. But there were dissenting voices. One girl nicely conflated ethnicity and nationality.

'We are all Chinese, so they should speak Chinese!'

'And there are more of us!' said the girl next to her.

Battle commenced. Wang Dong fired a fresh salvo.

'Do you think that is right? Why can't they speak their own language?'

A small girl wearing a sweatshirt with a picture of a raccoon on it stood up and said:

'I don't like it when the minorities talk together in their own language. It makes me feel strange.'

Part of me could understand. I remembered what it was like when I had first come to China and could understand nothing, how paranoid I had been, imagining every look and laugh to be aimed at me.

Wang Dong's desk mate – a short girl with bobbed hair who may have been his girlfriend – got to her feet and said, 'Why must they learn our language? We cannot speak theirs.'

Several sets of feet shifted uneasily, perhaps in protest: English lessons were not supposed to be about politics. A skinny boy in a tracksuit replied, 'We are all Chinese, yes? If we want to make our country stronger, everyone must work together. But we need to be able to communicate with each other. If we all speak different languages we cannot do this. It would be like the tower of babble.'

'Babel,' I interjected.

'Yes, like the tower of babble. There would be no unity. The minorities can keep their own language but they must also have good Chinese.'

He had a point. Perhaps if more Uighurs were fluent in Chinese this might promote understanding. However, there was a thin line between bridging the gap and assimilation. In a few generations the Uighurs could be like the Hui, integrated to the point of near invisibility. There was also the question of what the Han were prepared to do to create this often longed for unity. How many were willing to learn Uighur?

At the end of the lesson I summarised the main arguments and called for a vote. Hands dawdled up then shot quickly back down. The result was a three-way split, with a third of the students agreeing that people should be allowed to learn in their own language, another third disagreeing, and the remainder uncertain or uncaring. We hadn't exactly saved the world, but it was a start. I wondered what else I could do.

107

'GOOD MORNING, CLASS.'

'Good morning!' they chorused.

'I'd like to start by asking you a question. Has anyone here ever been to England? Anyone?'

They woefully shook their heads.

'Oh, right. Well, even though none of you have been, you still probably have some ideas about what England and the people there are like. Things that you learnt from books or films or talking to other people. Now, most people in England have never been to China, but they also have some ideas about what Chinese people are like. What do you think their ideas of Chinese people are?'

'Friendly,' said one girl.

'Hard-working' said another.

'Yes, perhaps. But there are other ideas too. Some people in England say that the Chinese are very short.'

They laughed.

'And others say that the Chinese are inscrutable. That means they are hard to understand.'

They frowned.

'Some also say that the Chinese people cannot think for themselves, that they can only obey.'

Their faces fell.

'But of course I know that isn't true.'

Then rose again.

'*Some* people may be like this. But are *all* Chinese people like this? No, of course not. So, often our ideas about other people are not completely true. We call such ideas stereotypes. Stereotypes.'

I wrote the word on the board in blue chalk.

'Now, as many of you know, I used to be a teacher in Hunan province. Do you think that many of my students in Hunan have ever been to Xinjiang?'

There was a chorus of 'no's.

'No, that's right, very few. So most have never met a Uighur person before. They probably have some stereotypes about Uighur people. What do you think their stereotypes are?'

'They live in tents and ride horses all the time.'

'That they can't speak Chinese.'

'They are beautiful and good singers.'

'That this is a primitive place.'

I had to give them credit. They had managed to come up with some stereotypes that weren't even their own. I prepared myself for the touchy-feely bit that was a complete lie.

'So, my students in Hunan don't know much about Uighurs. But you all live here, so you do. So what I'd like you to do is imagine you have a friend in Hunan who you want to write a letter to. In the letter you should try to explain some things about Uighurs to your friend. But be careful when you write to use words like 'many', 'most' or 'some', otherwise you'll just be writing another stereo-type. And remember, the aim of this is to help them to understand.'

This was probably clear as mud but I started them off anyway. Pens were borrowed and exchanged, sheets of paper cadged. For the next 20 minutes they wrote. These were some of the results.

Although it's true that many Uighurs and Kazaks can dance well, the same is not true of all Xinjiang people. For us Han Chinese, although we would like to accept your compliment, we have to say we can't do it so well, at least not all of us. Also, usually the dancers on TV are professionals who practice a lot.

In the past Uighurs had to ride horses when they wanted to go to places. But now there are cars and bicycles here. Riding camels and horses is now more a part of tourism than daily life.

The Uighurs are a symbol of Xinjiang. They are the main inhabitants here. Many Uighurs are friendly, though some of them are fond of drink. Maybe you think Uighur people are rude and not very good but this is wrong. We can't say that all a people are bad just because of a small group of bad people.

I thought back to what Madina had been saying about wanting respect above all. The students weren't quite there, but I began to feel that some of them might in the end understand. It was almost grounds for optimism.

108

I WANTED TO repeat this exercise with the KU class, given they were not short of stereotypes either. The problem was that I couldn't ask them to write to my old students in Hunan, and there were no other large Uighur communities outside of Xinjiang that I knew of. Eventually I decided that they were adults and thus should be able to analyse their own beliefs. I explained what stereotypes were and then asked them to think about their own. Unsurprisingly, this direct approach was less successful. Even the best piece had a whiff of irony.

> In most Uighurs eyes, most Chinese people are honest and when they are honest it is usually based on their own interest. They easily break their promises unless their interest is assured. But I don't agree with people who have the above idea. According to my own experience of working and studying with Chinese, it's true that some are like this but not the whole nation. It's all about the misconceptions that we have of them. In order to get rid of these ideas we need to change our minds and communicate with them so that we may live in harmony. If they are as dishonest as we think, how can they have succeeded so much? It is clear to us that the Chinese got such great achievements through co-operation with other nations, and that their honesty has played an active role.

The other efforts weren't exactly great leaps forward either.

Stereotype 1) All Chinese people eat every organism

It's not true. They couldn't eat everything. But I don't know what they don't eat.

Stereotype 2) All Chinese people have small eyes, small noses and are not beautiful.

False. Not all Chinese people have small eyes, small noses but it's very common. You can find beautiful Chinese people, but few, and you must pay attention.

In retrospect, it was naïve of me to expect such a blunt exercise to make people give up their long-nourished stereotypes. Thinking about the content of their stereotypes would not remove the basic sense of grievance against the Han. I tried to believe that it represented some kind of start but it was too difficult. Clearly there was little that could bridge the rift.

109

SHORN SHEEP MUTTERED in the shade; streams trickled their assent.
As for the ripening crops, the heat left them mute. My bicycle drew
a treaded fuse through the dust. It was one of those days when you
know you have to go somewhere, even if you don't know where that
is. Hence my cycling round the sun-bleached countryside, mouth
full of dust, happy to be moving.

The tarmac had finished an hour ago; there was only a stony strip
of dirt to follow. This was understandable: the houses were ten minutes' cycle apart; tractors were the main traffic. When I stopped to
rest, silence was quick to fall. Grasshoppers winked in and out of
vision, teleporting through the grass.

Another bicycle approached through the shimmer of the haze.
Its rider crisped into focus as a middle-aged Uighur man. He was
unshaven and his right eye clouded. I said hello and shook his hand.
He looked me up and down, seemed satisfied, then produced a red
apple that was as hard as a cricket ball. I thanked him in Uighur,
but had to switch to Chinese.

'Hot, isn't it?'

'A little.' He patted his sweater and jacket. 'Where are you going?'

'Not sure.'

His look suggested that he thought this impossible.

'Are you going to the fight?' he said, perhaps only to reassure
himself that I was not so completely insane as to be out in this heat
for no good reason.

'The fight? Oh, yes,' I said.

He nodded in approval, gestured down the road ahead, said
something I didn't catch, then cycled off with a wave. After a few
moments, I followed.

THE TREE THAT BLEEDS

The track ran on through purple swathes of lavender. Soon the path widened before a huddle of buildings that might have been a village. A cracked mosque flaked beneath a stand of poplars, its crescent-topped minarets leaning toward heaven. Remnants of decoration lingered round its shuttered windows: curling strands of golden grape that approached a pattern. A dog snoozed in the entranceway. When I got off my bike, it woke and started to bark. Its owner appeared – a long beard under a green *doppa* – and cuffed it into silence. It glared at me and crouched, malevolent but chained. I asked the man if he was the *imam*; he said he was and invited me in. I declined respectfully, said I had a fight to go to.

I cycled on till I saw signs of a gathering: a hundred bicycles leaned against the side of a fenced-off yard. Shouts and calls came from inside. I could see a large crowd of men gathered around something. At the gate I paid a sour-looking man four yuan and entered. Makeshift bleachers were arranged around three sides of a small arena. Men were standing or sitting on these long wooden benches, pointing and shouting, brandishing fistfuls of money, all because of the two black and scrawny birds pecking at each other. It was the monthly cockfight.

I sat down next to a small boy chewing a twig, and that was where I remained for the next hour, despite the fact that it was the hottest part of the day, and my head was uncovered, and the sight of all the pecking and blood was unpleasant. Thankfully, none of the fights were to the death: after each round the birds were wiped down and given a pep talk.

I stayed because of the miracle that was taking place all around me. It was the Han man in front of me talking to the old Uighur on his right. He said something which made his neighbour laugh. The Han man clapped the Uighur on the back then said something else which made him collapse in fresh attacks of laughter. To my left a couple of Kazakh young men were joking with a Han and two Hui. To my right a Hui man was conferring excitedly with the Han next to him, pointing to the more bloody of the birds and saying

'You see? Too slow.' His neighbour nodded his agreement. The atmosphere was excited but without tension. They were here for one purpose, to watch these scraps of beak and feathers going at each other. Finally, here was something that Hui, Han, Uighur and Kazakh could enjoy together; just for once they were united, bound as brothers by blood.

110

BUT 'SPORT' WAS not the answer. When the 2002 World Cup dragged itself into view, there was more than the usual predictable excitement: this was the first time that the Chinese team had managed to qualify for the tournament, a feat that some attributed to their increased ball control, others to the fact that Japan and South Korea – the two other major Asian sides – had automatically qualified, meaning that there was less competition for the usually mediocre Chinese side.

Whatever the reasons for their qualification, their first game, against Costa Rica, was eagerly awaited. The general mood among many Han seemed to be one of ludicrous optimism: they were not just going to win the first game; they were going to win the tournament. Many Uighurs were looking forward to the game for rather different reasons, including some hitherto unsuspected of being football fans.

'Are you going to watch the game Murat?'

'Yes, of course. Maybe it will be wonderful.'

'In what way?'

'Well, the Chinese will lose very badly because their bodies are too little and weak. Uighur bodies are much stronger. If there were Uighurs in the team maybe they could win. But they will not let us play. All the team are Han. This is their mistake.'

He looked like he could live with the humiliation of the Chinese team.

'So, who will you support?'

'Turkey. They are a people like us. They are a good team, especially Hassan. He is very fast.'

The afternoon of the game arrived. All lessons were cancelled.

It was apparently the students' patriotic duty to support their team. I sat in a crowded classroom with a television turned up to full volume. Play began and at first the Chinese team looked like they might have a chance. They passed well in midfield; their defence looked tight. But then there was a streak of blue and red and it was 1–0 Costa Rica. The students sat in the ruins of their optimism, moaning or in shocked silence. Play continued, with the students cheering on their team, applauding whenever they got possession.

They took the second Costa Rica goal better, merely shaking their heads. When the final whistle blew, one of the students ran to the map on the wall. She located Costa Rica then wailed, 'But it's such a *small* country!'

The mood amongst Uighurs was one of unsuppressed glee. Turkey had also been beaten, but by Brazil, and they had managed to score a goal. Hassan, the scorer, was proclaimed a hero. It was a glorious defeat.

III

EDIPIM INTRODUCED ME to another hero, or what was left of him.

'Nick, are you free now?'

'I suppose so.'

It was Sunday and very, very early.

'Would you like to go the tomb of Sadur?'

'Very much.'

When we met the sun had yet to burn the mist. We took one bus, changed to another, then had to walk the last few kilometres. This was time enough for Edipim to tell me all she knew about the great man, which didn't take very long.

Sadur ('the brave') was born in the Yili valley in 1798. His early life was unremarkable, mostly spent farming and having children. But sometime in his thirties he became involved in the resistance against the Qing invaders, and soon rose to prominence as a guerrilla leader. He was captured numerous times but always managed to escape. Despite this dangerous life, he managed to survive to the age of 73, finally dying in 1871. This was all she knew. But she was positive that he was a great hero, if only because he was a Uighur who had fought against the Chinese. That he had not been fighting the Han Chinese but the Manchus – a people from present-day northeastern China, who ruled the country during the Qing dynasty – didn't seem to matter.

'We're here.'

A seven-foot gilt-edged portrait stood by the roadside. The man wore a grey tunic and cape. His beard and eyes were black and fixed upon some distant point. His hand was on his sword, which was partly out of its scabbard. A throng of less heroic (though equally armed) men could be seen behind him. This then, was Sadur, or someone's idea of him.

A tarnished gold plaque announced that this was, 'An official site of historical importance'. A young boy in a blue tracksuit slouched beneath the sign. We were on the verge of walking by until he said we had to pay. He wasn't the most likely custodian of a folk hero's tomb – a large purple bruise lurked under his right eye –but if he was an impostor then at least he had had the sense to steal the tickets as well. He pocketed our money then tore two off with a semblance of care. Then he headed off down the road, back in the direction of town.

The path was flanked by pink roses. We stopped at a small, white-washed building that housed a museum. Something about the place was troubling me. The government had spent a moderate amount of money on a place that glorified a guerrilla leader. How could they tolerate, let alone promote, a site devoted to the life of a man who had perpetrated acts of dissent similar to those they had arrested and executed people for?

Some kind of answer was inside. Scenes from Sadur's life hung around the walls. In one picture Sadur had just slashed a pigtailed Manchu with a scimitar. In another, he was being wheeled away in a cage, watched by a herdsmen, his daughter and several fascinated sheep. A third picture had him fleeing through the woods, bleeding and pursued. Running above all these pictures was a large banner which read, in both Chinese and Uighur, 'Love your nation, learn from great men!' The captions for the pictures talked of Sadur's 'fight against feudalism' and 'his heroic struggle against the Qing land-lords'. The aim was clearly to write Sadur into a Marxist-Leninist version of history, thereby diluting his potential to be a nationalist icon. All that mattered was that he was a member of an exploited class rebelling against his feudal oppressors. He, like Ahmetjan Kasimi, had been posthumously recruited to the great revolutionary cause.

Edipim pointed to a picture on the end wall. A rather different Sadur, broader and beardless, sat on a prison bench. The ruins of a melon lay between his feet. Next to him were three small cakes that looked like Danish pastries.

'Nick do you know the story of Sadur and the melon?'

'No, but I'd like to.'

'One time when he was captured some people sent Sadur a melon. But there was a knife hidden within the melon. He used it to escape.'

'What about those?' I pointed at the cakes.

'Oh, those I do not know. Maybe some kind of fruit.'

We left the museum and resumed our walk towards the tomb. The sun was hot and we quickened our pace to reach the shade of the trees. When I saw the tomb I understood its need for shelter. It rose up from the ground like a lump of pink ice cream. His dates were picked out in mint-sized white pebbles. We stood in silence, our eyes feasting.

I walked around the side of the tomb. A second set of pebbles spelt August 2nd 1999. I asked Edipim what that date signified.

'That was when the tomb was restored. Before that none of this was here. Many people had forgotten about Sadur. But after the problems in 1997 there were some who remembered.'

Yes, I thought, including the government. It seemed there were two Sadurs buried there: one, a Marxist hero who had fought to establish the socialist dream of the present; the other, a champion of his people. The truth was likely somewhere in between, but where exactly, perhaps no one could say.

I certainly couldn't. The longer I stayed in Yining, or Ghulja, the less I knew. The names referred to the same geographical space but beyond that shared nothing: they were labels for parallel universes, where the meaning of each past and present act was equally con-tested. To imagine the future required an act of projection, but whether it was the place as seen by the government, or by the Uighurs, it was hard to imagine that things would improve.

Edipim was equally optimistic.

'If things continue as they are, things will only get worse. Maybe one day there will no longer be any Uighur people. And it is not only the Chinese. Some of our people don't think about the future. They are lazy. They do not care. But the biggest problem is that we have no one to lead us. If there is anyone like Sadur he is probably in prison.'

We sat in the shade and drank water. It occurred to me that if there was any chance for the Uighurs, it lay in people like Edipim, the young and well educated, those who cared about their people but who were not too mired in devotion or hate. So yes, perhaps there might be a chance, but only if she and others like her stayed. From what I had seen, first with Tilawaldi, then amongst the KU class and others, the reverse appeared to be happening. In the early 1990s, the brain drain had operated eastwards: it was estimated that for every professional who settled in Xinjiang, six left for the more developed coastal provinces. Now the drain was directed west, to Canada and Europe. I asked Edipim about her plans in that direction.

'My father and my uncle want me to go to America. But there are many good things for me here in Ghulja. As well as the English classes, there is also Noterhajim's school.'

'What's that?'

'It is a school for children who have no parents. Have you been there?'

'No, but I'd like to. Do you think it would be possible?'

'I will ask Noterhajim. But I think the children would like to meet you.'

'Maybe they haven't seen many foreigners before.'

'No, actually some young Americans go there every month. Are they your friends?'

'Not exactly.'

112

I RAISED AN EYE; it hurt. Memories of football and beer bobbed to the surface. An image of Michael Owen firmed into focus. Oh yes, that was it. England had beaten Argentina 1–0. I had got very drunk. A Kazakh man had shouted, 'Your country is so beautiful!' then thrown his arms around me. Not a bad night. The main thing now was to do nothing, to spend the day at home in bed, drinking water and possibly vomiting.

The phone screamed from the corner. I picked it up and Tursun's voice punched into my ear.

'Hello, Nick! What are you doing?'

'Not much,' I said weakly.

'Good! I have some free time. Let's go to my brother's orchard.'

I pictured a slow afternoon under the boughs, the light dappled all around as I sat eating fruit and losing badly at chess. I thought I could bear it. But just to be on the safe side I asked,

'Will I have to do anything?'

'No, don't worry, it will be fine. You're not sick are you?'

'Not really. But sort of.'

'I don't understand.'

Tursun was leaning on the gate when I arrived, talking to the tallest Uighur man I'd ever seen. This was his other brother Mehmet. He wore a green diamond-check pullover and blue jogging trousers. Life, or all that reaching upwards, seemed to have stretched him. We shook hands, then two of his friends appeared, and there was more handshaking. Then Hamit appeared on an antique bicycle; the shaking resumed. Finally we entered the long lines of the orchard. Apricots glowed from the branches, which spread a latticed shade on the ground. I slumped gratefully against a trunk.

Mehmet and his friends didn't own the orchard. Instead they had a five-year lease on it, for which they paid the astonishingly low figure of 300 yuan each year. They sold most of the produce to fruit sellers, and sometimes had enough to send to Urumqi. That year the high winds had made for a low harvest, bringing a lot of fruit down before it was properly ripe. Mehmet didn't use any pesticides which meant that the apricots were not exactly supermarket material: their skins were scabbed by brown encrustations, with not one smooth or perfect globe among them. But they had a gum-aching sweetness and were so juicy that the first bite was enough to flood one's chin. We sat and munched until our teeth hurt. Then Tursun brought the chess set out – the one I coveted – and set about giving a painful lesson in the guise of a game. I had definitely improved and could now drag out a game for up to an hour, chiefly by defending tediously, all the while hoping for a silly mistake that I knew would not come. It took Tursun a little longer, which led to more in-game commentary ('Yes, this pawn is a problem, so I must eat it. Can you stop me? No. You cannot') but he still won in the end.

The sun began to set. Mehmet and his friends slipped out. They had been gone for ten minutes before I realised they had gone to pray. Tursun alone remained.

'What about you?'

'Now, I do not.'

'What about Fridays?'

'Maybe a little. Sometimes. Now I must be careful. If I start going, people may say things. I must wait if I want to have my passport.'

Hamit came back first. I asked him why some people took longer than others to pray.

'Maybe they are in a hurry. Maybe they have things to do. A man who fears God more will take longer, he will pray more carefully.'

'What about you?'

'I don't pray fast or slow. Just normally.'

And then the inevitable, and quite justified question.

'And you? Do you believe?'

'No.'

'Why not?'

'Well, why do you believe?'

'Because God created everything. All people.'

'Yes, but why do you believe this?'

He looked baffled. I was questioning a manifest truth, something self-evident.

'Because it is written in the Qur'an. It has many facts.'

'Such as?'

'Mohammed said that mountains have roots. For a long time, no one believed this. Now science has found this is true.'

Tursun chipped in unexpectedly.

'Yes, and not just mountains. All people. Their root is God.'

Tursun and Hamit walked me back into town. On the way we heard that China was losing 4–0 to Brazil, which gave them a chance to practice their irony, a topic we had just covered in class.

'I've never felt more patriotic!'

'A big pity!'

'I'm so sad I may fall down!'

'Really a big shame!'

113

THE ORPHANAGE LAY on the road to the river, an imposing building set well back. Its upper storeys had a Russian feel; its lower ones were more like a car park. Edipim stood by the gate, talking to a man with the unmistakable languor of a caretaker. She looked upset.

'Hi Edipim, what's the matter?'

'Oh Nick, today has been a terrible day. Two girls ran away last night. Noterhajim has spent the whole day looking for them.'

'Did he find them?'

'Yes, thank God for that.'

'Why did they run away?'

'They missed their mothers too much.'

'Their mothers? I thought this was an orphanage, you know a place for children with no parents.'

'Many of the children have parents who cannot take care of them. Maybe they use the drugs or drink too much or are in prison.'

'What will happen to those two girls?'

'Noterhajim says that if they do that again he will make them leave. But you should have seen these girls. One had not seen her mother for two years. She cried and cried and I had to hold her until she stopped.'

Noterhajim stood on the steps outside. His stomach bulged over his belt. A slab of moustache obscured his upper lip. He looked like a man used to getting his own way. I thought there was a certain resemblance to Sadur but when I pointed this out to Edipim she just laughed and said 'Oh no, Noterhajim is much fatter!' He shook my hand and welcomed me, then launched into what sounded like a furious criticism of Edipim. His fist shook, his finger pointed. But then he laughed and laid a paternal hand on her shoulder.

Noterhajim was responsible for both the funding and management of the foster home. Though originally from Yining, he had spent many years away doing business, mostly in Kashgar. He had been started the place in response to the growing number of Uighur children living on the streets, most notably the ubiquitous shoeshine kids. There were currently about 200 children in the foster home. In addition to caring for their basic needs, the home also tried to provide the children with sufficient education for them to find jobs when they left at 16. This aspect of the home was something that the local authorities took an interest in. The home had to conform to the same basic regulations as any other school, particularly in respect to the content of classes. There could be 'nothing religious or harmful to social and ethnic unity'.

Unfortunately, the authorities' concern did not extend to funding. The teachers were paid so little they were virtually volunteers. A quick glance at the staff pictures in the entrance hall confirmed that they were all Uighur.

A bell signalled the end of class. The corridor flooded with children, all of whom were Uighur. I asked Edipim if there were any Kazakh or Hui children in the home. She shook her head. I asked if one would be allowed and she said probably not.

'He would be the only one and might find it difficult.'

'That might be true at the beginning but that's no reason not to try.'

'Maybe they don't need it. How many Hui or Kazakh boys have you seen shining shoes?'

She had a point. The tide of children broke against us, shouting and excited. Some of this enthusiasm was probably due to seeing a foreigner, but the main reason for their excitement was immediately apparent. They swarmed around Edipim, shouting hellos, soliciting hugs and kisses. Those unable to get near enough to her made do with the small consolation of staring at me. After a few minutes the bell rang again for class. Most took no notice until Noterhajim came and roared at them; then they scattered to their classrooms.

We went into Edipim's classroom. The children clapped and shouted more and less intelligible versions of 'Hello, how are you?' A boy at the front stood up and said in English 'Hello, my name is Josef. What's your name? What is your job?' I told him then shook his hand. The class applauded wildly.

'Have you been teaching them English?'

'Yes, two times every week. Many of them like it.'

It was ironic that of all the Uighur children in Yining, it should be these kids, the most underprivileged, who got the chance to learn English. Some of them were quite good. Another boy asked where I was from.

'England. And you? Where are you from?'

'East Turkestan' he said and grinned.

The class cheered and Edipim had to pretend to be cross. She managed to stop the class degenerating into a separatist rally by proposing that we sing some songs. The motion was passed; the singing began.

'This is a duck, that is a goose, yes I know, yes I know, this is a duck, that is a goose.'

We followed this with *Happy Birthday*, *We Wish You a Merry Xmas* and my own personal favourite, *Head, Shoulders, Knees and Toes*. Then Edipim asked the children if they had any questions for me. They asked if I liked Ghulja, if I could speak any Uighur, if I liked *polo*, whether I knew David Beckham. They looked crushed when I replied that I didn't, so I hastily added that I did like football. The children immediately begin asking Edipim something in Uighur. She turned to me and said they wanted to play football. As soon as I agreed the class ran out, heading in the opposite direction from the pitch. They returned laden with pots and buckets of water, the need for which became apparent once we reached the pitch. My foot sank into an inch of dust. The children spent the next ten minutes trying to damp the dust down to a non-lethal level. While we were waiting I put it to Edipim that she was an obscenely good person. She blushed and said she hadn't always been. I imagined, or hoped for, news of some scandalous indiscretion but all I got was a story about her throwing a stone at a Chinese woman when she was 12. The woman was cycling past with a basket of eggs. The stone struck the women in the head; she fell off, as did the eggs. Edipim's mother slapped her and made her apologise.

A collective whistle signalled that the pitch was ready, or as close it could be. Play began. Some of the kids were awesomely good for 11 or 12, whereas I was crap for any age.

My lungs gave out after half an hour. I coughed up dust, then sat down to rest. Edipim looked shocked.

'Nick! Look at your trousers!'

'What?'

'They're so dirty!'

'That's OK. I can wash them.'

'You're not a Ghulja boy.'

'That's true.'

'No, I mean the Ghulja boys are very clean. I don't think there is a boy in Ghulja who doesn't have a comb in his pocket.'

It was true that most young Uighur men were well turned out, even if they did dress like their fathers— the same thick jackets and patterned sweaters, the same absence of T-shirts or trainers. Whether they had chosen to dress like this or were simply stuck with their fathers' cast-offs was yet another unknown.

114

ON THOSE WARM, summer mornings, when one breathed in deep, there was the smell of manure. Every inch of college soil was covered in it. A group of officials from the education bureau was coming to inspect the college, and the leaders had demanded there be grass to welcome them. These lush lawns would undoubtedly convince them that Yili Teachers' College was fulfilling its pedagogical mandate (and certainly was not an institution characterised by corruption and inequality). But I didn't really care. I was leaving in a week. There were just a few things I had to take care of, one of which was Colin.

A little chat about his missionary activities was overdue. I didn't imagine that I would be able to have the same kind of frank exchange as I had had with Gabe (who had long since departed), because we certainly weren't friends. I had built up so much resentment against him for what he had been doing that I wrote a letter to him just so I could vent.

> I know what you are up to, and to pretend that you are not engaged in missionary activities is an insult to my intelligence and a sure sign of your inflated sense of your own abilities. What is it object to? The Christian faith? Not *per se*. It's more the arrogance of coming into another culture, one with its own existing traditions, imagining that you have so much to teach instead of learn, and furthermore, the deceit, getting people when they're down, giving them false hope, taking spiritual advantage of them.

Having gone through the 'charges' against him, I settled some scores.

> Don't imagine for one moment that I believe a single word you say about anything. You have already demonstrated a willingness to

deceive and lie when your fragile sense of worth is threatened. When you tried to arrange the class when I was at the wedding; when you said you had never seen those books before, when you claimed to be good friends with the police: all of these are symptomatic of your inability to accept that many people simply do not like you and that many of us are more capable/likeable/secure than you.

For the last few months I had been avoiding him, at least as much as was possible, given that we taught in the same department and lived in neighbouring blocks. One reason I hadn't said anything to him before was that I didn't think he had managed to influence the students much. The only student who showed any sympathy for Christian ideas was a hapless boy who also thought that the Nazis weren't so bad except for the killing. But I didn't want to leave without making it clear to him that I knew what he was doing. I didn't expect him to stop, but I did vainly hope that it might introduce some reasonable doubt.

My opportunity came when he dropped round some letters he wanted me to post when I got back to England. I was nervous and unsure of how to begin, despite the fact that I had been rehearsing this conversation for weeks. But it was then or never so I stumbled something out.

'Colin, you should know what some people outside the college are saying about the foreigners here, some people in other hospitals are saying that we are all engaged in missionary work.'

He seized my words.

'Other hospitals? What do you mean?'

'Um, well, in one hospital. But with people saying such things, I think we all need to be careful not to do or say things that might be misinterpreted.'

'I don't think there is a problem. No one here is doing anything they shouldn't be. Who do you have in mind?'

'Are you trying to tell me that those four young Americans aren't here for missionary purposes?'

'No, they're just here to learn the language. And they're only here for a short time. Brad's parents are only helping him stay for a year.'

'Well, whether or not some are people doing missionary work, there is a *perception* that people are. And even if there is no evangelising going on, it doesn't hurt to be careful. And that's why I wanted to talk to you.'

He shot me a wary look.

'Because I was looking in class '99's diaries and I found that some of them had written about going to see a film about Jesus at your house. They also wrote that you told them some things about this too.'

Multiple emotions ghosted across his face, and to my surprise, I saw fear. It was the first time I had seen him falter, and though a part of me enjoyed this, it also gave me pause. He and his family had been living in Yining for almost four years. It was their home in a way it would never be for me. It was where his children went to school, where they had many friends. I had never properly considered that he might have something to lose.

Perhaps this was why I said,

'Now, I know that of course it was probably entirely innocent. But someone else could misinterpret that, don't you think?'

'Who wrote that?'

'A couple of students.'

'What are their names?'

'I forget.'

'Well, we often have students coming round to our house. I can't remember every time they do. But the last time some students from that class came round they just watched cartoons.'

'So you're saying they were mistaken?'

'That's right.'

And I probably would have left it there. Of course he wasn't going to admit to anything. It had been stupid to expect otherwise. We weren't friends in the way that Gabe and I had been; only rarely do people confess when confronted.

I had no other cards to play, and was sure that he would change the subject. Instead he leaned back, then said calmly:

'The police aren't worried about religion. They're only worried about political trouble.'

'What makes you say that?'

'The college had a sports meeting a month ago. One of the athletes had been in prison for a year for being in an underground church. But people were still clapping and cheering him when he won.'

'Yes, but it wasn't the police doing the clapping. And they *did* put him in prison. I'd say that suggests the police *are* concerned.'

'No, one of the people there was a policeman. But the real problem here is rumours. They spread so quickly, and things get easily twisted.'

I nodded cautiously. He went on.

'And rumours can be very dangerous. They can come back on people. When we were in Lanzhou, there was a young teacher there who claimed that another teacher was trying to convert his students. The police heard about this and came to investigate. In the end they found that the teacher who had made the accusation had been saying things to his students about how China wasn't truly socialist and that the problem was the government. In the end, it was him who got arrested and deported.'

Was this some kind of threat? I tried to recall if I had ever said such things. I couldn't be sure. I looked at him. He looked at me. Then he remembered that he had to pick his daughter up from school. He thanked me for agreeing to post the letters then left. That was the last time I saw him.

Later that night I sat on my balcony, watching the storm slowly roll towards the city. The clouds flickered pink with summer lightning. Several hours of seething looked to find expression.

I found catharsis in a match. The first book I burnt was called *A Swedish Gospel Singer*. On its cover there was a drawing of a blonde girl wearing a crucifix with her mouth open and musical notes floating out. Inside was a story, written in simple English, about a

Swedish girl who loved to sing. One day, whilst passing a church, she heard a wonderful sound that moved her in a way she'd never known before. When she went in the congregation welcomed her and asked her to join their Gospel choir. It was through these songs she learnt about Jesus, his compassion, his sacrifice, the love he felt for all.

I began by placing the book in a tin bucket, to which I added newspaper. Then I took the bucket out onto my fourth floor balcony. It was not quite dark, so I waited and looked into the other apartments where people were cooking or watching television. Once it was dark, if they happened to look in my direction, they would not see the smoke, only the light from the flames. I did not think this would bother them; it probably would not seem as if my flat was on fire. I turned my gaze to the snow-topped mountains that formed the north wall of the valley. Their peaks faded from white to grey, to a blue that throbbed in the dusk. As soon as it was dark I bent to the bucket and struck a match. The flame was reluctant to lick at the cover, so I struck another match and held it till the cover caught. It took almost a minute before the fire ate through to the pages. I had yet to learn that a book burns better without its cover, and better still if its pages are torn.

After this I burnt *Heroes of the Faith*, *The Greatest Miracle in the World*, then *Our Lord, Our Lamb*. Over the course of that night I burnt 70 books. I enjoyed watching the flames. I had had the books in my flat for a long time, without knowing how to get rid of them. I had thought about simply throwing them away, but was certain that someone would see me. In the end I decided that burning the books was the only way to be sure. That there would be more books; that at best it was no more than a comma in the path of their efforts, these things did not matter. All that mattered was that I had been able to destroy something of theirs.

It was definitely time to leave.

115

NEXT MORNING I showered the smoke from my hair. I dressed and ate breakfast. Then I went and did my best to grass Colin and the others up.

Previously this had consisted of just telling random people. I hadn't wanted to speak to anyone official for fear that they might delve into the company I kept, or the non-official class I taught. Now that I was leaving, there was nothing to stop me. In hindsight, this seems reckless, but at the time I was too angry to think clearly.

Miss Cai was the place to start. She was the gatekeeper for all the college officials and probably knew a lot of people in the police and local government. I doubted that she would be pleased to find so many foreigners doing something expressly forbidden. She might lose face if it was known that foreigners under her supervision had engaged in such illegal activities, but it would probably be worse if this information came to the police from someone other than her. Despite our disagreements, I didn't want anything bad to happen to her.

When I entered her office she was sat at her desk, sharpening a pencil. We swapped pleasantries, then I got to the point.

'Miss Cai, there's something I've been wanting to ask you for a long time. I haven't been able to before but now that I'm leaving I suppose I can.'

She smiled sweetly and for one insane second I imagined her thinking I was about to propose to her.

'I remember when I first arrived we had a conversation about some of the special rules in Yining. Especially about religion. I assume you've given the same talk to all the other foreigners?'

'Yes, all of them. These are important rules.'

'Yes, well, maybe they didn't understand you properly.'

'What do you mean?'

'I mean that most of them are doing missionary work. They are trying to convert people, not just students but also people outside the college.'

'Yes, we know this.'

'You know?'

'Yes, the police and the leaders here have had meetings about it.'

'But if you know, and it is illegal, why don't you stop them?'

'Although we know, we cannot prove it. They are very careful. We do not have proof. Maybe if we had proof we could do something.'

'What kind of proof?' I asked, already in dread of the answer.

'If they gave information about religion to someone in order to make them believe. Maybe if they gave a person a book. That would be proof.'

A book. Oh yes. I knew where there were some of those.

'Um, right, well. I just wanted to make sure you knew.'

'Thank you for telling us. How's your packing going?'

'Fine. No problem.'

116

MURAT WAS UPSET to hear of my imminent departure.

'So you are leaving? I think this is a mistake.'

'In what way?'

'You have stayed for one year. Maybe now you are used to living here. So it is too soon for you to go. Perhaps if you stayed longer you would meet a nice girl and get married. That would be good for you.'

'Yes I'm sure it would. But what about you? What are your plans?'

'Have I not told you the good news? Allah has chosen to give me another child. The doctor says it may be twins.'

'That's great. Congratulations.'

'And I will also continue my teaching. This is very important. Now that China has entered the World Trade Organisation there is a good chance of it breaking up. Because there will be many problems.'

'Well, it's possible I suppose.'

'It will happen. And then Uighurs will need English to do business and negotiate with America and England.'

'Yes, they will.'

'If you stayed, you could help us more. But I know you have not seen your family for a long time. I know you miss them. Maybe you should go.'

'Thanks, Murat.'

'You're welcome.'

Just before we parted it occurred to me that I would probably see him at Kuresh's wedding. But when I asked if he was going, he said he would not.

'Didn't he invite you?'

'He did but I will not go.'

'Why not?'

'Because there will be dancing. Boys and girls who are not married will dance together. This is wrong and forbidden. Good Muslims will not do this.'

'Don't you ever dance?'

'I only dance with my wife and only at home. And it is not only me who will not go. Erkin, Ismail and Yusuf will also not go either.'

And so we said our goodbyes. Although we promised to write, neither of us did.

117

THE DAYS WERE long and heat hazy. The fields were full to bursting. Fans worked the air in split shifts. We would have paid for rain.

Tursun and I ambled beneath the trees. Earlier he had phoned to say he had a surprise for me, and it was this we were heading towards. We were in the small streets of a Uighur neighbourhood just off the square. A stream of snowmelt ran cold to our left. We walked and talked, our words tempered by the awkwardness of knowing that a farewell approached. We passed children with ice cubes in their mouths. They spat them into their hands, waited for their tongues to warm up, then replaced the cubes.

A crowd was gathered at the next crossroads in a shouting circle. Tursun shouted, 'It's a fight, come on!' And it was, sort of. But it was neither cocks nor people fighting. At the centre of the conflict was an angry bull that had escaped. One man was waving his jacket in front of it, matador style. Another man was gingerly trying out an impromptu lasso. The bull took no notice of either. It lurched towards the spectators; they scattered and regrouped five feet further back. Someone probably would have been gored had the bull not taken sudden exception to a bicycle stand. They toppled in a long line and when some of their bells rang it only angered the bull further. The beast started trampling them, which led to its hooves getting tangled in the spokes. This gave the man with the rope a chance to finally get it round its legs.

'Did you see that?' shouted Tursun excitedly. 'It was like that film, *The Gladiator*.'

'Did you like it?'

'Very much. It was wonderful. He stood up to authority, he did not give in. He was like *Braveheart*. He was also very great.'

'Like Sadur?'

'Sadur! Sadur is a children's story. And there is no Sadur today.'

'Does that mean that there is no hope?'

'Oh no, one day the Chinese will go away. But we won't need to fight them. They will be destroyed by their own corruption.'

We were now lost (well, I was) within the twisting streets. A dog stuck its head out of a doorway, prepared to bark, then thought better of it. Tursun stopped and knocked at a green metal door. After several moments he knocked again. This time a muffled shout came from within. He grinned at me.

'He was probably sleeping.'

'Who?'

'Don't you know?'

He pushed the door and entered. I followed him into a cluttered yard. Pots of paint and varnish sat clotting in corners; wood shavings covered the ground like a perm; black hinged boxes hung from washing lines, their paint still sticky-looking.

An old man in a red *doppa* shuffled from the shadows. He greeted us warmly. then said something to Tursun, who after thanking him, turned to me and said,

'Your board is ready now. Would you like to see it?'

'My board?'

'Your chessboard. And the pieces too.'

The old man disappeared then returned with two parcels wrapped in white cloth. He laid them on an old tree stump and opened the larger of the two. The board was massive and my first thought was to wonder how I would get it home (in the end I had to send it). But then I was lost in its checks, their jet black and creamy white beneath the shining varnish. It was a new version of Tursun's board, perhaps the way it had looked 20 years before. Then there were the pieces. The second bundle opened to reveal an elegant huddle. The bishops were pointed spires, the pawns broad and squat. The wood had been stained lightly enough for the grain to remain visible, thin lines packed close as isobars. They were made from poplar. Every time I play with them, I think of those long streets where the trees seemed to converge. How the silver of their trunks was bright against the blue.

Tursun spoke to the old man for a few minutes, then translated for me.

'He said that to carve all the pieces only takes half a day, but the knight' – his hand traced a horse's head in the air – 'takes almost a day by itself.' He paused then continued. 'Now, let us play the first game on this board. It will be our last game but maybe when you play on this board you will remember our friendship.'

We set up the board; I was white. Pawn to king's four. I tried to do all the things that Tursun had taught me. I anchored my rooks in the centre of the board; I kept my bishops on the long diagonals; I poked holes in his pawn structure. And after almost an hour, Tursun stuck out his hand to offer me the coveted prize of a draw. He probably could have beaten me, but it was a nicer way to part.

The only thing that remained was for us to say goodbye. We joked our way through it. He said he see me in London; I said he could come to my wedding. But just before we parted he grew serious.

'If people ask about us when you go home, tell them that we're not terrorists. We just hate the government. The Chinese are not so bad. But sometimes we forget the difference. That's all.'

118

OUR PREPARATIONS were complete. Kuresh had bought two cows. My books were boxed and waiting. The invitations had been sent. My bags sat packed and ready. The restaurant and band were booked. All that remained was for him to get married and for me to leave.

My last sunset was an orange blaze that built till it was gold. The light segued to saffron yellow then navy. The pavement outside the Grand Pavilion restaurant began to fill with people.

Half an hour later there was still no sign of the wedding party. One man declared he had had enough of waiting. He started up the stairs into the restaurant then stopped when he realised no one else was following. He rejoined his wife who curled her lip but said nothing.

A line of Volkswagen Passats glided into view, their windscreens almost obscured with plastic carnations and ribbon. It was like the motorcade of some minor king. Kuresh and his wife stepped out of the first car, she in a dress of layered blue veils, he in a green *doppa*, black trousers, and camel-coloured jacket. Cameras flashed, a cheer rose, the royal couple entered.

Inside the restaurant circular tables were arranged around the walls. The guests began to fill their circumferences. I was looking around for a familiar face to sit next to when Kuresh called out to me.

'Hey boy! Come over here, this is your place.'

He insisted I sit next to him, a place that should have been the best man's. I tried shifting a few seats along but he was having none of it.

'You are one of my good friends and you are leaving tomorrow. We will not see each other for a long time. We should spend this time together. Anyway, this is my wedding so you must do what I tell you! Yes?'

'Yes.'

Waitresses began to circulate, first bringing tea then small plates of cold vegetables. There was no sign of alcohol, which although I didn't really expect, I still vainly hoped for. I made a poor attempt at a joking inquiry.

'In the past we used to drink a lot at weddings. But there were too many fights. And since the trouble, people are more strict. I will not. But I want my friends to enjoy themselves.'

He lifted the tablecloth and pointed. Three red boxes sat underneath one of the chairs, each containing a bottle of *baijiu*. It was going to be a blurry night.

Hot dishes began to arrive, steaming dishes of lamb and potatoes. There was a whistle followed by a thump from a microphone. A small spotlight lit up a man with the worst mullet I had ever seen, a curled crest at the front, a permed waterfall behind. He called for our attention, then launched into a deafening speech that the speakers distorted. The bride was presented with several armfuls of flowers; the mullet shouted the names of those who had bought bouquets.

An accordion wheezed into action, followed by a keyboard. The spotlight swung over to Kuresh and his bride. They got up and moved to the centre of the dance floor. A red sash was tied around their waists, forcing them to dance close to one another. They began to dance, slow and dignified, their eyes fixed on each other. Even when a bright stream of liquid string was squirted at their faces, their expressions of devotion did not falter.

The music continued till the cans of string were empty. Then the bride and groom returned to their seats, dripping blue and green. There was applause, the flash of cameras, then the music resumed at a much faster tempo. Gentlemen offered their hands to ladies. The dancers were all given handkerchiefs, white for men, red for women. Then they began a courtly Morris dance, stepping to and from each other, waltzing, turning, twirling. It was hard to see what Murat and all the other 'good Muslims' found so objectionable about this. It was as chaste as a church disco.

Furtive glances were exchanged; then the bottle was opened. We filled our glasses under the table, then drank a discreet toast to Muhammad. Then we drank another. The *baijiu* burned its way to my gut. I fervently hoped that this would be the last time I would ever drink it. The mullet began booming again. People clapped and looked in my direction. I smiled and asked Kuresh what he had said.

'He said we should all welcome our Russian friend.'

'That's nice.'

'And he said you will show us all a special Russian dance.'

I was halfway through refusing when the spotlight swung on me. I was caught in the headlights with nowhere to run. Three hundred pairs of eyes watched me walk to the centre of the floor; if the bottle of *baijiu* had been to hand I would have downed it, then used it to fight my way out. Music burst forth, Russian and impossibly fast, a *Sabre Dance* played in the key of amphetamine. The hands connected to the eyes began to clap in time. I attempted to borrow their sense of rhythm. I placed one hand on my heart and out-stretched the other. I threw my head back. Then I started to stride around, my extended hand twirling like a propeller. The clapping faltered. I stuck both hands out and tried to whirl. A few people came onto the dance floor and tried to copy what I was doing; I pitied them. I prayed for the music to end, which after an eternity, it did. One apoplectic climax and I was free. I bowed and acknowledged the probably ironic applause. More competent dancers took the floor whilst I headed for the drink that I deserved.

But my intoxication would have to wait. When I got back to the table, someone was in my seat: Erkin, the good Muslim who certainly wouldn't attend such an immoral gathering of dancing, was shaking Muhammad's hand and congratulating him. I went over and said hello. I asked if he had come alone.

'Yes, Murat and the others would not come. But Kuresh is a good man and I have known him a long time. But...'

He gestured at the dancers gliding by.

'Look at them! They are all madmen! Mad!'

They swept on regardless. Erkin composed himself.

'I heard there was a Russian dancer here. Did you see him?'

'Yes. He left.'

Erkin stayed another ten minutes. As soon as he had gone, we brought the *baijiu* back out. Quickly, things began to blur. Features slipped from faces. I stuck the eyes and noses back but upon the wrong people. Seated round the table now were Edipim, Ismail, Hamit, Erkin, Madina, Yusuf, Tursun, and, of course, Kuresh. I sat and drunkenly reflected that they were, if such things can still be said, profoundly good people. When I told them this they smiled. They wished me a good journey.

119

DAY HAULS ITSELF over the mountains. The sun's first rays sweep through the valley, over the fields and flocks. They pause at the river, check their reflection, then continue on. They reach orchards, the orphanage, fruit and children wake. The light gets caught in the main square, where every inch of chrome and tile fills itself to excess. A white glare builds to melting point; the light rushes on. Down the street of Ahmetjan, down Liberation Road. The rays turn right into the college, stop to ask directions, then hurl themselves through your window. You wake and protest; your bus isn't until the afternoon. The alcohol adds its voice but to no avail. You have to get up.

The curtains part onto a wall of saw-toothed mountains. Old men are hanging caged birds in the trees below. The peddlers' cries bounce off the walls. Go now, walk the streets.

Rooks are massing somewhere near, cawing anxiously. The endless details of the streets impress themselves on you: an alley full of shoes; the sight of loaves being exhumed. Stalls of dried reptiles and roots. Children throwing stones at a green bottle. A woman is trying to sell a cow's head; an old man has a jar of snakes. There is the gleam and jingle of horse bells, steam from a vat of *polo* and always, always, that blue weight pressing down.

And when you think of Yining now, it is not the injustice or hate or general sense of division that comes to you first. It is these sights that recur, these and other marvels.

You return home, gather your bags, bid goodbye to the dust of your flat. You insert yourself into the bus, which for once leaves on time. The fields blur by in brown and green divisions till the land starts to rise. As you creep up the valley you slip into sleep. And when you wake, in the warmth of the dark, you are far away.

Afterword

FOR ALL THAT we know of change – that it is both unpredictable and inevitable – there is often a need to deny it. This is particularly true of change that occurs in our absence. In the years that followed my departure from Yining, the place and the people I knew there remained static in my mind. Perhaps this is a consequence of writing an account: the process of organising memories fixes things in amber. They are preserved, but at the cost of life, the messy flux of it. Although I received the occasional email, or, quite remarkably, phone call – one from Kuresh on Christmas Day morning, when I was too groggy with sleep to speak of anything of substance – most of this news was about people getting new jobs, going to university, or having marital problems. It updated my view of the person in question, but told me little about the broader picture. When I did ask more pointed questions – about religion, the missionaries, the atmosphere in town – they were seldom responded to. This was no doubt because these were sensitive topics; people (with good reason) were wary of their communications being monitored (the other reason is that whilst a blunt question is hard to ignore in person, it is easy to do so by email).

The little that I managed to glean – through the odd remark, and via the news (on which Xinjiang very rarely appeared, except in connection with Guantanamo Bay, where several Uighurs were imprisoned), suggested that the Chinese government had not altered its policies regarding religious and cultural expression. In 2005, Nurmemet Yasin, a writer, was sentenced to ten years' imprisonment for publishing a story allegedly 'inciting separatism'. His story told of a blue pigeon that travelled far from home. When it returned, different coloured pigeons captured him and locked him in a birdcage. Although the other pigeons fed him, the blue pigeon opted to commit suicide rather than remain imprisoned in his hometown. Because many pro-independence Uighur groups use a blue flag, Chinese authorities read the story as referring to Uighur resentment of the government's policies in Xinjiang. The court tried Yasin in closed hearings; some sources claimed he was denied access to a lawyer.

Despite the maintenance of this awful status quo, there were few reported incidents of protest, violent or otherwise, during the next few years (which is perhaps in itself not especially revealing, as it could be interpreted as a sign that Uighur dissatisfaction lessened, or that the security clampdown which followed the 9/11 attacks discouraged further expressions of dissent).

The first reports of major conflict appeared in January 2007, when the Chinese Public Security Bureau claimed to have raided a suspected terrorist training camp in the mountains near the Pamir Plateau in southern Xinjiang. According to official sources, 18 individuals, whom Chinese State media referred to as 'terrorists', were killed and another 17 captured (however, Rafael Poch, a Spanish journalist, after investigating the incident, found no evidence that there had been such a camp).

In the run-up to the 2008 Olympics, the government began publicising its efforts to ensure security. The police claimed to have raided an apartment in Urumqi and shot dead five men who they said were planning a 'holy war' against the Han. They also reported blocking an attack by three airline passengers who were planning to crash a Beijing-bound plane.

However, as in the raid on the camp in the Pamirs, there was no external confirmation of these incidents, and no group claimed responsibility. The World Uighur Congress claimed that these incidents were being used to give the government an excuse to crackdown on Uighurs.

There is at least some evidence for the attacks that were said have taken place just before, then during the Olympics. The first took place in Kashgar, when 16 Chinese police officers were killed after two men rammed a truck into a group of police officers jogging near their barracks, then threw explosives at the police station. Although no one claimed responsibility for the attack, officials said the ETIM was responsible. However, it was also suggested that the attackers had a particular grievance with the police (something that could well apply to many similar incidents), and were not part of any organised group.

The next incident occurred on 4 August, two days after the start of the 2008 Olympics, when homemade explosives were thrown at a dozen government sites in Kuqa city in southern Xinjiang. A group of assailants attacked a police station, as well as government offices, supermarkets and hotels. One security guard died and ten assailants were killed in the unrest, with police chasing down and firing at some of the attackers. Again, no one claimed responsibility for the attack, and this time the Chinese government said they did *not* believe the ETIM were responsible.

The violence in Urumqi in July 2009 was the largest incident since the protests in Yining in 1997. However, it differed from both this incident, and also the attacks in Kashgar and Kuqa in 2008, in one crucial manner. Whilst these incidents were directed at government officials or the police, much of the violence in Urumqi appears to have been racially motivated, i.e. directed against the Han, who had by far the most casualties. Unsurprisingly, this was disputed by the World Uighur Congress, who claimed that the Uighur death toll had been considerably higher, but had been deliberately underreported by the government so as to make Uighurs appear the aggressors.

(Another possibility, which no one seemed to consider, was that the figures were accurate, but reflected demographics rather than ethnic targeting. Urumqi is about 75 per cent Han, and 15 per cent Uighur (the rest are Hui, Kazakh and Kyrgyz) Given that most of the violence appears to have been in central, mostly Han areas, it would have been surprising if the Han had not been the major victims)

But whether or not the violence was racially motivated, this is how it was perceived. On 7 July 2009 a crowd of Han Chinese armed with iron bars, meat cleavers and shovels attacked Uighur neighbourhoods in Urumqi. One man, clutching a metal bar, told the

AFP news agency: 'The Uighurs came to our area to smash things, now we are going to their area to beat them.'

Police eventually dispersed the mob with tear gas, after there had been considerable property damage. During the following weeks, Han and Uighur neighbourhoods were regularly patrolled by troops; some estimated that 20,000 soldiers had been brought into the city. Unsurprisingly, many Uighurs left the city, fearing further reprisals.

Although the government stressed that life had returned to normal, relations between Han or Uighurs remained strained. In mid-August there were reports that people in Urumqi had been attacked with hypodermic syringes. Although there were no casualties, and no one seemed to have been injected with any dangerous substance, these 'needle attacks' caused such hysteria that many falsely reported injuries, which increased public fears. As the stabbings continued, Han residents began to claim they were being targeted. On 3 September, large groups of Han Chinese assembled at junctions throughout the city, calling on the government to protect them. The police maintained order, but the crowds returned the next day. The police then used tear gas to disperse the crowds, which led to five deaths and fourteen people injured. The authorities announced that they had charged four suspects, all Uighur, three of whom were said to be drug users. Officials warned that anyone convicted of further needle attacks could receive the death penalty. However, it remained unclear who was responsible for these attacks, or what their motivation was.

When I returned to Urumqi in April 2010, it was partly in hope of finding answers, not just to this question, but to several other mysteries about the events of July 2009. There was still no satisfactory account of how the initially peaceful protest of 5 July turned into a night of murder. Nor was it clear why, on 7 July, the thousands of police and soldiers who had been brought into the city had not stopped the Han mob earlier.

I hoped that some of my old contacts might be able to shed light on these questions. But it proved hard to find people after so long, not least because internet access was blocked. For a week I roamed the streets of Urumqi, watching and photographing police and soldiers behind parked cars. I struck up conversations in shops and restaurants, hoping that talk about kebabs or the weather would shift to more dangerous ground.

I had pretty much given up on the afternoon that I went to Kentucky Fried Chicken. I was half way through a bucket of wings when a voice said, in English, 'Do you like chicken?'

I looked up and saw a Uighur man, tall and in his early 20s. A cold sore shone above his lip, which had a faint cloud of moustache.

'Not much,' I said. 'What about you?'

'Chicken is good' he said, then introduced himself as Alim. He asked where I was from. When I wiped my mouth and told him, he nodded his approval. Then he asked what I did for a living. I told him I was a journalist who sometimes wrote about China. Usually this made people withdraw, but Alim only smiled.

'That is very good' he said. 'Do you have free time?' Oddly, my first instinct was to say no. It was not that he frightened me – he could not have been less threatening – more that I was taken aback by his eagerness. After all, we had been talking for less than a minute. But I had hardly spoken to anyone in the past week, other than shopkeepers, taxi drivers and hotel staff, so I said yes, I had time.

'Now I have to pray,' he said. 'Then I must do something for my uncle. So–' He paused to look at his phone. 'At four o'clock, I will meet you on Erdaoqiao. By the camel.'

He could also have said 'by the eagle'; tourists take pictures with both in a small square opposite the new Grand Bazaar. In 2002, the Bazaar had been a sprawling, chaotic maze of stalls that sold leather goods, knives, carpets and pomegranate juice; now it was a series of strip-lit cubicles inside a faux-Islamic building.

'I will go first' said Alim and left. For the next hour and a half I wandered through alleys where Uighurs were selling shoes, fabric, and sheep's heads, or welding large sheets of steel. Men with twisted limbs asked for money. An old woman sold plastic combs on a tray hung round her neck.

By a quarter to four, I was standing next to the camel (it was the eagle's day off). I counted police and soldiers, then police cars (six) and riot vans (three). By day these drove around the Uighur neighbourhoods; at night they patrolled the streets outside Xinjiang University, where most of the student protesters had come from.

When Alim arrived he walked past me and muttered, 'Let's go'. I followed him down a small street where two young Uighur girls were selling plastic belts. We passed a mosque covered in grubby white tiles, in front of which a man was fixing a puncture. Alim turned down an alley lined with broken televisions, which narrowed and then swung right. He stopped at a door and knocked. There was no answer, so he knocked again. 'Please wait a minute,' he said, then brought his tongue to his sore.

The door opened onto darkness. 'Please come in,' said Alim. I hesitated, and then entered.

Inside a light was switched on, showing the space to be a large storeroom full of carpets and rugs. We took off our shoes before going into a second, smaller carpeted room, whose walls were bare except for a large photo of Mecca. Alim was wearing orange and white striped socks that made me think of clown fish.

We sat down on blue cushions spread around a low table piled with nuts, dried fruit, sweets and hunks of nan bread. A middle-aged woman, hair wrapped in a pink scarf, came in with a teapot and bowls. 'My aunt,' said Alim as she poured the tea, after which she left. I had experienced such hospitality in hundreds of Uighur homes before, and it was perhaps the familiarity of the situation that kept me from wondering why he had brought me there in such secrecy. But then he reached over to a small black briefcase. He opened it and brought out a laptop, which he placed on the table.

'First you should see this.'

On screen I watched a blur of movement. A crowd of people were running and shouting, at night, between apartment buildings. The camerawork was shaky, for the person holding it was running as well. I heard excited shouts, then a scream. The person filming slowed to walking pace as they approached a small group of people standing around something. They parted and I saw a Uighur man lying on the ground, his hands and face covered in blood. There was more shouting, and then the crowd and cameraman were moving again, back between the apartments until they came to a parked ambulance. Inside, another Uighur man was lying on a stretcher. The camera panned away, then moved forward, till five or six other bodies could be seen. They were on the ground in front of the ambulance, bloodied and totally still. Then a man stepped forward and kicked one of them, till he was pulled away by a policeman, the first I had seen thus far. At this point the video ended. I looked at Alim who only said, 'Again?' On second viewing it was clear that the blur of motion at the beginning was that of the Uighur man being pursued. It was also clear that everyone, bar the dead and injured, were Han Chinese. As they stood around the body, someone shouted, 'Another one', either because they were keeping score, or as a suggestion.

We were silent after the clip ended. However many violent films one has seen, however desensitised one feels, the sight of a real person being killed evokes a horror uncomplicated by thought. Later I wondered how many times Alim had watched the clip; if even his intense hatred had its own plateau.

'That was on 25 May,' he said. 'In Shaoguan, in Guangdong province. The government forces many Uighurs to work in factories there. Almost 100,000.'

'It *makes* them go?' I said, surprised. China has a huge pool of migrant labour (around 130 million people, according to the Chinese National Bureau of Statistics), who flock from the countryside to the cities. Usually the possibility of well-paid work is incentive enough, which is most likely true for both Uighurs and Han alike. However, Alim claimed that some Uighurs, especially from the south of Xinjiang, are threatened with fines if they don't go.

'They want to separate us', he said. 'This' – he pointed at the screen – 'was in a toy factory. There were over 8,000 Uighurs working there. After a man wrote some lies about a girl who was raped, over 2,000 Chinese attack them. Seventeen Uighurs were beaten to death. But the government say only two.'

I nodded, but was unsure; it is difficult to tell the difference between someone who has been beaten to death, and someone who has merely been beaten into unconsciousness.

'And the police did not stop it. They do not arrest anyone. For them, it does not matter if some Uighurs are killed.'

Xinhua had said that there had been 13 arrests, but it only announced this *after* the July riots in Urumqi, which begged the question of when these arrests had taken place.

'From 26 June to 3 July, almost all the Uighur websites respond to this event. They began to change the colours of their websites to light gray one by one for mourning.'

Alim said that on 3 July Rebiya Kadeer (a Uighur businesswoman jailed in China, but later released into exile in the US, who heads the World Uighur Congress) called on Uighurs to protest, a message spread via discussion boards and instant messaging programs.

'Then someone sent a picture message which contained exact place and time of demonstration. We promise to be in people's square at 5:00pm. I was awake all the night up to prayer time [*fajr,* the pre-dawn prayer]. After pray, I went to sleep and waked up at about 11 am. Then I had to help my friend move house. There were many boxes. I was very tired!'

He grinned in a boyish manner, as if we were not talking of demonstrations or killings. And there was a part of me that wanted to hear more about the move. Before seeing that video, all of it – the mob in Guangdong, the riots in Urumqi, the killings – had been comfortably abstract. When Alim continued, he was still smiling, which made me hope that he was going to tell me about his friend's new house, perhaps that it was on the tenth floor and the lift was broken.

'When I come to the square, many are already there. Because 5 July was Sunday, so they come early. When the police see many people gather, they try to separate them. A policeman knock a girl's breast, so others began to shout at him and other policemen come and order them back. The police took pictures and videos, they act violently, shout at all people, arrest about 30. Then more and more people come. I join them and we increased soon to more than 1,000. Look, I will show you,' he said.

From 20 storeys up, we watched a crowd of thousands. They had blocked one side of the street, and would no doubt have spilled onto the other had there not been a barrier that partitioned the road. The protestors' whistles were loud and echoing. No police were in sight.

Then the film cut to a scene at ground level, in the midst of the crowd. At first the camerawork was shaky, so that all I could see were people walking quickly. Their faces were blurred, their speech unclear, then I saw a face I knew. Alim was waving his arms in the air and shouting. I wondered why he had chosen to keep a copy of a film that so clearly implicated him. But this question was pushed aside by the expression on his face. Instead of anger or fear, there was joy.

'The police try to stop us but we broke through. Then they stop us and push us back. After that they arrest two or three of us. Every time we ran back they chased us, but not so far, so we gather again.'

His expression as he said this was almost the same as on screen. There was the same kind of elation, the same sense of release.

'Then large numbers of PLA [People's Liberation Army] soldiers began to come and act as if they are in battle. This made people angry. At about 6:30 some people started to throw things at the soldiers.'

'Did you also throw things?'

He nodded. 'I will not do that again. But we were so angry.'

I asked how the stone throwing had led to the looting and murders; if it was true (as was rumoured) that much of the violence was carried out by street traders – the people selling belts, shoes, underwear, inner soles, tights, and key rings from tarpaulins on the pavement that you see in most cities in China. Though unemployment is a problem throughout the country, Xinjiang has particularly high rates, especially amongst Uighurs. This makes the fact that the *bingtuan*s are almost 90 per cent Han a particular source of resentment amongst Uighurs.

But Alim did not believe that the violence could be solely explained by economic frustrations.

'They did some of it,' he said. 'But even without them, it would happen. There are too many other things.'

I asked if it was true that the violence had been directed against the Han, expecting him to deny this, to dismiss it as an attempt on the part of the government to discredit the protestors. But without hesitation he said, 'Yes, it is true. Many Chinese were killed. But also 80 or 90 Uighurs are killed by police. They do not say this on television or in newspaper. They only talk about the dead Chinese.'

The newspapers and TV had been selective in other ways; none of my Han friends outside Urumqi knew anything about the revenge attacks on Uighur neighbourhoods on 7 July.

'And there is another thing,' said Alim. 'The newspapers say we were shouting *Sha Han Hui Mei*. It means "Kill the Han, exterminate the Hui". But this is Chinese slogan, not Uighur. And to make this kind of slogan you must be very educated person. If we say this in Uighur, it would not sound like this. We did some shout some things on the protest but it was "Justice" or "Wake up".'

I asked why they had shouted the latter.

'Because most Uighurs do not understand what is happening. They think that if they do not do some political thing there will be no problem. It is because of this that we are not so strong. If you have a heart, there can only be three ways: you are arrested, dead, or you go abroad.'

We were interrupted by a crash from above. Alim shifted on the cushions and said, 'It is just my friend' but did not seem convinced. We waited, but heard nothing more, and so Alim continued.

'That night I stop two young men who were beating a Chinese

very badly. They would kill him if I did not. Several days later, I did not know why I do this.'

The attacks on 7 July changed his mind. That the Han mob had not been quickly stopped led to suggestions that the police were more concerned with not angering Han residents than protecting Uighurs. There were even rumours that the police and military had played a role in assembling the mob.

Alim was in no doubt of this. 'They were shouting slogans. They said *Mei Wei Yang Han*. It means, "Exterminate Uighur, make the Han Stronger". This is not something they say on their own, someone must tell them to say it. Look, this is proof.'

We watched footage of several hundred Han men standing on the street, most of them armed with sticks, bats or metal poles. They milled around, smoking and talking on their mobiles, obviously waiting for something. This went on for several minutes, during which I caught the occasional flash of a policeman's blue shirt, saw the white dome of a soldier's helmet, but always at the edge of the crowd. Perhaps they believed that a group of armed men were a curious sight that only needed to be watched.

The camera panned right and stopped on an army truck. A soldier climbed out the back, holding a metal pole, which he then passed down to the crowd. They yelled and cheered when he passed down another, as if he was awarding them a prize.

And for Alim, the sight of this soldier handing out two metal poles was proof that the army was complicit in the killings. When I suggested that this could have been an isolated incident, he was quickly sceptical. In his eyes, all Han were equally bad.

Though relations between Han and Uighur have never been good, it was clear that the July riots had worsened the situation, an assessment Alim shared. When I asked if he thought the protest should have taken place, he said, 'Then we had no choice.' He raised a hand, then let it drop. 'Now we also have no choice.'

At the time this seemed a gesture of resignation, an admission of defeat. It was a convenient end for the narrative of brutality and protest that our talk suggested. For my part, I believed that the protestors' anger was legitimate, the result of decades of religious persecution and prejudicial economic policies. The fact that the protest later sparked into violence (albeit with provocation) did not invalidate the reasons for that anger. Having reached this neat conclusion, I was content for our conversation to shift away from the riots. For the next half hour we spoke of literature. Alim said he loved Dostoyevsky 'because it shows the mind'. He said that in a Muslim country the people must be educated. 'If they do not, it is better that the people do not believe.'

And if I had left then, my memory of Alim would have been quite different. Next day, on a bus heading westwards to Yining, I would still have remembered his cold sore, his grin, but they would have belonged to someone who made sense to me. As I looked out onto a plain of black gravel, at saw-toothed mountains that rose on each side, I would have recalled his anger, his dislike of the Han, but this would have been tempered by the sense that he regretted the events of last July. I would have thought, *That is a moderate man.*

But then the door opened and another man came in, stocky, clean-shaven, older than Alim, in his mid-30s I guessed. He greeted us in Uighur, then shook hands with me. 'This is my friend,' said Alim, in English. 'He is good at organising things.' The man smiled and shrugged, but made no other reply, which made me unsure whether he spoke English. Neither he nor Alim offered his name, for reasons that quickly became clear.

'It is true what I say,' said Alim. 'This man can organise 100 people. Sometimes a thousand. Everyday I ask him to organise another protest but he says it is not effective.'

For a moment, I was taken aback that one of the organisers of the 5 July protest was quietly sitting in front of me. It was like meeting a famous person one has hitherto only seen on TV, except that he had to be the opposite of famous, or he would not have been anywhere except in prison, or dead: 26 people had already been executed for their part in the riots. If I had been less stunned, I would have asked why he thought it 'not effective'. Instead I blurted out what seemed like an innocuous question.

'What do you think the main changes have been since the riots?'

I expected Alim to state the obvious, namely the number of police and soldiers in Urumqi. Instead he said, 'The changes? The biggest is that many Chinese respect us now. They are scared of us. They have seen our strength.'

His grin told me what he thought of this, but I asked anyway.

'Yes,' he said. 'It is good thing,'

'Are you sure? Don't you think that things have gotten worse?'

'No,' he said. 'They are better. But let me ask you something. What makes you happy?'

He smiled throughout my banal answer – 'cats… waterfalls… good weather' –then said, 'Did you see the news?' About Qinghai?'

I nodded. An earthquake, several days before, had killed more than a thousand people.

'When I see this I am happy because many Chinese are dead. Maybe it is bad for me, but I am.'

I pointed out that most of the dead were Tibetans, not Han, an objection that did not seem to trouble him. Then he said, 'I have a question for you. Do you think the peaceful protest can work?'

'Yes,' I said, without hesitation. It seemed axiomatic.

'I thought so too,' he said. 'But now I do not think so. *He* does not think so. We try many times but they do not listen. Just arrest and kill our people.'

I tried to formulate reasons why peaceful protest was the *only* viable means of resistance, but as I did so I kept seeing an image of a tall, beautiful Asian woman stepping out from a crowd of protestors. I watched her walk slowly, calmly, towards a line of riot police, who ordered her to stop. When she did not, they raised their guns and took aim, but still she advanced, smiling, until she was so close that they seemed certain to fire. Then music swelled and they stepped aside and all was right in the land.

But this was not a sequence from life. It was from a film, or dream, and I could not imagine it happening in China. In the end, the best argument I could come up with was a negative one. I offered the negligible comfort that the Chinese government treated the majority of protests the same, regardless of the ethnicity of the protestors: demonstrations by Han farmers and unemployed workers have been quashed with as much force as those in Xinjiang (the exception is when the protestors are prosperous, middle-class citizens with a non-political complaint. In 2007, a protest in Xiamen, in Fujian province, against a proposed chemical plant made the government reconsider its plans). Although this was true, it wasn't much of an answer. In retrospect, I can see that it must have seemed like I was telling Alim that he shouldn't complain about being oppressed because *everyone* was similarly oppressed, from which it was only a short step to arguing that this oppression was therefore acceptable.

Alim had a good answer for this.

'My brother is in prison now. And he' – Alim indicated the man in the corner – 'he has been in prison five times in ten years.'

'What for?'

'For nothing. There is no trial, you are not the guilty man, but they keep you for two months, maybe half a year.'

The routine abuse of judicial power in China has been well documented by Human Rights Watch and Amnesty International. People 'disappear' and are never heard from again. In Yining I had heard many stories of angry young men like Alim being taken away by the police. Sometimes they were returned to their families after being tortured. Occasionally their bodies were found in the countryside.

Alim shook his head. 'The only thing to do is fight. If I had a perfect bomb that could kill 100, or 1,000 I would use it. Or if we have 1,000 Uighurs with AK47s. If they kill 1,000 Chinese it can work.'

He was almost breathless with excitement. But before he could continue, the stocky man leaned forward and spoke to him in Uighur. Then he turned to me and said, 'I am sorry. My English not good. But I will tell him.' He continued in Uighur, for almost a minute, then Alim translated.

'He says we want to go to Afghanistan before. To take several hundred and make a camp. Maybe stay for three, four years and train 1,000 people. We only need to kill 1,000 Chinese and the others will leave.'

'What if they don't?'

'I think most of them will. If not, we must kill 1,000 more,' he said calmly. 'Then they would go. The Chinese are not brave.'

'Maybe. But isn't there a difference between ordinary Chinese people and soldiers? What have they done to you?'

'If they are here in Xinjiang, they are guilty, unless they are the sick, women, old or the child.'

I pointed out that the rioters had killed a number of women.

'That was a mistake' he said, and paused, with what I hoped was regret.

'Even if you did that, you'll still be outnumbered. And if you start killing ordinary Chinese, the conditions of Uighur people will only get worse.'

'It doesn't matter, their condition is already low. They are used to the simple life, they can live on three breads a day.'

'What if they retaliate, and kill ordinary Uighurs?'

'Their condition is now so bad. They are already dead.'

His hatred was so implacable that the deaths of thousands of Uighurs seemed an acceptable price. My first instinct was to tell him that this was morally wrong, and that whatever the Chinese government had done, it could not justify ethnic cleansing. But although it was strange and horrible to debate the murder of thousands, I thought the best argument I had against violence was that it wouldn't work.

'If you start killing Chinese people, it makes it easier for the government to do what it wants. It will be like after September 11.'

I went on to suggest that any further acts of terrorism would only reduce support in America. This was not a prospect that troubled Alim.

'Will they help us? Do they help the Tibetans? They are too scared of the Chinese to do something.'

I could not disagree. There seems no chance that any solution to the Xinjiang will come as a result of external pressure. Decades of activism and pressure against the Chinese government has had virtually no effect on their policies in Tibet.

I asked Alim to imagine how he would feel if thousands of Han Chinese were murdered by his hypothetical army. Not because I thought it would work; just to try and make him confront it as something more than an abstraction.

To his credit, he did consider the question. His tongue explored the sore. Then he leaned back and said, 'I would feel better. In Qur'an it says there is life in revenge for killing your brother.'

When I asked which verse that was from, Alim said he did not know. And perhaps it did not matter. The fact he thought it was from the Qur'an was enough. In the face of his anger, his desire for revenge, I had nothing to say.

It was then that the organiser leaned forward and spoke to Alim in Uighur. Alim reached in his pocket and took out a pen, which he handed to him. Next the organiser drew an arrow on a piece of paper.

'There are three ways for us' he said, and drew two more arrows pointing in different directions. 'One way,' he said, and then his English ran out. But Alim knew what to say.

'The first way is help from abroad. From America or Britain.' He looked at me pointedly – as if it was somehow my fault – then crossed out the arrow.

'This will not happen. No one will make the Chinese government do something. The second way is peaceful protest. We get closer to government. We hope they change our conditions.'

He drew a line through this.

'The third way is Taliban. In 2010 nothing will happen. But you should be here in 2011. If you are here then, you will see something.'

He put the pen down and sat back, and there was an air of challenge in the gesture, as if he was daring me to object. But I had no more counter-arguments. Although I could not condone terrorism, neither could I pretend that the other options had much chance of success.

'Do you have any other questions?' said Alim.

With a sense of failure, I told him I did not. The organiser shook my hand and left, followed a minute later by Alim and myself. Outside it was dark, and the street was unlit. We went in separate directions.

But next day, on a bus speeding west, I came up with a fourth option. As the land rose on other side, funnelling us to a mountain pass, I thought about other forms of resistance. Though the Uighurs could not fight, or protest, they could still survive. They could pass their language and culture on to their children, so that when Chinese government policy changed, as it one day must, Uighurs would still retain a sense of themselves as a people. By the time we were bumping along the frozen edge of Sayram Lake, its surface so white that it blinded, I was convinced that this was the *only* reasonable option. I decided I had to call Alim, not because it was something he hadn't thought of, a revelation that would make him renounce violence, more because I wanted to prove to him that I had an answer to his challenge (albeit one that even at the time felt limp and somewhat patronising).

I rang Alim as we reached the lip of the valley. He did not answer, so I left a short message outlining my idea. Then the bus was curving round the hairpins that led to the valley floor. It took an hour on a muddy road that made the bus lurch, lean, and sometimes threaten to fall. Then we were on level ground and moving fast again. Sheep drifted on the hills. Racks of honey jars glowed amber in the day's last light. On entering the valley, there were obvious signs of massive Han influx. There were factories and new apartment complexes where there had been (as the cliché goes) only fields.

As we neared the outskirts of Yining city, I saw a large army base to the right, where soldiers stood at attention in front of a line of riot vans. Then the bus conductor came round and asked for everyone's identity card.

'What for?' I said.

'They want to see them.'

He pointed to a large structure ahead, which at first looked like a tollgate, but as we slowed I realised was a checkpoint. Then we had stopped and riot police were getting on board. Two stood at the front of the bus, while another walked down the aisle. When he got to me he paused. He asked where I was from. When I told him, he asked to see my passport, which the conductor duly produced. He flicked through it till he reached the photo. He looked up at me, then back to the photo. My phone chimed into life. I was not able to look at the message, as I and the other passengers were too busy getting off the coach, taking our luggage out of the hold, opening it for inspection. Police dogs watched from the side of the road as we unpacked our underwear.

After 20 minutes, we were allowed to get back on the bus. Entering town, on the west end of Liberation Road, was like coming into any other place in China. There was now a long row of neon lit hotels, karaoke bars, and restaurants. It had always been a Han part of town, but eight years ago the buildings had been smaller, like those on the Uighur streets.

We pulled into a new bus station that had been built round the corner from the college. Everyone who entered, even just to buy a ticket, was searched and scanned with a metal detector.

I had difficulty finding a hotel that would take foreigners. Previously, I had had a resident's permit, which let me stay anywhere; without it I was reduced to working my way down Liberation Road. At each intersection, there were police and armed soldiers sitting in makeshift shelters by the side of the road. They looked at me, and each time I expected to be called over, to have to produce my passport. Instead they smoked and looked tired and it occurred to me that they had been sitting there for months, probably since last July.

Eventually, just before dark, I remembered a place near the square where friends had stayed when they came to visit (it being against regulations for them to stay with me). It was only when I sat in my hotel room later that I read Alim's text. It said, 'Your idea is for us to give up. We do this every day.'

Next morning I went to the college, where the first thing I saw was a line of riot shields, helmets and batons at the front gate. I wondered who they were intended for use on. Inside there were many new buildings, but also, I was glad to see, all the old Russian ones as well. I went to the English department, but was told by one of the secretaries that it had been moved to another building. On the walk across campus I thought of the dean's grin, his hairpiece; how, when I walked into his office after eight years' absence, he would probably just say, 'Hello, naughty boy!'

I climbed the steps to the fourth floor and saw a large picture of myself and the students from '99 class. It had been blown up from a small photo, and was so pixellated that I barely recognised myself. I went into the office and asked one of the teachers – who I did not know – if Dean Geng was in.

'No,' she said and looked surprised. 'Don't you know?'

'What do you mean?'

'He died four months ago. From drinking.'

She didn't know any more. 'A pity,' she said.

I left the building, then the college. There was no reason to stay.

I spent the next several days walking around and talking to people, meeting up with old friends. And if that sounds somewhat vague, it is intentionally so. Whilst it is safe to write what people said and did eight years ago, in the current climate, with so many troops, and increased surveillance, I'm not sure that changing the details of people's identities will protect them enough. It doesn't seem worth the risk.

What can be said is that Yining, like many other towns in Xinjiang, has been subject to continuing Han immigration. The developments in the valley, and on Liberation road, are part of a trend that is likely to continue. The passenger railway line between Urumqi and Yining is almost completed, and will only hasten the influx of people from inner China. In itself, this is not necessarily a problem. If one accepts that at least some of the problems between Han and Uighurs have their roots in poverty and unemployment, it is hard to object to developments that might ameliorate this. The issue is whether or not the benefits of economic development will be equally shared. A study in 2004 found that the regions in Xinjiang with the highest GDP, and greatest concentration of industry, were predominantly those with the highest proportion of Han in the population. In particular, southern Xinjiang, which is still mainly Uighur, has had significantly less investment in industry, so most have to rely on cotton whose market price is highly unstable.

But it would be inaccurate to say that the government is unwilling to spend money in Uighur areas. In Yining, some of the most dramatic changes can be found in the Uighur neighbourhoods. In my mind, their streets were still muddy and dark, treacherous throughout winter and spring, a place where the most common vehicle was the horse and cart. So it was with a shock of non-recognition that I took in their hard surfaces, street lamps, and new signs, these last in both Chinese and Uighur. On some of the streets on the far side of the square there are even sitting areas and ornate streetlights. Unsurprisingly, these changes were popular with almost everyone I spoke to. The man who gave me a lift on his truck; the boy pulling a cart laden with bread; the schoolchildren cycling home: each said that conditions were better.

It is probably to my discredit that this made me unhappy. Never mind the obvious improvement: it just wasn't as picturesque. A more substantial objection was the fact that a large brick gate had been erected on one of the streets near Han Ren Jie. Next to it was a large notice in Chinese, Uighur and English that announced that this was a 'Folk Tourism Spot':

> There's no mansions and high buildings, but tiny bridge over a sparkling steam, and on the far bank, a pretty little village. She is just like an allopatric princes with purdah, and sleeping deeply, peceful [sic], concine [sic] and mystery, to let yourself be seduced into love her, and be charmed...

The main Uighur neighborhood (whose population, according to the notice, is 100,000) has thus been designated as a kind of sight-seeing area. It would be an understatement to say that this was unpopular with some of my old friends.

'It is a fucking cage,' said one of them, whose grasp of the vernacular had greatly improved. 'And they demolish some people's homes to make it look like this.'

Similar 'improvements' have taken place in Kashgar, where the old town is being demolished, except for a small portion that will be kept for tourists. The destruction, and then repackaging, of Uighur communities in this fashion, can surely only be detrimental to their cultural identity.

But despite these changes, much was as I remembered. The small mosques; the rows of poplars; the humming from the pigeon's whistles. The sky was blue and clear each day; the King of Kebabs still deserved its name. After lunch I cycled through the streets of the market, trying to remember what was down each alley. Looking at the rugs, the carpets, the barrows of fruit and vegetable stalls, the trousers hanging from an obliging tree's branches, the bottles of scent, the perfect circles of nan, I felt that I was back to stay. I would buy some apples and take them home to my flat and then, after having dinner in the *Old Hui* or *The Fragrant Garden*, prepare my lesson for next day. After that, a game of chess, or a drink on my balcony, till the mountains swallowed the sun. And this time I would not let myself be driven crazy by missionaries (assuming there were still some in town). I would work harder at learning Uighur, spend more time with people who didn't speak English, maybe finally make it to the mountains that taunted me.

But I was just a visitor, as I perhaps had always been. When you are revisiting a place you once knew well, you compare the present with the past. One approves of the things that have not changed, and in those unfortunate cases where someone has changed, or a restaurant has been knocked down – as the *Old Hui* and *the Fragrant Garden* had been – one grudgingly amends one's memories. Though

I could not escape the conclusion that the town was becoming more like other places in China, and its Uighur community increasingly marginalized, I was certain that if I cycled out into the countryside, towards Yarkiki Togruk and the Tree That Bleeds, I would have an afternoon of seeing things as they were.

The town dwindled fast, then it was just fields. I passed a Han graveyard where there were signs of recent visitors: burnt incense sticks, empty *baijiu* bottles, bowls of rancid food. These were for *Qing Ming*, the yearly cleaning of graves, when spirit money is burnt for the souls of one's ancestors. Further on, there was a Uighur graveyard where sheep were grazing. Their shepherd waved to me.

I blurred through a village where children screamed when they saw me, perhaps in delight, and it was hot, and I had not brought water, but the more I cycled, the more I saw, and the better that made me feel. Admittedly, there were new army barracks, and signs for *bingtuans* I didn't remember, but I cycled quickly past these, not least because, on this occasion, I wasn't sure that the area was open to foreigners.

When I next looked at the road markers I was 20 kilometres outside town. I was tired, dehydrated, almost hysterically happy. All that remained was to see the magic tree.

I cycled on, overtaking an old Uighur man whose bicycle was making a tortured sound. The sound of his scratching chain quickly faded, and though I could not see the tree ahead, it was nonetheless clear in my mind: the red ribbons, the spread of its branches, the ring of glass round its trunk.

After ten minutes it was obvious I had remembered its location wrong. The stone markers said 22, then 23 kilometres; I could not have missed a tree in the centre of the road.

I cycled on another five kilometres before realizing I had never come so far before. Contrary to reason, I continued on; it was only when the road marker said 30km that I turned around. Despite my aching legs, I cycled quickly, as if the tree were somehow in danger of leaving, and really, I should not have cared, because it was not a shrine I had worshipped at. It had no significance in my secular world. But still I pedalled, feeling somewhat lightheaded, and the road was straight and no tree came toward me; as the kilometres counted down my sense of panic grew. Eventually there was a speck in the middle of the road that began to expand, that acquired a form, but it was not a tree, it was the old man labouring on the bicycle that complained. When he came within earshot I said hello, raised my hand, then braked, and though he looked at me in puzzlement, he did the same. I told him in Chinese where I was from, that I had once taught in the college, and at this he nodded, because this was something many people knew.

Then I said, 'Do you know about the shrine? It's on this road, isn't it?'

He looked at me blankly, then pushed his hand under his cap, then, when I repeated myself he said something in Uighur I didn't understand. When he said it in Chinese, I still didn't know. Finally he raised his hand, then brought it down quickly, chopping at the air.

There could be no doubt. The tree had been cut down.

Further Reading

The Mummies of Urumchi (2000) by Elizabeth Wayland Barker

Situating the Uyghurs between China and Central Asia (2007) by Ildiko Beller-Hann, M. Cristina Cesaro, Rachel Harris & Joanne Smith Finley (eds.)

China's Last Nomads: The History and Culture of China's Kazaks (1997) by Linda Benson and Ingvar Svanberg

The Uighurs: Strangers in their own land (2010) by Gardner Bovingdon

Down a narrow road: identity and masculinity in a Uyghur community in Xinjiang (2009) by Jay Dautcher

The Xinjiang conflict: Uyghur identity, language policy, and political discourse (2004) by Arienne M. Dwyer

News from Tartary (1936) by Peter Fleming

China's Minorities: Integration and Modernisation in the Twentieth Century (1994) by Colin Mackerras

Violent separatism in Xinjiang : a critical assessment (2004) by James A. Millward

Eurasian crossroads: a history of Xinjiang (2007) by James A. Millward

'Negotiating Locality, Islam, and National Culture in a Changing Borderlands: The Revival of the Mashrap Ritual Among Young Uyghur Men in the Ili Valley' (1998) in *Central Asian Survey* 17(4) by Sean Roberts

Governing China's Multiethnic frontiers (2005) by Morris Rossabi (ed.)

Oasis Identities (1998) by Justin Jon Rudelson

A History of Inner Asia (2000) by Svat Soucek

Xinjiang: China's Muslim borderland (2004) by S. Frederick Starr (ed.)

Shadow of the Silk Road (2007) by Colin Thubron

Wild West China: the taming of Xinjiang (2004) by Christian Tyler

Index

Some other books published by **LUATH** PRESS

Letters from the Great Wall

Jenni Daiches
ISBN 978 1905222 51 3 PBK £9.99

Eleanor Dickinson needs to see things differently. To most her life would seem ideal; 33 years old, a university lecturer in a respectable relationship. But Eleanor is dissatisfied: she's suffocated by her family and frustrated by the man she has no desire to marry. She has to escape.

In the summer of 1989, she cuts all ties and leaves behind the safe familiarity of Edinburgh to lecture in the eastern strangeness of China. But as the young democracy movement flexes its muscles, Eleanor is soon drawn into the unfolding drama of an event that captured the world's attention.

What freedoms will be asserted in this ancient nation, shaped both by tradition and revolution? And will Eleanor discover what really matters in her life before the tanks roll into Tiananmen Square?

Daiches manages her double narrative with dexterity... this is an accomplished book.

SCOTLAND ON SUNDAY

The Shard Box

Liz Niven
ISBN 978 1906817 62 6 PBK £7.99

This collection of poems eloquently captures the contradictions and multiple identities of modern China.

Liz Niven has a keen eye for detail and a light touch that delivers an unexpected intensity; taking on ancient traditions and contemporary issues, this selection is in turn humorous and poignant and illustrates China as it is rarely seen. From the intimacy of the tea ceremony to the lives of the migrant workers in Beijing, nothing is as you would expect.

The Shard Box is a testament to the poet's emotional honesty, her willingness to explore and engage. It is a book that will linger with the reader long after it is finished.

These are not travel poems; they are 'Chinese' poems with a very strong Scottish accent – humorous, sympathetic, enlightening and involved. They demonstrate how valuable the reflective nature of poetry can be in engaging with another culture.

TOM POW

Details of these and other books published by Luath Press can be found at:
www.luath.co.uk

Luath Press Limited
committed to publishing well written books worth reading

LUATH PRESS takes its name from Robert Burns, whose little collie Luath (*Gael.*, swift or nimble) tripped up Jean Armour at a wedding and gave him the chance to speak to the woman who was to be his wife and the abiding love of his life. Burns called one of 'The Twa Dogs' Luath after Cuchullin's hunting dog in Ossian's *Fingal*. Luath Press was established in 1981 in the heart of Burns country, and is now based a few steps up the road from Burns' first lodgings on Edinburgh's Royal Mile.
Luath offers you distinctive writing with a hint of unexpected pleasures.

Most bookshops in the UK, the US, Canada, Australia, New Zealand and parts of Europe either carry our books in stock or can order them for you. To order direct from us, please send a £sterling cheque, postal order, international money order or your credit card details (number, address of cardholder and expiry date) to us at the address below. Please add post and packing as follows: UK – £1.00 per delivery address; overseas surface mail – £2.50 per delivery address; overseas air-mail – £3.50 for the first book to each delivery address, plus £1.00 for each additional book by airmail to the same address. If your order is a gift, we will happily enclose your card or message at no extra charge.

Luath Press Limited
543/2 Castlehill
The Royal Mile
Edinburgh EH1 2ND
Scotland
Telephone: 0131 225 4326 (24 hours)
Fax: 0131 225 4324
email: sales@luath.co.uk
Website: www.luath.co.uk